Letters of Light

Letters of Light

*Arabic Script in Calligraphy,
Print, and Digital Design*

J. R. Osborn

HARVARD UNIVERSITY PRESS

Cambridge, Massachusetts
London, England
2017

First printing

Library of Congress Cataloging-in-Publication Data
Names: Osborn, J.R., author.
Title: Letters of light : Arabic script in calligraphy, print,
and digital design / J.R. Osborn.
Description: Cambridge, Massachusetts : Harvard University Press, 2017. |
Includes bibliographical references and index.
Identifiers: LCCN 2016046675 | ISBN 9780674971127 (hardcover : alk. paper)
Subjects: LCSH: Arabic language—Writing—History. | Arabic language—Written
Arabic—History. | Communication and technology—Arab countries.
Classification: LCC PJ6123 .O83 2017 | DDC 492.7/1109—dc23
LC record available at https://lccn.loc.gov/2016046675

Inscribed with and for a Host of Characters,
Each with its own personality.

CONTENTS

NOTE ON TRANSLITERATION

Since this book seeks to introduce issues of Arabic script to nonspecialist audiences, I have used a simplified form of transliteration that minimizes, as much as possible, the diacritical marking of Latin letters. Thus, the term *khatt* appears instead of *khaṭṭ, mushaf* instead of *muṣḥaf,* and *masahif* instead of *maṣāḥif.* An exception is made for the names of Arabic letters. Letter names display full diacritical marks, including long vowels and sublinear dots for hard consonants (for example, *bā', jīm, ḥā', khā, qāf, kāf,* etc.). An apostrophe (') is used for both *hamza* and *'ayn.* Figure 1.1 in Chapter 1 presents the Arabic alphabet (or *abjad*) along with the Latinate names used for all letters. Since the book addresses Ottoman Turkish as well as Arabic contexts, it also contains numerous Turkish terms. Turkish terms and Ottoman Turkish titles retain modern Turkish spelling. Occasionally, the modern Turkish spelling of an Arabic term differs from common Latinate transliteration of the same Arabic term. Turkish, for example, refers to the classical style of *thuluth* as *sülüs.* In such cases, Arabic transliteration is preferred. Whenever alternate Turkish spellings are provided, such as the list of Ottoman scribal styles in Chapter 2, they are indicated as such. These inclusions are meant to assist scholars who often wrestle with multiple Latinate spellings of words that appear the same in Arabic script.

Letters of Light

Introduction

Past Scripts and Future Visions

This book looks to the past in order to inform the future. New media technologies have shaped, and continue to shape, Arabic script. The reed pen, the printing press, lithography, typewriters, word processors, and networked computers have all left their mark. *Letters of Light* tells a story of those changes. It follows a cast of characters—the letters and shapes of Arabic script—on a long journey from the tenth century to the twenty-first. Historically, it tackles questions of scribal practice, textual modernization, the perceived "delay" in Islamic and Arabic printing, and movements of script reform. In the contemporary realm, it addresses challenges of Arabic computing and the design of digital Arabic fonts. The overarching argument is that the former elucidates the latter. Digital questions of script design can be understood only within the specific scribal histories that precede them. We must familiarize ourselves with earlier practices in order to make smart decisions about the shape of script on current media technologies and technologies that are yet to come. In this regard, the book is directed as much toward contemporary practitioners and future designers as toward scholars and students of history. It addresses readers and users of Arabic script from Dubai to Detroit and from Amsterdam to Aleppo.

Written communication is currently in flux. Textual roles and responsibilities, practices of reading and writing, and the processing and transmission of textual content have all shifted with digital technology. New forms of text abound: status updates of 140 characters, scrolling tickers on newscasts and public transit, automatic translations of foreign words, computer code written for devices rather than human readers, and ideographic emoticons that replace letters and words. These new forms unsettle, but do not replace, traditional media. Old forms of writing circulate and coexist alongside the new. On any given day, we are likely to jot down notes by hand, read printed typography, type on a keyboard, tap letters on a mobile device, and print from screen to paper. We are also beckoned by flamboyant neon signs, entranced by textual animation, and intrigued by the complexity of graffiti hiding under bridges. In a world dominated by visual media, writing too is visual. Scripts and letters display shape, size, color, direction, and decoration. The aesthetic range and visual variation of written characters is enormous. And a new look or font is merely a drop-down menu away.

Across this diversity and variation, written scripts maintain a semblance of cohesion. Arabic script remains Arabic script across manuscript, print, and digital registers. And Latin letters are equally Latin in handwritten, printed, and screen-based varieties. Scripts endure across technologies, and technologies of script also endure. Handwriting never ceased, even as printing arose as a mass medium. And both media continue apace in the digital era. The current book traces the cohesion of Arabic script across three moments of technological transformation. It asks what is preserved, and what is lost, when Arabic script adapts to new technical systems. The theoretical frame is one of comparative media and technology, and the specific focus is Arabic script as a writing system and a visual technology.[1] Visions of technology bring to mind printing presses and personal computers. These technologies transmit, distribute, and share written content with readers and users. The scripts that hold content are not always considered technologies in their own right. Scripts are interstitial. They occupy a middle position in the trajectory from distributive technologies to final reader. Scripts are transmitted by other technologies. Yet they too are designed, constructed, and built as material artifacts. Throughout history, script design has operated at the intersection of ideas. Writing records ways of living and experiences that have meant something.[2] Technologies of script shape the how and what of that "something."

The following presentation adopts a periodization of roughly five hundred years. In the tenth, fifteenth, and twentieth centuries, new media technologies altered the appearance and shape of Arabic script. Each of these moments represents a communication "revolution," in which the increased circulation of text accompanies new methods of designing and inscribing written characters. Elizabeth Eisenstein applied the phrase "printing revolution" to the spread of movable type in fifteenth-century Europe. Five hundred years later, the twentieth-century computer revolution dethroned print as the dominant mode of textual production. The story of Arabic script prefaces these sweeping and oft-debated technical transitions with an earlier "revolution": the development of *al-khatt al-mansub* in the tenth century. *Al-khatt al-mansub* is a highly regulated method of forming proportional Arabic letters. It formalized identifiable and repeatable styles that are as distinct as digital fonts (for example, Palatino versus Times New Roman), and it supported a deeply robust, durable, and influential tradition of scribal and calligraphic writing. The formal consistency of *al-khatt al-mansub* makes tenth-century handwritten Arabic as legible today as it was a thousand years ago. Latin handwriting, in contrast, changes dramatically in as little as a hundred years. Understanding the durability of *al-khatt al-mansub* clarifies the challenges that faced Arabic script when it encountered the later revolutions of printing and digital communication. The story presented in the book is the story of adapting proportional Arabic script to new technologies.

The book's periodization foregrounds script technologies—*al-khatt al-mansub*, movable type, and digital fonts—rather than cultural practices that surround them, such as the circulation of written text, changes in literacy, genres of writing, and reading practices. *Letters of Light* seeks to play a much-needed interdisciplinary role by treating Arabic technically and aesthetically while remaining accessible to readers of diverse academic backgrounds. It weaves discussions of calligraphy, typography, printing, computer history, and digital culture within a holistic and wide-ranging tapestry. For scholars of communication and media, the study offers a comparative perspective on book and digital history in a non-Western setting. By detailing the technical considerations of a non-Latin script, it provides a much-needed contrast to studies of writing drawn primarily from the Latin alphabet and Euro-American contexts. For scholars and students of the Middle East, the chapters follow Arabic script across diverse technologies. Those who study Arabic calligraphy are rarely familiar with the technical challenges of Arabic printing, those who study Arabic print history may possess only a cursory understanding of scribal structure, and often neither group is versed in digital history and the coding of Arabic script for computers.[3] *Letters of Light* synthesizes these discussions in order to identify recurrent issues and broader themes. Although the presentation is historical, the contributions look equally to the future. For practicing designers and technologists, the study offers a framework for reconsidering the technical possibilities of script design in digital environments.

A focus on script produces a different sort of a book than studies bounded by historic, geographic, linguistic, or ethnic communities.[4] Scripts cut across languages and cultures; they cut across technologies and textual content. But why *Arabic* script? And *which* Arabic script? Arabic script answers the first question through its prevalence and durability. The script has a global history, and it remains one of the most widely used writing systems in the world. Few writing systems transect so many geographic, religious, political, technological, and cultural categories. Arabic script conveys the blessings and prayers of more than 1.5 billion Muslims worldwide, and it operates as the official script of more than twenty-five countries, many of which use it to transcribe languages other than Arabic. The script's characters have touched all corners of the globe, from China to California and Indonesia to Istanbul. Languages as diverse as Arabic, Persian, Ottoman Turkish, Urdu, Kurdish, Berber, Swahili, Hausa, and Afrikaans—along with a wide variety of other languages—have all employed Arabic letters. Arabic script is widely diverse. It is sacred; it is profane. It is classical; it is contemporary. It has served as the mark of empire and the voice of colonial resistance. Arabic script appears in holy books and mass-marketed periodicals. It is meticulously hand drawn in calligraphic celebration, and it is rapidly texted in social media revolutions. Following the script across such diverse landscapes produces neither an art historical examination of calligraphy nor a social and political study of media effects, neither a literary history nor a formal linguistic analysis. But the study touches on all of these areas. The technology of Arabic script has played, and continues to play, a multiplicity of roles.

As to *which* Arabic script is featured, the answer is subtler. As much as possible, the book uses the term "script" to refer to Arabic as a general writing system and the term "style" to refer to a particular variety. The study's broad historical examination of Arabic script is balanced by its focus on a particular style: *naskh*. The *naskh* styles are a subgenre of Arabic script and adhere to the rules of *al-khatt al-mansub*. They maintained particular significance for Muslim communities during the Abbasid and Ottoman eras, they are regionally dominant in the central Middle East, and they remain the most common form of Arabic script in print and online. *Naskh* styles represent Arabic and related languages across the Middle East and within the global Arabic diaspora. But they are only a subset of the visual and stylistic variety that Arabic script has exhibited across time and space. The eastern and western regions of the Arabic and Muslim worlds developed distinct styles with unique appearances and histories. These styles—the eastern style of *nasta'liq* and the western style of *maghribi*—do not necessarily adhere to the formal rules of *al-khatt al-mansub,* and they therefore fall beyond the scope of the current study.[5] Likewise, the historical styles employed by Arab Christians and the related script of Syriac are not addressed, nor are the styles of Sub-Saharan Africa and East Asia, where Arabic script has played equally important roles.[6] The geometric *Kufic* styles, which precede *naskh* and remain prevalent in architectural inscriptions, are only lightly addressed. When discussion of *Kufic* and other styles does occur, they serve primarily as structural foils to *naskh.* Much important work has been done on all these styles— *nasta'liq, maghribi, Kufic,* and beyond—and every effort is made in the notes to direct scholars to relevant studies. But the focus falls squarely on the *naskh* style of Arab and Ottoman Muslim communities.

The argument unfolds over ten centuries. It begins with the formalization of *al-khatt al-mansub* in the tenth century, and it ends with the adoption of Unicode, an encoding standard for digital text, in the twenty-first. *Naskh* occupies a position of prominence in each of the examined communication transformations, and the long scope necessitates some degree of generalization. The transitions of the tenth, fifteenth, and twentieth centuries highlight wide-ranging technological and aesthetic shifts. Limitations of space prevent detailed examination of the contexts—and the often heated debates—that surround particular variants of *naskh* and their unique backstories. More specifically, the first two chapters connect the technical revolution of *al-khatt al-mansub* in the tenth century (Chapter 1) with the prevalence of *naskh* styles in Ottoman scribal practices of the fifteenth century (Chapter 2). This five-hundred-year jump brings the first transformation into contact with the historical era of the second: movable type. Focus then turns to the ramifications and spread of movable type printing. In Europe, the new technology spread quickly (Chapter 3); in Ottoman lands, adoption followed a more gradual and nuanced pace (Chapter 4). Although Hebrew, Armenian, and Greek printers had been operating in Ottoman Istanbul since the sixteenth century, Ottoman Muslims did not apply movable type to Arabic *naskh* until the eighteenth century. In the final transition, the legacy of movable type encounters digital computing. Arabic script reform debated *naskh*'s compatibility with modern technologies (Chapter 5), and digital design opened new frontiers in the reproduction, representation, and circulation of Arabic script (Chapter 6). A brief coda generalizes the lessons of Arabic script for the future of digital text more broadly.

Letters of Light places Arabic script at the center of technology history. If the Ottoman context is emphasized more than others, this is due to Ottoman prominence and its relationship to Europe during the rise of print. The Ottoman trajectory unites the story of *naskh* across all three transitional eras. Ottoman scribal practice refined and applied the proportional styles of handwritten *naskh,* the Ottoman administration negotiated the adoption of print technology, and modern Turkey jettisoned Ottoman *naskh* in favor of Latin letters. Among its other arguments, the book holds a mirror to European print history. In doing so, it replaces one center (Europe) with another (Ottoman power), and it brackets Ottoman printing between the scribal transformations that preceded it and digital transformations that followed. The appearances of scripts are constantly evolving. But script aesthetics become especially noticeable during technological transitions. At such moments, scripts cannot remain transparent holders of content. The shape of scripts *must* be considered whenever they encounter new technologies of inscription and reproduction. What features can adapt and change to new technologies, and how much should they change? What features cannot change without sacrificing familiarity and recognition? What are the fundamental and essential features of a script's structure? Answers to these questions were renegotiated during the technological transformations of the tenth, fifteenth, and twentieth centuries. As Arabic script encountered new technical possibilities and new technical constraints, its appearance and structure shifted.

The first transition occurred during the Abbasid period and continued through the Ottoman era. Chapter 1, "The Layers of Proportional *Naskh*," and Chapter 2, "Ottoman Script Design," examine the scribal system that evolved with technologies of reed pen and paper. Both chapters emphasize the communicative role of stylistic variety. The tenth century saw an explosion of materials written in Arabic. Following the Abbasid adoption of paper, more texts were written and shared than ever before.[7] By the end of the tenth century, the Baghdad library housed well over ten thousand volumes. A similar scale of written production did not occur in Europe until the sixteenth century, more than one hundred years after the spread of print. *Al-khatt al-mansub,* the proportional system attributed to vizier Ibn Muqlah, helped organize the flood of written material. It is a formal method of script design that geometrically constructs Arabic letters in relation to the primary measure of the *nuqta,* or rhombic dot. Differing *nuqta* measurements and proportional relationships define identifiable scribal styles. And Arabic scribes employed these stylistic differences to communicate the genre, audience, or intended role of written messages.

Chapter 1 begins with a quote from *The Fihrist of al-Nadim,* a bibliographic index completed in Baghdad around 990 c.e. Ibn al-Nadim presents an incredibly detailed discussion of writing systems and stylistic variety. He assumes reader familiarity with scribal diversity and the connection of particular styles with particular forms of content. Ibn al-Nadim's list of styles ranges from those used exclusively for sales of land to those of administrative utility and those reserved for copying the Qur'an. The chapter then presents the visual marks and layered structure of Arabic script. Arabic script is not simply a horizontal line of letters strung one after the other. Layers of significance emanate above and below the primary line of characters. These layers evolved over time to differentiate consonants, vowels, and additional features. A final section examines three pillars of Arabic calligraphic tradition, each of which symbolizes a significant shift of *naskh:* Ibn Muqlah, Ibn al-Bawwab, and Yaqut al-Musta'simi. Ibn Muqlah developed *al-khatt al-mansub;* Ibn al-Bawwab beautified the system and applied it to copying the Qur'an; and Yaqut emphasized the communicative interplay of multiple proportional styles.

Chapter 1 introduces a number of themes that reoccur throughout the book: stylistic and scribal variety, the aesthetic differentiation of secular and sacred content, and the seven-layer model of Arabic script.[8] Arabic script transcribes both the holy Qur'an, a uniquely sacred book, and everyday writing, secular and profane. Visual and stylistic differences demarcate the two realms. Many technological changes in Arabic script and *naskh* styles were first applied to secular content before being transferred to Qur'anic copying. *Tashkil* marks for vocalization, *al-khatt al-mansub,* and movable metal type were all adopted for secular purposes before being applied to the holy text. The Qur'an was not printed locally until 150 years after the Ottoman Muslim adoption of print for secular texts. This differs significantly from European Christian tradition, which quickly applied printing to the distribution of Bibles. Another major theme challenges the now commonplace presentation of Arabic letters with four positional forms. The four-form model parcels cursive Arabic letters into four variants: isolated, initial, medial, and final forms. Arabic script is necessarily cursive and contextual. Letter shapes vary in response to surrounding and nearby characters. But the range of *naskh* variation does not easily generalize into four predetermined forms. The seven-layer model suggests an alternative model of Arabic script that alters the way in which the script interfaces with technology.

Chapter 2 expands upon these themes through an exploration of Ottoman scribal practice. This is the chapter that deals most directly with questions of calligraphy. The label of "calligraphy" filters Arabic script through the qualitative lens of artistic judgment. This inadvertently downplays the communicative role of stylistic differences, and the chapter's opening section suggests design as a better analytic framework for scribal practice. Scribal choices and the diverse styles of Arabic script provide historical examples of applied graphic design. A catalog of styles follows, comparing the classical *naskh* styles of *al-aqlam al-sittah* (the six pens) to other Ottoman styles and forms. Entries identify aesthetic and design differences, as well as differences of use. All styles are illustrated by the celebrated calligrapher Mohamed Zakariya. Although the list is far from exhaustive, the selection demonstrates the range of formalized and identifiably distinct styles. A final section analyzes Ottoman scribal practice through the lens of typographic design. The collection of scribal styles is imagined as a toolbox of fonts, which are deliberately applied to textual copy. Similar design considerations inform both typography and scribal practice. Both practices align particular styles of lettering with particular types of content.

The second technological transition began with Johannes Gutenberg during the fifteenth century, and its societal effects in Europe are well documented.[9] This is the adoption, invention, and spread of movable type printing. Print played a key role in the formation of European modernity and the historical developments of capitalism, secularism, and nationalism. As mechanical reproduction and mass circulation destabilized traditional centers of textual and religious authority, the printing press interfaced with the Protestant Reformation, the European Renaissance, and the Scientific Revolution. Printed works became items of commerce, which heralded even greater changes to come. Sales of vernacular works dethroned Latin as the primary written language of European scholarship, and printed vernaculars demarcated new ethnic and national borders. None of these changes occurred overnight; they slowly blossomed from the fifteenth through the nineteenth centuries. Nevertheless, printing undoubtedly accompanied the geopolitical shift toward European ascendance. Europe's economic, political, military, and technological reach increased dramatically from the late fifteenth century onward. During the same period, historical centers of Arabic and Islamic power declined. The emirate of Granada capitulated to Christian Spain in 1492 C.E., and the tide of Ottoman expansion faltered during the seventeenth century. Unlike Christian Europe, Muslim societies did not immediately embrace movable type. Scribal modes of production maintained a position of prominence for a longer time in the Middle East, and Muslim printing did not pick up steam until the eighteenth century. Chapter 3, "European Printing and Arabic," and Chapter 4, "Print in Ottoman Lands," explore the ramifications of the print revolution for Arabic script.

Chapter 3 analyzes early attempts at printing Arabic script in Europe. The chapter opens by contrasting the printed Bible and the hand-copied Qur'an. The Bible, a cross-referential collection of texts, was quickly printed in a variety of languages and translations. Christian Protestants in particular argued that the biblical text should be made available in local vernaculars. Similar arguments of printed translation did not transfer to the Qur'an. The Qur'an is necessarily Arabic, cannot be translated, and it was carefully protected from alteration by meticulous practices of proper copying. The cursive structure of Arabic script was also problematic. Arabic script's connected cursive line needed to be parceled and segmented before it could be set as movable type. But these challenges did not prevent enterprising European printers from printing Arabic texts, including the Qur'an, in hopes of lucrative returns. Movable type abstracted cursive Arabic as a series of discrete, repeatable, and reusable forms. This process concretized the four-form model of isolated, initial, medial, and final variants as distinct metal sorts. Regularized variants benefited typesetting while greatly simplifying the formal and contextual rules of *al-khatt al-mansub*. The chapter concludes with discussion of the letter connections of cursive *naskh*. It draws a parallel between simplifications of the Arabic four-form model and THE LIMITING OF LATIN SCRIPT TO CAPITAL LETTERS. Although capitalized text remains legible, it deviates from the expected rhythm of rising and falling Latin letters. For readers accustomed to a cursive and scribal rhythm, the four-form model reduced Arabic to a similar unfamiliar and unsettling range. European printers failed to recognize Muslim and Arabic preference for handwritten script as a structural criticism of movable type's static appearance.

Chapter 4 continues with print but shifts to the Ottoman perspective. In 1727 C.E., Ottoman bureaucrats Ibrahim Müteferrika and Said Çelebi opened the first Ottoman Muslim print shop. The eighteenth-century launch of Ottoman printing appears delayed when compared to the initial innovation of Gutenberg. When compared with the rise of national presses and the deployment of printed material for state purposes, however, it aligns nicely with European developments.[10] Thus, the perceived "delay" in Arabic and Ottoman printing may have less to do with print technology per se and more to do with what was printed and how that technology operated from the fifteenth to the eighteenth century. The Müteferrika press was the first to typeset *naskh* in Ottoman lands, the first to cater to local Muslim readers, and the first to direct print in service to the Ottoman state. Yet Ottoman constituencies printed in scripts other than Arabic long before Müteferrika. The Ottoman *millets* (defined religious communities) utilized distinct scripts, and many of the *millets* practiced printing. Hebrew characters were printed in Ottoman lands before 1500 C.E., and the printing of Armenian, Greek, and Latin followed. These non-Arabic printings complicate notions that Ottoman society simply resisted print technology. In particular, the chapter targets the alleged printing bans of Sultans Bayezid II and Selim I. These unverified decrees continue to haunt discussions of delayed Ottoman printing. The chapter posits rising Ottoman power and a well-regulated scribal system as an alternative explanation. During the early centuries of print, Ottoman civilization was reaching its peak while Europe was in political and religious disarray. Ottoman administrators may not have wished to disrupt time-tested practices of textual authority already working in their favor. As Ottoman political influence began to wane, attitudes shifted, and the second half of the chapter chronicles the highly bureaucratic process of establishing the Müteferrika print shop. Müteferrika's formal petition argued that print provided a means of preserving Ottoman glory, and the press championed scientific, educational, and military modernization. Much like *al-khatt al-mansub,* movable type entered Ottoman society as an administrative and secular tool.

The third technological transition occurs in the twentieth century, as movable type printing was duly unsettled by digital production. Chapter 5, "Questions of Script Reform," and Chapter 6, "Arabic Script on Computers," straddle this technical divide. Chapter 5 plays a role similar to that of Chapter 2. It explores the legacies of the previous transition (printing) at the birth of the next (digital text). Cases of Arabic type typically contained more than five hundred metal sorts, almost double the standard number of Latin typefaces. This complicated typesetting and reduced efficiency. And the discrepancy between Latin and Arabic sorts spurred ongoing debates of Arabic script reform. Chapter 5 explores these debates in Turkey, where a new Latinate alphabet ultimately replaced *naskh* as the preferred mode of printed and written exchange, and Egypt, where a sponsored competition to simplify Arabic script reviewed multiple proposals without selecting a winner. A key argument in these presentations is that symbolic associations of Latin script with European progress and modern technology were as important as purely technical considerations. These symbolic and connotative readings of Arabic and Latin script resonate with scribal practices in which stylistic differences communicate diverse genres and functions.

For Turkish reformers, Ottoman *naskh* symbolized scribal elitism, technological stagnation, and societal decline. Latin script, in contrast, offered the sleek characters of modern communication, mass media, and technological progress. By adopting Latinate letters, Modern Turkey dramatically announced its alignment with European modernity. Reformers in the newly independent Arabic countries similarly sought the modern and symbolic benefits of new communication technologies. But they also perceived Arabic script as a symbol of local heritage, ethnic identity, and postcolonial resistance (contra both Ottoman and European power). The most successful Arabic proposals—such as Nasri Khattar's Unified Arabic Alphabet and Ahmed Lakhdar-Ghazal's Arabe Standard Voyellé-Codage Arabe (ASV-CODAR)—once again championed modern secular communications as stylistically and functionally distinct from scribal production. The chapter's final section raises the question of lithography, an alternative print technology that can accurately replicate handwritten forms. Lithography challenged movable type's reliance on discrete characters, and it was quickly adopted as a preferred method of printing Arabic script in regions without a history of movable type.[11] More significantly, lithographic printing was widely applied to printing the Qur'an. This reinscribed the visual and stylistic distinction of sacred (handwritten and lithographic) and secular (movable type) content.

Alongside debates of script reform, digital computing technologies began altering the written landscape yet again. Chapter 6 explores the digital revolution in light of Arabic script. It explains how Unicode, an international standard for encoding all the world's writing systems, handles the various characters and layers of Arabic script. Digital history, much like histories of the book and printing, implicitly builds on Latin script as the dominant model of written communication. Keyboards, like movable type, are optimally suited to writing systems with a limited number of commonly repeated elements. The one-to-one mechanical relation of characters and typewriter keys inspired numerous projects of Arabic script reform. Digital computing helped halt this trend. Computer keyboards map keys to coded sequences, and the multiple cursive variants of Arabic letters no longer required separate keys. The appropriate form is computationally selected as strings of code program the rules that link keyboard inputs to contextual outputs and variant forms. A discussion of Arabic encoding schemes—perhaps the most technical section of the book—explains the process and the particular challenges posed by Arabic script. These include the large number of Arabic variants, the contextual changes that arise from a letter's position, and right-to-left directionality (which reverses the left-to-right directionality of Latin script, as well as the dominant coding languages that employ Latin script).

Chapter 6 concludes the book with a discussion of Arabic fonts. Two case studies illustrate the design of digital Arabic script: The Khatt Foundation for Arabic Typography's 2007 Typographic Matchmaking project and DecoType's Advanced Composition Engine (ACE). Typographic Matchmaking paired teams of Dutch and Arabic designers to create Arabic script companions for Latin fonts. Digital texts circulate on the global Internet, and project participants sought aesthetic consistency across the fonts of multilingual and multiscript texts. The project shared cross-cultural typographic knowledge, extended successful Latin fonts to Unicode's block of Arabic characters, and released five new professional-quality Arabic typefaces. Typographic Matchmaking raised the prominence of Arabic design by placing it on a stage with digital Latin script. DecoType's ACE, in contrast, operates on a more abstract level of computation. It is a unique font-rendering technology modeled on careful analysis of handwritten Arabic script. ACE is not simply another Arabic font. It is a software program that reimagines how computers handle and represent Unicode characters. Most font-rendering engines connect predesigned images of character glyphs, sliding them together on a line like a digital version of movable type. ACE forgoes this method to draw the strokes of Arabic script. This allows more faithful rendering of the cursive *naskh* line and the multiple layers of Arabic script. DecoType's ACE challenges us to imagine alternative protocols of computerized text, character encoding, and script rendering.[12]

Letters of Light adopts the persistence and durability of Arabic script as its foundation. It binds scribal production, printing, and computing side by side. With each transition, new technologies reframed the appearance and role of *naskh*. All three transitions—the formalization of *al-khatt al-mansub* in the tenth century, the spread of movable type printing from the fifteenth century onward, and the rise of digital computing in the twentieth—dramatically altered the production and circulation of written content, and all three had wide-ranging societal ramifications. Yet similar questions of scribal form recycle with each turn of the wheel. And the recurrent questions are different for Arabic script than they are for Latin or any other script. Our instinctive ideas of writing are heavily colored by the writing and notational systems with which we are most familiar.[13] *Letters of Light* looks beyond the Latin alphabet to open new vistas. It touches on questions of graphic design, Islamic art, the cultural history of the Middle East, technology studies, linguistics, language reform, and computer history. These diverse threads are woven together in a new synthesis of Arabic script history. In doing so, the work draws heavily on secondary sources, which are reanalyzed through the lens of comparative media. The author encourages further studies drawn from the primary archive. All the scribes, designers, printers, technologists, and other characters introduced in the book deserve more careful and nuanced examination. All too often, examples of Arabic script are generalized in global studies of communication and media. If parts of *Letters of Light* are guilty of the same, it is my hope that the holistic approach will push back equally against earlier generalizations. This book champions both the continued relevance of Arabic script in our digital world and the reinsertion of non-Latin scripts into global histories of communication.

The third and final technological transition discussed in the book continues to unfold around us. Digital text and technology influence all corners of the world, and few places have been more rapidly affected than the Middle East. The twenty-first century has seen Middle Eastern social media revolutions, incredible urban development in the Persian Gulf, the rise of global Arabic media networks, and new waves of Islamic thought. These developments intersect with new media forms and novel digital designs. The study of Arabic script sheds useful light on current debates, precisely because Arabic and

Islam remain pertinent to so many global issues. As Arabic letters adapt to new messages, new landscapes, and new technologies, they invite us to reconsider the history of communication and reimagine its possibilities. The future of media will arise in dialogue with changing theories of language, script, and representation.[14] *Letters of Light* contributes to this endeavor by approaching Arabic script writ large. It introduces the script to scholars of media and book history who are more familiar with European and non-Arabic contexts. And it invites Arabic specialists to cross the disciplinary and topical boundaries of calligraphy, printing, and digital design. Students of scribal culture and calligraphic practice can compare these realms with developments in Arabic printing. Likewise, those examining the societal effect of print can reconsider those changes alongside preceding scribal shifts and subsequent digital ones. And scholars, designers, and technologists of the digital era can explore the long tail of Arabic script in earlier media.

Digital fonts, printed sorts, and handwritten scripts all stand together on the contemporary stage of written communication. Multiple forms of writing and script coexist and interact. As we stretch the digital canvas even further, we have a unique opportunity to reclaim lost practices. Developing font technologies facilitate the accurate representations of scribal forms and non-Latin scripts better than ever before. We can now begin a typographic reading of scribal practice and a scribal-informed approach to digital type. The diverse histories of script usefully inform the texts that remain unknown to us, the yet-to-be-discovered futures of writing. Digital script can adopt an overwhelming number of styles through the simple selections of a drop-down menu. More and more users than ever before have a favorite font, and coders and designers are increasingly working with foreign and unfamiliar character sets. How these changes will be written and represented in future communications is yet to be seen. We cannot predict where letters and scripts will go next, but we can study where they have been. Light, as a metaphor for knowledge, shines through the form of written characters. In our digital age, that light continues to shines forth from monitors and digital screens. This book is dedicated to those who will give shape to the future letters of light, with their path illuminated by the past.

Chapter One

The Layers of Proportional *Naskh*

*I*n 936 C.E., the vizier Ibn Muqlah lost his hand to political enemies. The Abbasid vizier would later be celebrated as the father of Arabic calligraphy. Some accounts report that he tied a reed pen to the stump of his right hand; others say that he began to write with his left. Still, his enemies hounded him. Ibn Muqlah's possessions were confiscated, his tongue was removed, and he died under house arrest, unaware of the recognition he would later receive. Ibn Muqlah is now remembered as the official who standardized Arabic script. He devised a proportional system for the geometric construction and measurement of Arabic letters. The new system laid the foundation for a lasting tradition of Arabic and Islamic calligraphy, and it continues to inform the design of Arabic fonts in our digital age. The import and strength of Ibn Muqlah's proportional system—or at least the system attributed to him—are undeniable. Despite his political difficulties, the vizier left a lasting mark on the shape of Arabic script: "It was poured upon his hand, just as it was revealed to the bees how to make the cells of their honeycombs hexagonal."[1]

Ibn Muqlah's new system of writing, *al-khatt al-mansub,* was a technological and geometric breakthrough. It formalized *naskh* as a genre of proportionally identifiable styles, and it set the stage for a robust tradition of Arabic calligraphy. But the initial innovation was more prosaic than artistic. *Al-khatt al-mansub* produced formal stylistic variants, much akin to the collection of fonts that populates digital devices. Differences of proportional style, like choices of font, dress a text for an intended audience. Thus, the typeface used for the current book subtly conveys an air of academic austerity; it does not resemble the letters used in children's books. The application of handwritten styles operates similarly. Differences of proportion, size, and appearance indicate the genre, audience, or function of a text. Visual traits signify the origin of a written message or the intellectual genealogy of its author. Specific styles of Arabic script marked political administrations, and new styles marked their successors. The proportional system of Ibn Muqlah—a system for which he lost his hand and ultimately died—formalized styles of *naskh* as communicative vehicles.

Styles of Arabic Script

In the tenth century, Ibn al-Nadim ambitiously cataloged "the books of all peoples, Arab and foreign, existing in the language of the Arabs, as well as of their scripts."[2] His *Kitab al-Fihrist* references thousands of texts—many of which have since been lost—listing authors, titles, genres, brief descriptions, and sometimes specific bibliographic information, such as the size or the number of pages. Ibn al-Nadim prefaces his grand bibliography with a discussion of scripts and notational systems. An introductory section presents at least sixteen different systems of writing. These include scripts used for Syriac, Persian, Hebrew, Greek, Chinese, and Russian. The Latin alphabet is mentioned as the script of the Lombards, Saxons, and Franks. The various scripts are differentiated according to the direction of writing, the form and types of characters, and the tools of inscription. Nadim discusses diverse methods of sharpening writing implements, compares the Arabic reed pen with the brushes of Chinese scribes, and weighs the affordances of various substrates: clay, papyrus, parchment, and paper. Although scripts are organized according to nation, emphasis falls on stylistic differences of design and use rather than language. Every writing system, or script, is a collection of subscripts, or styles, and unique styles are further specified according to appearance, function, and technology.

Ibn al-Nadim constructs a typology of stylistic variation. He lists well over twenty varieties of Arabic script; three forms of Syriac; seven styles of Persian; and at least three styles of Greek script. Greek scribes in Abbasid Baghdad, for example, employed one style for sacred scripture, another style for official correspondence, and a third style—a specialized shorthand reserved for "kings and the most eminent scribes"—for quick transcription.[3] Ibn al-Nadim presents each of these stylistic differences as communicatively significant. Arabic script is presented with even greater, and more specific, variety. In one particularly detailed passage concerning styles of script, Ibn al-Nadim writes:

> Among [the Arabic scripts] there is a style called Ashriyah, derived from the Sijillat al-Awsat handwriting. With it are written emancipations of slaves and sales of land and houses and other things. Among them is a style called the Mufattah, sprung from the Thaqil al-Nisf. The Mumsak style, with which they write on the half-size sheets, is derived from it. Three styles grow out of it: a style called the Mudawwar al-Kabir, which the scribes of this period call the Ri'asi and which is written on the half-size sheets; also derived from it is a style called the Mudawwar al-Saghir, a general-utility script with which are written records, traditions, and poems; and a style called Khafif al-Thuluth al-Kabir. It is written on the half-size sheets, being derived from Khafif al-Nisf al-Thaqil. From it there springs a style called the Riqa', which is derived from Khafif al-Thuluth al-Kabir and with which are written signed edicts and similar things.[4]

To modern readers, the specificity is shocking. And for current purposes, the specific names are less important than the fact that the author takes time to list them. Ibn al-Nadim expects reader familiarity with the diverse implications of stylistic variation. Styles of script indicate particular uses and different genres of written messages. Styles are classified into families of common origin, they differentiate according to function, and they relate to particular sizes of paper. This detailed typology highlights the complex scribal milieu in which Ibn al-Nadim circulated. The style of Arabic script operated as a secondary code, alongside textual content. Through the choice of style, scribes could "connote professional or social attitudes beyond the mere content of his or her message. . . . The *type* and *size* of a script and its amount of diacritics become an important manifestation of the sender's attitude towards the addressee."[5] Scribes write for different reasons, for different audiences, and with different tools. Reporting from within that milieu, Ibn al-Nadim sees no reason why they should therefore share a common style of script.

The contemporary parallel to Ibn al-Nadim's multiple styles is the digital font. Although fonts partake of a common alphabet, they carry distinct histories, imply distinct meanings, and indicate distinct roles. If Ibn al-Nadim were to examine the textual possibilities of a modern computer, he would likely be fascinated by the sheer variety of fonts. A single machine can display any number of writing systems and scripts, from Arabic to Chinese to Hebrew to Armenian to Latin. Narrowing the focus to the Latin alphabet and written English, Ibn al-Nadim might first note the twenty-six letters of the alphabet. He would then discuss the directionality of the writing: a progression of characters that flow from left to right and lines that run from top to bottom. And he would comment on methods of input, for example, typing as the movement of the fingers across the keys and how this differs from handwriting with a pen. Ibn al-Nadim might be pleasantly surprised that the visual space of the screen does not limit the number of words or the scope of the text. He would reserve his greatest fascination, however, for the sheer number of fonts. Ibn al-Nadim would painstakingly list each font, including italic and bold varieties, alongside guidelines for their proper use: the serifs of Times New Roman are said to assist the reading of printed passages, Helvetica works well for titles and text at a distance, Verdana is primarily a screen font, Comic Sans detracts from the seriousness of a message, and so forth. Modern texts are written for a variety of purposes. And Ibn al-Nadim would see no reason why they should therefore share a common font.

Styles of script, like fonts, are material artifacts. They have shape, size, color, and texture. Differences in style, appearance, and form help readers navigate the written landscape. This is as true today as it was in the tenth century. Arabic scribal practices deliberately employed the communicative potential of material and aesthetic variation. For early Islamic writers, the primary example is the separation of Qur'anic copies from all other writings. If the Qur'an is ontologically different from other texts, then it should look, feel, and operate differently than other writings.[6] The primary distinction separating sacred and secular content occurs time and again with Arabic script. Hieratic styles are repeatedly contrasted with secular styles of administrative decree and everyday communication. In the manuscript era, differences of pen, style, and form separated the two channels. The Arabic term for a Qur'anic copy, *mushaf* (plural: *masahif*), specifically references its codex form.[7] The codex form distinguished Qur'anic *masahif* from other texts, which commonly were written on scrolls. Early *masahif* were further distinguished by both the scale and the shape of the letters. Qur'anic styles were larger than other styles, and the size of the text was emblematic of its status. During the era of print, the sacred-secular distinction became a technological one. Handwritten *masahif* distinguished the Qur'an from secular printed works. The Qur'an was not printed by an Islamic administration until the nineteenth century, four centuries after printing of the Bible and well over a century after Islamic authorities first deployed print for secular purposes. Visual and technological practices separating sacred and secular content continued well into the twentieth century. In 1938, Abdullah Yusuf Ali published what would become one of the most popular English translations of the Qur'anic text.[8] Whereas the English translation is printed with movable type, the Arabic text reproduces the handwritten calligraphy of Pir Abdul Hamid with photolithography. The handwritten line distinguishes the Arabic copy as something unique and beautiful. And that uniqueness is doubly lost in translation: the translation from Arabic to English and the translation from handwritten style to movable type.

The visual distinction of Qur'anic styles from other varieties of writing was already common by Ibn al-Nadim's time. The *Fihrist* dedicates an entire section to identifying and classifying styles of script suitable for copying the Qur'an.[9] In the seventh century, when Umayyad caliph Abd al-Malik famously replaced iconographic imagery on Umayyad coins and monuments with religious and Arabic phrases, the distinction began to blur. Although Abd al-Malik's script-only designs were visually novel, the move was initially criticized. Religious scholars frowned on the use of Arabic script on political currency.[10] Muslims and non-Muslims alike could handle coins inscribed with Qur'anic phrases, which challenged the purity expected of religious text.[11] By employing Arabic as a political marker, Abd al-Malik undercut the visual and stylistic distinction between sacred and secular authority. The implicit problem—how to differentiate sacred and secular content—was answered by a design solution: stylistic variety. Specific styles and formalized design templates insulated Qur'anic copies from secular texts. The basic stylistic distinction bifurcated Arabic script into two categories, *Kufic* and *naskh*. The former grouping displays solidity and formality; the latter displays more cursive fluidity. Although the two categories are overly generalized, their visual distinction signals a much deeper current of stylistic and visual variation.

The hieratic *Kufic* styles appear rigid, stately, and bold. They emphasize geometric structure and horizontal extension: "slow-moving and dignified, exacting in their application and requiring skill to read, they bore the connotation of eternity and visually defined Islam's perception of the holy book."[12] The category name derives from the city of Kufa, which became famous for the early beauty and precision of its Qur'anic script. Ibn al-Nadim associates a number of early styles with the city or locale in which they were written.[13] Pairing stylistic differences with the names of localities may also have allowed early Muslim readers to gauge the provenance of Qur'anic *masahif* with which they came into contact. Ibn al-Nadim specifically identifies the Makkah (Meccan) script through its *alif* (which bends slightly to the left).[14] But the fame of *Kufic* script won out, and the name now labels a wide category of overtly geometric, decorative, and bold-shaped Arabic styles. The *naskh* styles, in contrast, display slimmer lines and the gestural trace of handwritten flow. Their fluid cursivity enabled the quick and efficient transcription of spoken content, as well as multiple copies of bureaucratic texts. By the end of the first Islamic century, *naskh* styles had branched in a variety of distinct usages and appearances. When Ibn al-Nadim describes more than twenty recognizable styles of Arabic script, the vast majority are soundly bureaucratic: a script for economic transactions and sales of land, scripts of correspondence from caliph to emirs in outlying regions, scripts used for exchanges between kings of equal stature, and so on.[15] Further examples are plentiful.[16] A specialized chancellery cursive, with thin lines and elongated verticals, indicated correspondence between regional governors and bureaucratic record keepers. Slightly thicker characters indicated bilingual notifications. And a separate protocol style displayed multiple letter variants, irregular letter connections, and a high degree of abbreviation. Protocols circulated within a highly selective circle in which both readers and writers shared familiarity with idiosyncrasies of style and content. Abbreviations and irregularities designed protocol styles as intentionally cryptic. For those outside the intended circle, the difficulty of the text protected against misuse and forgery.

Functional differences were further reinforced by material differences. Styles were related to the size of the pen and the size of the sheet on which they were written. Grand pronouncements were written with broad pens on large sheets; less prominent correspondence employed thinner pens, small sheets, and more condensed layouts. The largest of the standard Arabic writing sheets was *tumar,* which measured roughly 74 by 110 centimeters, and the grandest of the pens was *qalam al-tumar* (the pen of *tumar*).[17] During the Umayyad caliphate (661–750 C.E.), *tumar* specified decrees issued directly by the caliph. The prominent display of large characters and broad strokes, as well as the sizable expenditure of parchment on which they were written, communicated the grand stature of these decrees. *Tumar*'s political importance established it as the base measure by which smaller sheets of paper and, by extension, smaller pens were measured. The size of the sheet influenced the size of the pen, the size of the pen influenced the line width, and the line width introduced stylistic variation. *Thuluth,* which went on to become one of the most famous of the *naskh* styles, translates as "one-third." The name derives from the size of the *thuluth* pen, which measures one-third the width of the *tumar* pen.

By the Abbasid period (750–1250 C.E.), stylistic differences had solidified into distinct communities of practice: religious scholars, chancery scribes, and professional copyists. Qur'anic copying was the most conservative. It emphasized precise preservation and strove to protect the Qur'anic revelation from alteration or abrogation. Qur'anic *masahif* were inscribed by religious scholars deeply familiar with Qur'anic content, and the design was highly codified. *Masahif* pages were oriented horizontally (what we now call "landscape" orientation) and displayed an odd number of lines per page. The size of the text box was fixed across pages. A consistent ratio of length to height (for example, 3:2) preserved consistency throughout any given copy. Text boxes divided into three or five lines of writing per page, and the lines were subdivided by a series of interlines. Spacing of the interlines, in turn, was determined by the size of the pen. The resulting relationship ensured that letter size remained consistent throughout the text. Proportions of page width to page height, subdivided by line and spaced by interlines, created a formalized template.[18] The system appears to have been deliberately created to visually and materially signify the uniqueness of the Qur'an. It does not resemble the textual formats employed for other religious traditions.[19] The formalized design of Qur'anic *masahif* set them apart from all other texts, both sacred and profane.

A separate scribal community answered textual demands of the Abbasid state. Chancery scribes recorded official correspondence and administrative decrees. Notably, however, Abbasid scribes did not employ the grand Umayyad style of *tumar*. Instead, the Abbasid chancery adopted a new style of highly cursive *tawqi'* style as the signature script of official pronouncements. *Tawqi'* visually distinguished the new dynasty from earlier *tumar* texts of the displaced Umayyad. Stylistic differences signified competing channels of political authority, just as a broader visual distinction separated religious authority from temporal authority. Professional copyists composed a third community of scribes. These writers were neither religious copyists nor chancery scribes. They transcribed the words of poets and scholars, translated foreign works, and generally served as secretaries for hire. Like members of other communities, the professional copyists employed distinctive styles of Arabic script. These copyist bookhand styles may have emerged from the chancery, but they evolved to copy a wide range of texts. They were functional styles and did not represent specific political affiliations. The bookhand styles strove for legibility. They were less geometric and less formalized than *Kufic* varieties and would go on to become the general category of *naskh* styles of script.[20]

As multiple styles of script circulated side by side, the Abbasid era witnessed an unparalleled explosion of writing. More texts were written and shared than ever before. And paper provided the technological infrastructure that allowed this to occur. Islamic sources apocryphally trace the arrival of paper to the capture of Chinese prisoners in Central Asia. By 751 C.E., papers mills were operating in Islamic Samarkand, and Baghdadi paper production began during the legendary reign of Harun al-Rashid. By the end of the ninth century, papermaking was booming in Baghdad, and the Abbasid administration adopted paper for its official record keeping and correspondence.[21] Less than a century later, the Baghdad library housed well over ten thousand volumes, from administrative records to literature and scientific reports. A similar scale of written production did not occur in Europe until the sixteenth century, more than one hundred years after the spread of printing. Paper drastically reorganized Islamic scholarly practice. And Abbasid Baghdad may have been the first place in history where an individual could survive, and be paid, as an independent author.[22]

Paper provided an effectively limitless surface for writing, and the abundance of space allowed scholars and artists to experiment with new notational systems and spatial representations, including mathematics, maps, mechanical diagrams, star charts, and biological illustrations.[23] Earlier writing surfaces were much more limited. The heaviness and fragility of clay limited its portability. Papyrus, another option, was brittle, prone to cracking, and imported from Egypt. Its cultivation ebbed and flowed with the agricultural cycles of the unpredictable Nile. A third option, parchment, was expensive due to the limited availability of animal hides and their high demand for a number of uses, from clothing to armor to roofing to storage. Paper provided the best of multiple worlds. It was portable, durable, and much more economical than other options. And it could be locally sourced and produced from linen and scrap, thereby saving animal hides for other uses. As a result, book culture flourished, literacy increased, and the level of scholarly exchange was elevated. The explosion of paper surfaces meant that more texts could circulate, more readers could read them, and more scribes could write them. The results would have lasting effects on the written grammar of Arabic script and *naskh* styles in particular.

The Layers of Arabic Script

The stylistic variation of Arabic script built on a common foundation. Although styles remained visually and recognizably distinct, they shared similar features. These similarities—the common features that unite a writing system across styles—can be labeled "script grammar."[24] If linguistic grammars are the structures formed by linguistic elements to convey meaningful messages, script grammars are the consistent structures formed by written elements to represent meaningful messages.[25] Visual marks must be differentiated and recognized as different before they can be read as meaningful. Certain visual differences— those of script grammar—denote linguistic differences. Other visual differences connote meaning. Stylistic varieties modify and tweak script grammar according to genre, audience, and role. In order to appreciate how diverse styles of Arabic script function communicatively, it is necessary to establish a shared basis of Arabic script grammar.

The primary unit of script grammar is the grapheme: the smallest unit of semantically relevant visual difference. In alphabets and *abjads,* like Arabic script, graphemes are often—but not necessarily—letters. Arabic letters are differentiated through the use of horizontal, vertical, and rounded strokes, as well as the later addition of dots placed above and below the primary forms. Strokes and dots combine to form the Arabic *abjad* of twenty-eight letters. Unlike an alphabet, an *abjad* does not contain vowels, although three Arabic letters—*alif, wāw,* and *yā'*—play a dual role as both consonants and long vowels. The Arabic character set also includes a few special shapes: the *lām-alif* ligature, which combines the separate letters *lām* and *alif* into a unique ligature; the *hamza* sign, which represents a phonemic glottal stop; and the *tā' marbutah,* a word ending that signifies feminine nouns. Additionally, a collection of optional *tashkil* marks represent vocalization. Arabic script grammar governs the arrangement of these various visual components. It stipulates that characters run from right to left, that letters connect cursively, and that those letters connect in a particular way.

Within a word, most Arabic letters share cursive connections with both preceding and following letters. But six letters connect only with the preceding
letter—they do not cursively connect with the following letter. As a result, visual spaces can occur within words as well as between them.

The isolated form of a letter is a rather rare occurrence in written Arabic.
The cursivity of the script connects letters into shared shapes or letter
blocks. A letter block consists of at least one, but usually a number of graphemes, strung together without a visible break. Since spaces occasionally
occur after letter graphemes, an individual word may consist of one, two, or
more letter blocks.[26] More importantly, the specific shape of an Arabic letter
will vary according to its position within a block. Arabic letters adopt different forms in the beginning, the medial, and the end of letter blocks. However, the common presentation of Arabic letters in a table of four forms—
isolated, initial, medial, and final variants—is somewhat misleading. (See
Figure 1.1.)

The four variants shift in response to specific connections and surrounding
letters. Cursive letter connections subtly influence the connecting forms. For
example, four-form letter tables display the medial form as a static shape in isolation, despite the fact that the medial form—by definition—never occurs in
isolation. The medial form is highly contingent upon the letters and forms that
precede and follow it. Many Arabic letters display multiple variants in the medial
position, and the type of connection may alter from letter to letter. In handwritten
Arabic script, multiple instances of the letter *jīm* stack vertically; Arabic script
grammar both allows and proscribes the vertical connection of subsequent
jīm. The four-form model, in contrast, provides a single shape for medial *jīm*.
It suggests that multiple instances of *jīm* connect horizontally along a shared
baseline rather than stacking vertically. As we will see in later chapters, the
horizontal consistency implied by the four-form model benefited technologies
of print. But it inaccurately represents the script grammar of handwritten
Arabic. We might even go so far as to say that the table of four variants was a
printer's aid, which has retroactively come to define the script.

Within a letter block, individual Arabic letters may connect horizontally or
vertically. Additional marks are then layered above and below this primary line.
The layering of signs constructs a two-dimensional space of meaningful relationships. Arabic script expands outward from the primary ductus, and readers
navigate both the line of primary text and the applied layers of additional sig-

English Name	Isolated	Final	Medial	Initial
alif	ا	ﺎ	ﺎ	ا
bā'	ب	ﺐ	ﺒ	ﺑ
tā'	ت	ﺖ	ﺘ	ﺗ
thā'	ث	ﺚ	ﺜ	ﺛ
jīm	ج	ﺞ	ﺠ	ﺟ
ḥā'	ح	ﺢ	ﺤ	ﺣ
khā'	خ	ﺦ	ﺨ	ﺧ
dāl	د	ﺪ	ﺪ	د
dhāl	ذ	ﺬ	ﺬ	ذ
rā'	ر	ﺮ	ﺮ	ر
zā'	ز	ﺰ	ﺰ	ز
sīn	س	ﺲ	ﺴ	ﺳ
shīn	ش	ﺶ	ﺸ	ﺷ
ṣād	ص	ﺺ	ﺼ	ﺻ
ḍād	ض	ﺾ	ﻀ	ﺿ
ṭā'	ط	ﻂ	ﻄ	ﻃ
ẓā'	ظ	ﻆ	ﻈ	ﻇ
'ayn	ع	ﻊ	ﻌ	ﻋ
ghayn	غ	ﻎ	ﻐ	ﻏ
fā'	ف	ﻒ	ﻔ	ﻓ
qāf	ق	ﻖ	ﻘ	ﻗ
kāf	ك	ﻚ	ﻜ	ﻛ
lām	ل	ﻞ	ﻠ	ﻟ
mīm	م	ﻢ	ﻤ	ﻣ
nūn	ن	ﻦ	ﻨ	ﻧ
hā'	ه	ﻪ	ﻬ	ﻫ
wāw	و	ﻮ	ﻮ	و
yā'	ي	ﻲ	ﻴ	ﻳ

Figure 1.1. The four-form model of Arabic script

This common presentation of Arabic letters shows each letter with four forms: initial, medial, final, and isolated. The Arabic *abjad* has twenty-eight letters, each of which changes shape according to its position within a cursive letter block. (Table produced in Adobe Creative Suite, with the help of Unicode.)

nificance. Layers of script wrap around one another like skins of an onion. First, primary letterforms are strung together in a series of letter blocks running from right to left. This is known as *rasm*. Next, *i'jaam* (typically *nuqta,* or dots) are placed above or below the primary line of *rasm*. These two layers (*rasm* plus *i'jaam*) represent letters, and both layers are required for the visual presentation of contemporary Arabic script. The additional layers are optional. They represent vowels and vocalization, recitational cues, and even decorative motifs. Their presence or absence depends on a document's genre, its expected audience, and its textual role. Educational texts, for instance, are more likely to include vowel markings. And contemporary Qur'anic *masahif* often contain full vocalization, including the highly specific cantillation marks that guide Qur'anic recitation. In a careful examination of Arabic script grammar, type designer and script historian Thomas Milo identified seven distinct layers. (See Figure 1.2.) The layers move from the center outward.

1. *Rasm.* These shapes compose the skeleton script over which other layers are applied. Higher layers flesh out *rasm;* they provide body, specificity, and personality. Milo labels these shapes "archigraphemes," the foundational structures on which graphemes are built.[27] Although the Arabic *abjad* consists of twenty-eight letters, the script contains only fourteen archigraphemes. Classes of letters share the same archigraphemic form. The *bā'* class (the letters *bā'* and *tā'* and *thā'*) share a similar *rasm;* the *jīm* class (the letters *jīm* and *ḥā'* and *khā'*) share another. Moving beyond the Arabic language, other languages that adopted the script (for example, Ottoman Turkish, Farsi, and Urdu) often created new letters. But no new *rasm* were ever introduced; all new letters modified the basic set of seventeen archigraphemic forms. The skeleton script therefore supports expansion to cover any language, but it also limits the way in which expansion can occur.[28] The capacity to generate new consonants maintains visual stability across drastically different languages.[29]

2. *I'jaam.* These forms identify and specify graphemes that share a single *rasm.* For the Arabic language, they consist of *nuqta,* or dots, placed above or below the skeleton script. The addition of *i'jaam* is known as letter pointing (much like dotting the lowercase English letter i). In the *bā'* class, for example, the letter *bā'* points one *nuqta* below the basic

Layer 1: The *rasm* shapes of the skeleton script.

Layer 2: *I'jaam* (*nuqta*) specify consonants.

Layer 3: *Shaddah* marks consonant doubling.

Layer 4: *Tashkil* indicate vowels.

Layer 5: Cantillation marks specify precise verbalization.

Layer 6: *Muhmal* prevent erroneous copying.

Layer 7: Ornamentation balances the composition.

Figure 1.2.   Seven-layer model of Arabic script

Arabic script expands outward from the skeleton script *(rasm)* in layers of significance and specificity. The light gray marks indicate the new signs at each layer. In current practice, layers 1 and 2 are required, while the higher layers (3–7) are optional. (Image courtesy of Thomas Milo.)

rasm; the letter *tā'* points two *nuqta* above the *rasm;* and the letter *thā'* points three *nuqta* in a triangular shape above the *rasm. I'jaam* modify the archigraphemes of layer 1 in order to specify unique graphemes. They enable the Arabic *abjad* to build twenty-eight graphemic letters from seventeen archigraphemic forms. And the same seventeen forms can expand to cover new letters and other languages as necessary. Non-Arabic languages may layer additional *nuqta,* compose new combinations of *nuqta,* or recruit small versions of *rasm* shapes as *i'jaam.* Urdu, for example, expands the *bā'* class of letters to represent the sound of a heavy "t" (which is not present in spoken Arabic). The Urdu alphabet forms the new letter *ṭe* by pointing a small form of the letter *tā'* above the *rasm* shape of *bā'.*

In current practice, both layers 1 and 2 are required for Arabic script to be considered complete and legible.[30] And the majority of modern texts consist solely of these two layers. Abbasid *masahif* of the seventh and eighth century, however, rarely included *i'jaam.* They were inscribed only with *rasm* and targeted a highly specific audience of Qur'anic scholars. Readers were expected to be familiar enough with the text to identify unpointed letters from context. All the *rasm* forms of layer 1 appear in early Qur'anic copies, and no new forms developed once letters began receiving *i'jaam* (layer 2).[31] *I'jaam* provided a flexible system for constructing new letters without adding to or modifying the seventeen basic shapes. Modern texts—including modern *masahif*—always display *i'jaam* and *rasm.* And modern alphabets unite the two layers as graphemic letters. Indeed, Unicode encodes *rasm* and *i'jaam* together as complete graphemes; it does not specify unmarked *rasm* as distinct characters. The remaining layers (layers 3–7) are encoded separately. These forms modify graphemic letters, and they remain optional.

3. *Tashkil: shaddah.* Layers 3 and 4 guide the phonetic vocalization of Arabic script, and they are collectively referred to as *tashkil.* In Milo's model, layer 3 consists of a single mark, the w-shaped *shaddah* (which was originally derived from a miniature version of the *rasm* shape for the letter *sīn*). The *shaddah* indicates consonant gemination, or doubling, and it appears above the grapheme it modifies. Not all Arabic words contain the *shaddah,* but it is the only *tashkil* that may appear alone (without any other *tashkil*). When *shaddah* is present, it modifies

the placement of *tashkil* (specifically *kasrah*) in layer 4. It therefore warrants its own layer of analysis.

4. *Tashkil.* This layer consists of a variety of signs including the short vowels, or *harakat* (*fathah, dammah, kasrah,* and *sukun*), and the *tanwin,* which combine *harakat* with a final nunnation. All *tashkil,* except *kasrah* and its corresponding *tanwin,* are placed above the mark they describe; *kasrah* is placed below. Typically, *tashkil* respond to the graphemic forms of layers 1 and 2, appearing above or below the letters they modify. In the rare case of *kasrah* modifying the *shaddah, kasrah* is placed directly below the *shaddah,* which is itself located above the grapheme. Thus, the *kasrah* falls between the *shaddah* and the line of letters.

5. Cantillation (precise verbalization). This layer also contains *tashkil,* but Milo separates it due to its rarity and precision. It includes highly specific signs such as *maddah, alif khanjariya* (the dagger *alif*), and *waslah.* These rare marks serve primarily to guide Qur'anic recitation. They are identified as a separate layer because most vocalized texts do not contain them. Texts containing layer 5 tend to play a different, elevated, or much more precise role compared to texts in which they are absent.

6. *Muhmal.* This layer plays a protective and redundant role. Rather than providing new information per se, it blocks the erroneous placement of future *i'jaam.* For many classes of *rasm,* the unpointed form indicates one letter and the addition of *i'jaam* indicates other letters (for example, *dāl* and *dhāl, sīn* and *shīn, 'ayn* and *ghayn, ṣād* and *ḍād,* etc.). The unmarked letters are *muhmal,* and layer 6 prevents the later addition of *nuqta* or other *i'jaam* that alter their meaning and pronunciation. A miniature version of isolated *rasm* inserted below the main text blocks unwanted pointing. This both confirms the identity of the unmarked letter and prevents the addition of unwarranted *i'jaam* in later copies. The redundancy of layer 6 also prevents stains and paper defects from being read as part of the text. Protection from textual drift was particularly important in transmission of the Qur'an and the copying of *masahif.* In the displayed example, the unmarked letters *sīn* and *ḥā'* are confirmed by miniature forms of the same letters placed below the words in which they occur.

7. Ornamentation. Layer 7 consists of visual elements that fill spatial holes and decorate a text. Although these marks do not play a linguistic role, they support aesthetic communication. In rich calligraphic pieces, visual composition and balance are as important as the presentation of words. The marks of layer 7 may formally balance a composition or beautify its presentation. They are included only in the most decorative and dramatic presentations of Arabic script. But within the realm of calligraphic art, they are quite common.

The final number of layers in a given text depends on context, role, and intended audience. Most messages contain only the first few layers, just as the most common sentences share similar words. Yet just as linguistic grammar guides even the rarest of words, Arabic script grammar guides the interaction of all seven layers. Higher layers build logically on lower layers. Most contemporary texts contain only layers 1 and 2.[32] The presence of all seven layers signifies a highly structured piece of visual communication, and fewer layers are the norm. Interestingly, Qur'anic *masahif* provide the most common examples of both the fewest and the most layers. Early Abbasid *masahif* display only the *rasm* of layer 1. As noted, readers were expected to be familiar enough with the text to identify unpointed letters from context. As *masahif* spread to less specialized audiences, many of whom were not native Arabic speakers, the higher layers evolved to facilitate recitation and prevent copyist errors.[33] Most contemporary *masahif* display layers 1 through 6. Early Qur'anic *masahif* addressed to a specialist audience contain a single layer of script; for more recent copies, the audience is unknown, and every effort must be made to protect the text from misreading and erroneous copying.

The layered model of Arabic script breaks the standardized presentation of the four-form model into a collection of contingent signs. Stephen Houston has warned against the synoptic fallacy in which a writing system that develops historically comes to be seen as synchronically fixed and unchanging.[34] Arabic script, like all writing systems, altered in response to new technologies and new practices of writing. Over time, new layers were added and modified. The lowest layers of *rasm* are traceable to the earliest stone inscriptions, and the higher layers developed later. Ibn al-Nadim credits the trio of Muramir ibn Murra, Aslam ibn Sidra, and Amir ibn Jadra as the first to compose in Arabic script. According to his account—which is anecdotal rather than historical—layers 1 and 2 were present at the birth of the script, but different individuals designed them: Muramir designed the forms, Aslam formalized the cursive connections, and Amir contributed *i'jaam*.[35] Ibn al-Nadim's anecdotal account emphasizes the forms of Arabic script as invented and designed technologies. And like all technologies, the script adapted and developed over time. The addition of vocalization (layers 3 through 5) responded to the wide-scale adoption of paper, and the visual compositions of layer 7 accompany the formalization of calligraphic technique as an art of display.

The earliest attempts at vocalization (layers 3 and 4) began as colored dots rather than distinct shapes. Tradition attributes the practice to Umayyad grammarian Abul Aswad al-Duali (d. 688), who noticed that habits of spoken Arabic were changing. Al-Duali worried that this observed linguistic drift would affect the orally recited Qur'an and traditions of the Prophet Muhammad, which would no longer be properly understood. To rectify the situation, al-Duali located a scribe and began to recite. He instructed the scribe to place a colored dot above the letters he vocalized with an open mouth, a colored dot on top of the letters he vocalized through a closed mouth, and a colored dot below the letters he vocalized through puckered lips. Colored ink visually disassociated the vocalization marks from the primary text, assuring that they would be understood as helpful additions rather than abrogation of the original. Colored vocalization dots were opposed to the darker brown and black inks of *rasm*.[36] However, the practice required at least two inks and separate pens for each color. Dotting on top of a letter also demanded two passes: colored dots could be applied only after the base script had already dried.

The eighth-century polymath al-Khalil Ibn Ahmad al-Farahidi (d. 786) took it upon himself to address the issue.[37] He replaced differentiation by color with differences of shape and position. Al-Duali's colored dots were discarded, and al-Khalil designed a new collection of vocalization signs. These signs, which would become layers 3 through 6, included the *harakat* for short vowels, the *hamza*, the *tanwin*, cantillation marks, and the marking of unpointed *muhmal* letters. In order to preserve visual consistency, al-Khalil derived his new signs from miniature versions of the seventeen *rasm* forms. Thus, *shaddah* resembles a tailless *sīn*, *damma* derives from the shape of *wāw*, the *hamza* resembles a tailless *'ayn*, and the *muhmal* markings replicate isolated *rasm* at a smaller scale. These new vocalization marks were often written with a finer pen in order to preserve visual contrast and maintain separation from *rasm*. The new signs accompanied the spread of paper and the explosion of stylistic variety in the tenth century. Initially, they appeared only in nonreligious writings.[38] The copying of Qur'anic *masahif* remained more conservative and did not include them. But paper placed Qur'anic *masahif* before new eyes and unspecialized audiences. Al-Khalil's vocalization marks were adopted as useful educational supports, and the outer layers of Arabic script came to be seen as protective devices. This combination of technological change—changes to the substrate on which writing occurred (paper) and visual changes (the addition of new layers)—drastically reorganized Arabic scribal and scholarly practices. The *naskh* styles, which utilized the new layers, became increasingly common, while *Kufic* styles that eschewed them fell out of favor.

A Triad of Scribal Innovation

The tide of change leads back to vizier Ibn Muqlah. Despite the loss of his hand, the vizier drastically altered the construction and appearance of *naskh.* Tradition honors Ibn Muqlah as the inventor of *al-khatt al-mansub,* a new system of proportional script design. Under the new system, styles of script could be compared, classified, and analyzed according to proportional relationships. The new system did not add new layers of script grammar. Instead, it described and measured the shape of *rasm. Al-khatt al mansub* placed the formal variety of the *naskh* styles on a geometric foundation. Styles became recognizable types much akin to the variety of digital fonts that we employ today. Two other notable scribes, Ibn al-Bawwab and Yaqut al-Musta'simi, further extended the system. Although the exact contributions of all three scribes remain under debate, each serves as a symbolic and mnemonic stand-in for a significant shift in *naskh* design. By the end of the Abbasid era, this triad of scribes established the foundation of an immensely rich and abiding calligraphic tradition.

The career of Abu Ali Muhammad Ibn Muqlah, who died in 940 C.E., reads like the plot of a political thriller. Beginning as a tax collector, he climbed the ranks of the Abbasid administration to become vizier, and between 928 and 936, he served three Abbasid caliphs: al-Muqtadir (reigned 908–929 C.E.), al-Qahir (reigned 929–934 C.E.), and al-Radi (reigned 934–940 C.E.). Ibn Muqlah presided over a court that enforced a particular canonical reading of the Qur'an, and the competitive politics earned him a number of enemies. When those enemies inevitably came to power, the vizier was deposed, tortured, and placed under house arrest. To silence his communication, they amputated his hand and removed his tongue. Rather than forfeit, Ibn Muqlah continued to write, either by switching hands or, more dramatically, binding a reed pen to his handless stump. But the vizier never regained his former status. When he died in captivity, his body was thrown into an unmarked grave. His tumultuous life rose and fell like a flowing line of handwritten cursive: Ibn Muqlah was thrice vizier, thrice went to war, and thrice interred—first under house arrest, second in an unmarked grave, and finally, with a proper burial. The final flourish belonged to his supporters. Once the political winds shifted yet again, his body was exhumed and ceremoniously laid to rest.

Despite this political turmoil, Ibn Muqlah is best remembered for bringing order to chaos. The number of secular *naskh* styles grew steadily during the early Islamic period and Ibn al-Nadim presents a complex typology of multiple names and classifications.[39] Ibn Muqlah became the lens that channeled and focused this confusion into a lasting tradition. Scholars continue to debate the extent of his involvement, but the vizier's precise contributions are less significant than the changes he represents.[40] The proportional system of *al-khatt al-mansub* was incredibly powerful and consistent. Paleographer Alain George, who specifically criticizes Ibn Muqlah's role in formalizing this system, meticulously demonstrated the consistency of proportional measures across a variety of tenth-century texts.[41] Indeed, the debate surrounding Ibn Muqlah's specific contributions—much like the earlier search for verifiable examples of his handwriting—downplays the design significance of *al-khatt al-mansub*. The precise origins of proportional script are less relevant than the formal geometric constraints and semiotic field that it cultivated among Arabic scribes:

> Something changed in the tenth century. To put it more accurately, later times attributed to the early tenth century, and the vizier Ibn Muqlah, who died in 939 under tragic circumstances, a series of changes whose existence and effects can be visually demonstrated in manuscripts and other written sources from the eleventh century onward. The invention was a new method, a new approach, a new way for *khatt,* the orderly typology of ways to write. The new system was known as *al-khatt al-mansub,* "proportional script." In it, the module for constructing letters was the dot, or rather the square or rhomb, produced by a pen put on

paper and pushed open, then closed. A key, in the musical sense, to any piece of writing was given by the number of dots (three, five, or more) in the single vertical letter *alif,* and all other letters followed suit, thereby creating what was presumably lacking until then, a rationally thought out system of composing letters, words, pages, and, by extension, whole books.[42]

The revolutionary system of *al-khatt al-mansub* defines proportional relations that describe the shapes of Arabic graphemes. All letters are measured in terms of the *nuqta,* or rhombic dot, which is formed by pressing the nib of a reed pen *(qalam)* to paper. (See Figure 1.3.) The resulting *nuqta* becomes the base measure for the design of archigraphemic *rasm.* The height, length, and concavity of individual letters are all measured in number of *nuqta.* The height of the letter *alif,* for example, measures a specific number of *nuqta* stacked vertex to vertex, and the number of *nuqta* varies according to style of script: the *alif* of the *thuluth* style measures seven *nuqta* tall, the *alif* of the *muhaqqaq* style measures nine *nuqta,* the *alif* of copyist *naskh* measures five *nuqta,* and so forth. Horizontal, vertical, and curved segments are similarly measured in *nuqta.* The isolated *naskh bā',* for example, measures five *nuqta* wide, giving it a one-to-one proportional relationship with the height of the *naskh alif.* And the isolated *naskh yā'* begins with a short counterclockwise stroke measuring three *nuqta.* A second stroke bends clockwise from the end of the first. And a final stroke descends one *nuqta* below the bend before it finishes two *nuqta* to the left. The gap separating the bend from the tip of the tail is two-fifths the width of the *naskh bā',* or a two-to-five proportional relationship with the height of *naskh alif.*

Oleg Grabar insightfully compares *al-khatt al-mansub* to the formal typographic inventions of sixteenth- and seventeenth-century Europe. Like typographic guidelines, *al-khatt al-mansub* both (1) describes proportional variation across a diversity of styles or types and (2) assures geometric consistency within a particular style. Like the typographic point, the *nuqta* describes the size of letters. A twenty-point font is larger than an eleven-point font, and a nine-*nuqta alif* is taller than a seven-*nuqta alif.* Extending the analogy, modern Latin fonts are defined by proportional relations between baseline (on which the letters rest), x-height (which defines the height of lowercase letters), ascenders (which rise above x-height), and descenders (which fall below the baseline). Different fonts display different proportional relationships. A twelve-point font might measure

Figure 1.3. Letters measured in *nuqta*

Al-khatt al-mansub measures all letters in proportional relation to the *nuqta,* or rhombic dot. Both solid strokes and open spaces are measured in *nuqta* placed corner to corner. The *nuqta* is formed by pressing the nib of a reed pen *(qalam)* to paper. The size of the pen therefore shapes the size of the script. Also note that *nuqta* do not form a simple horizontal-by-vertical grid. The line of *nuqta* measurements will angle and curve in order to follow a stroke. (Image courtesy of Mustafa Ja'far.)

the x-height six points from the baseline, and another twelve-point font might measure the x-height at five or eight points. This simple difference alters the proportional appearance of letters across the entire font. Relations of *al-khatt al-mansub* operate similarly. But unlike the mechanical point, which remains constant across pages and devices, the size of the *nuqta* varies according to pen. In other words, the point is an absolute measure while the *nuqta* is a relational measure arising from the initial written gesture.

Al-khatt al-mansub formally describes script geometry. As a result, it allows the multiplicity of *naskh* styles to be defined, designed, and compared. Styles of script differ according to the height of the *alif* and the relational measurements of *nuqta*. Standardization occurred both within and across multiple letters of a particular style. Within a letter, distinct components (such as bowls, loops, and line segments) are measured in *nuqta*. Across letters, similar components repeat similar measurements. Just as the x-height is shared by all lowercase letters of a Latin font, and just as the descenders of p and q display structural similarity, the bowls and swashes of Arabic *rasm* display shared proportions for any given style. The *nuqta* measure for the bowl of the *rasm sīn* is the same as the *nuqta* measure for the bowl of *ṣād*. And the *nuqta* measure for the open counter (the "eye") of *rasm ṣād* is the same as the *nuqta* measure for the open counter of *ṭā'*. The system uniformly repeats proportional relationships across all letters of a particular style. Shared measures produced visual uniformity across multiple instances of the same letter as well as collections of distinct letters. Just like modern fonts, these proportional variations translate into stylistic differences.

The colorful tumult of Ibn Muqlah's life adds a coating of mystique to the origins of *al-khatt al-mansub*. And although it is tempting to interpret his punishment and downfall as the dramatic revenge of competing scribes, handwriting probably contributed very little to his fall from grace. The vizier was alternately exalted and exiled, and he eventually lost his hand, due to political affiliations rather than the radical nature of his penmanship. Much like the marking of *tashkil*, *al-khatt al-mansub* began in secular documents and only later moved into the religious and artistic realm.[43] The initial impetus was technical and administrative rather than aesthetic and creative. As a tenth-century government bureaucrat, Ibn Muqlah managed the chancery scribes responsible for court documents. And he likely supported the system in order to standardize penmanship. *Al-khatt al-mansub* provided scribal, administrative, and educational consistency across the quickly expanding Abbasid territory. Only later would calligraphy, writing for aesthetic effect, become synonymous with the harmonious and beautiful application of proportional rules.

The second of three masters, Ali Ibn Hilal al-Bawwab (d. 1022 C.E.), provides the symbolic linchpin that unifies the cold proportionality of *al-khatt al-mansub* with the beauty and grace befitting Qur'anic *masahif*. During Ibn Muqlah's time, Qur'anic copying was still handled by a distinct community of religious scholars who did not employ *naskh*. The use of *naskh* styles for both secular documents and Qur'anic *masahif* began only after the adoption, and perhaps as a result, of *al-khatt al-mansub*. Ibn Khallikan records that Ibn al-Bawwab rendered the method of Ibn Muqlah with elegance and splendor,[44] a claim echoed by modern scholars: "Ibn Muqlah no doubt beautified writing, but the beauty lay in geometric design and in mathematical accuracy. His was the art of the mechanical draughtsman. . . . Ibn al-Bawwab was an artist with an artist's eye for the rhythm and movement that find expression in the flowing line and graceful curve."[45] Ibn al-Bawwab symbolizes the application of *al-khatt al-mansub* for artistic beauty. He began life as the son of a porter, and he worked as a home decorator before becoming an illuminator, a librarian, and finally a scribe. According to legend, he discovered an unfinished Qur'anic *mushaf* in the style of Ibn Muqlah. Ibn al-Bawwab was so awed by the script that he scoured the library for the remainder of the text. When he could locate only twenty-nine of thirty *juz* (Qur'anic sections), he proposed a challenge: he would complete the copy, and if the newly added section was indistinguishable from the originals, he should be greatly rewarded. His patron emir agreed, and Ibn al-Bawwab set to work. He methodically located paper of similar provenance, meticulously copied the script, and borrowed the binding of another book. When he presented the complete *mushaf* before the court, neither the emir nor his trusted advisers could distinguish additions from original copy. As a reward, the scribe received a handsome supply of paper in order to further his craft.

Once again, the veracity of the anecdote is less important than its implications. The origin story links Ibn al-Bawwab with Ibn Muqlah, the symbolic stand-in for *al-khatt al-mansub*. It affirms the importance of emulating the proportional models of previous scribes, and it firmly establishes Ibn al-Bawwab as a copyist of Qur'anic *masahif.* If Ibn Muqlah stands for the adoption of proportioned script, Ibn al-Bawwab stands for the beautiful extension of proportioned *naskh* to sacred text. Ibn al-Bawwab's beginnings as a painter and illuminator provide an artistic foundation, which flowed into his handwriting.[46] His artistry beautified the rigidity of Ibn Muqlah's formal geometry. He also provides the example of scribal student par excellence. Through meticulous practice and replication, he mastered the style of Ibn Muqlah before developing it as his own. Ibn al-Bawwab's beautiful script arose through dedication, training, and practice. In his short epistle on handwriting, he reaffirms the importance of daily practice. The poem, which Ibn Khaldun included in his *Muqaddimah,* stresses the consequences of regular exercise: "Make patient imitation of your habit. . . . Do not be ashamed of bad writing, when you begin to imitate [the letters] and draw lines. The matter is difficult [at the beginning] and then becomes easy."[47] Finally, and most significantly,

Ibn al-Bawwab applied his artistic mastery of *al-khatt al-mansub* to the sacred Qur'an.

This important shift signifies the movement of *naskh* styles into the hieratic realm. Ibn al-Bawwab completed sixty-four Qur'anic *masahif*, one of which is preserved in the Chester Beatty Library in Dublin. Although he was not the first to copy the Qur'an in proportional *naskh* style, his copy remains one of the earliest surviving samples.[48] And the number of *masahif* written with proportional *naskh* increased dramatically after his example. Ibn al-Bawwab's copy, which remains easily readable after ten centuries, stands as a remarkable testament to the power and longevity of *al-khatt al-mansub*. In traditions with less formalized handwriting, readers often find penmanship less than a hundred years old difficult to decipher.[49] His design standardizes layout in a regular grid of fifteen lines per page. *Surah* headings display a larger, more ornate style than the *naskh* used for the body of the text.[50] Whenever these larger headings occur, they uniformly occupy the equivalent of two lines of body. Despite the fluid appearance of Ibn al-Bawwab's handwriting, the underlying geometry is meticulously preserved. The height and proportions of individual letters display amazing consistency from page to page. By superimposing ruling on the text, Alain George demonstrated that the tallest strokes, the compact forms, and the bases of letters all adhere to regular vertical intervals.[51]

Ibn al-Bawwab's copy encapsulates a number of changes that slowly altered the material format of earlier Abbasid *masahif*. First and foremost, cursive *naskh* styles, which had previously been reserved for secular and administrative documents, were now used for the divine text. The traditional separation of archaic *Kufic* styles, written and controlled by the religious *ulama,* and bookhands, utilized by professional scribes, was beginning to narrow. In order for this to happen, the *naskh* styles required formal standardization, which they received via *al-khatt al-mansub*. The repeatability and geometric formalization of proportional script protect Qur'anic *masahif* from abrogation and misreading. Although adoption was likely gradual, Ibn al-Bawwab provided the final exclamation point. With his beautiful example, the question of copying the Qur'an in *naskh* was all but answered. The book is small (measuring 19×14 cm), the paper pages are taller than they are wide, and the script is fully vocalized in line with al-Khalil's system. The text displays six layers of Arabic script grammar. *Tashkil* dance around *rasm* and bring the text to life, harmoniously balancing austere formality with regularly shaped curves. In addition, textual addenda provide vital statistics and verse counts, and the opening and closing pages are intricately decorated will full-page illumination. All these traits contrast with Qur'anic *masahif* produced before the ninth century. Umayyad and early Abbasid Qur'ans typically employed parchment, not paper; pages were wider than they were tall (landscape, not portrait); vocalization—if it occurred at all—used the colored dots of Al-Duali rather than the *tashkil* markings of al-Khalil; and verse counts were absent. These earlier *masahif* were intended for a specialist audience of familiar readers. Ibn al-Bawwab's copy, in contrast, is designed as a personal object for a private collector.[52]

As Ibn al-Bawwab became the exemplar for future calligraphers, Qur'anic copying became a customary exercise for aspiring scribes rather than the protected practice of a religious elite. Regular copying offered a means of improving one's handwriting, directed meticulous attention toward properly formed letters, and served as a popular devotional habit. Yaqut al-Musta'simi (d. 1298 C.E.), the third calligraphic figurehead, devoutly copied two *juz* per day, and he is rumored to have copied the Qur'an more than one thousand times. His dedication was famously displayed when the armies of Hulagu Khan sacked Baghdad in 1258 C.E. With the city burning around him, Yaqut sought solace in a minaret. As days passed, he covered all available scraps with writing. When the supply of paper ran dry, he cut linen from the edge of his robe and continued to practice. Yaqut's symbolic role signals the importance of practice and the expansion of *naskh* to a wider Muslim community. Yaqut began life as a non-Muslim. He was brought to Baghdad as a slave by the final Abbasid caliph, al-Musta'simi, who provided his surname, and became a scribe in the imperial chancery. He applied his skill, emulated the *naskh* style of Ibn al-Bawwab, and became renowned for the fineness of his lines. After the Mongol invasion took the life of his patron, Yaqut descended from his minaret and continued his distinguished career under the new rulers.

Yaqut is remembered as a prodigious teacher, and he applied his beautiful handwriting to Persian as well as Arabic texts.[53] Traditional accounts credit a new method of trimming the reed pen to him and consider it his primary innovation. Yaqut trimmed his pen at an oblique angle, which increased the width of the nib and thereby enabled greater contrast between the thinness of vertical strokes and the thickness of horizontal swashes.[54] The resulting lines infuse Yaqut's style with elegance and lightness of grace. The page becomes a melody of sleek ascenders, robust curves, and stylistic variety. *Al-aqlam al-sittah,* the six classical styles of *naskh,* were formalized around this time. Each style displays a unique set of proportional relations, and different pens with different thicknesses produce different styles. Yaqut mastered them all. And he combined them.[55] He was particularly adept at applying multiple styles on a single page. Running text would shift between lines penned in a large, stately style and lines penned in a smaller, more elegant style. His stylistic variation emphasized proportional relations across *al-aqlam al-sittah* as well as within them. For larger styles, layers of vocalization were often traced with a finer pen, which would dance within and around the more dominant line of *rasm.* The same fine pen might also trace the *rasm* of a smaller style. The result is a symphony of contrasts: thick and thin, big and small, vertical and horizontal, stately and bold, solid and sweeping.

The symbolic line running from Ibn Muqlah to Ibn al-Bawwab and Yaqut al-Musta'simi records a dual trajectory: the triumph of the *naskh* styles and the opening of Qur'anic *masahif* to a wider community of scribes and readers.[56] What began in an exclusive community of religious scholars, with unique hieratic styles and inaccessible formats, becomes the shared practice of professional scribes. The *naskh* styles of *al-aqlam al-sittah,* all of which adhere to *al-khatt al-mansub,* became the dominant mode of copying the Qur'an. Each of the three scribal figureheads symbolically marks a key moment in this trajectory. Ibn Muqlah brought geometric order: *al-khatt al-mansub* placed *naskh* on a proportional foundation of formality, uniformity, and consistent reproduction. Ibn al-Bawwab infused the system with the artistry and elegance of a divine text: his Qur'anic *mushaf* condensed a series of stylistic and formatting changes that opened the text to a wider reading public. And finally, Yaqut symbolizes the canonization of *al-aqlam al-sittah:* he celebrated the multiplicity of *naskh* styles, sharpened his pen, and epitomized the practice of daily copying.

The symbolic triumvirate signifies a popularization of Arabic script. Ibn Muqlah was a high-ranking official who served as vizier for three Abbasid caliphs. He was deeply involved in the legal and political debates of his day. Ibn al-Bawwab, in contrast, rose from the position of tradesman and librarian to become a renowned artist. He worked as a professional copyist for royal patrons and rich collectors. Finally, Yaqut al-Musta'simi was a non-Arab slave. He converted to Islam, devoutly practiced writing, and attained wide renown through the application of his acquired skill. Through his prodigious production and tireless teaching, Yaqut shared Arabic script with an increasingly multicultural Islamic world. His patrons included the last of the Abbasid caliphs and the first of the Mongol Turks who displaced them. He wrote in Arabic and Persian, taught his craft to Arabs and non-Arabs alike, and influenced generations of scribes.[57] Yaqut symbolically witnessed the downfall of Abbasid unity and the rise of competing regional factions. Although the Abbasid caliphate came to an end, proportional *naskh* endured.

Chapter Two

Ottoman Script Design

*W*ritten communication is never simply a transcription of spoken word to paper; it is always the *design* of a message. Like modern designers, Turkish scribes had a toolbox of styles from which to choose. The chosen style aligned with the audience, genre, and intended use of a document. Ottoman textual design began with the notational differences of writing systems. Characters of Arabic, Greek, Hebrew, Armenian, and Latin circulated side by side. Notational differences communicated alongside linguistic content. A courier need not read Arabic or Greek in order to know the destination of a message. Nor did these scripts imply a specific language. Ottoman design was multi-scripted, multi-linguistic, and stylistically diverse. Arabic script was the most common, but far from the only, representation of Ottoman Turkish. Turkish was also transcribed using Greek, Hebrew, Armenian, and even Latin letters. In 1851, Vartan Pasha published *Akabi Hikayesi* (Akabi's Story), which stakes a claim as one of the earliest Turkish novels. The novel consists of Ottoman Turkish prose transcribed in Armenian characters.

Today, spoken languages and written scripts typically are paired in hermetic union. This was not the case in Ottoman Turkey. Spoken vernaculars were not tied to a particular script. Arabic script transcribed texts for Ottoman Muslims. Greek and Armenian characters transcribed texts for different Christian communities. And Hebrew characters transcribed texts for Ottoman Jews. Each of these groups was semiautonomous. Ottoman scripts demarcated legal and religious jurisdictions, rather than linguistic divisions. A particular script did not signify a particular language. Hebrew script did not imply Hebrew language, nor did the Greek alphabet indicate that a text was written in Greek. Ottoman Jews who spoke Arabic wrote the Arabic language using Hebrew characters, and immigrant Jews from Spain used Hebrew script for Ladino (Judeo-Spanish). Greek script, which signified an Orthodox Christian audience, often transcribed Greek. But it was also used for Ottoman Turkish and, on rare occasions, Arabic. Greek-speaking Muslims, in contrast, might employ Arabic script, even when writing in Greek. Ottoman languages changed dress according to the circles in which they moved.

The multivalent relationship between script and language worked in both directions. Spoken languages (such as Ottoman Turkish) were transcribed in multiple scripts, and a single script (such as Arabic) transcribed multiple languages. Arabic script served the Ottoman Muslim community. And Muslim texts came in many languages. These included Albanian-, Bosnian-, and Greek-language texts, among others. But the most common by far were Arabic-, Persian-, and Turkish-language writings. Educated audiences expected familiarity with all three languages. Arabic was the language of the Qur'an, religious law, and classical scholarship; Persian recorded epic poetry, histories, and spiritual treatises; and Ottoman Turkish was the official register of the state. *Naskh* varieties of Arabic script transcribed multiple languages. But subtle proportional differences and stylistic variety shaped content for specific audiences and uses. The classical styles of *al-aqlam al-sittah* implied Arabic content as well as general knowledge. The hanging style of *ta'liq* indicated texts of Persian influence. And the regal uniform of the imperial *diwani* style was exclusive to Ottoman Turkish.

This chapter opens the toolbox of Ottoman stylistic variety. It begins by reframing the term *khatt,* which is often translated as "calligraphy," as a practice of design. It examines two master Ottoman scribes—Şeyh Hamdullah and Hafız Osman—in light of how and what they designed with *naskh.* Dominant styles are then listed and compared alongside distinguishing features and suggested uses. A final section analyzes the application of theses styles as a practice of scribal "typography." In Ottoman practice, scribal styles offered technical choices of design. Visual and aesthetic cues demarcated communities of readers and writers. The presence of Arabic, Greek, or Armenian letters encoded useful information regarding textual origin and target audience. Within the particular system of Arabic script, stylistic choices further specified genre and function. Styles such as *thuluth, naskh* proper, *muhaqqaq, ta'liq,* and *diwani* had distinct uses and implications. Styles of script, like current menus of multiple fonts, offered a plethora of design options. And Ottoman scribes, much like contemporary designers, employed these options in the connection of text and audience.

The Question of Calligraphy

Scribal beauty and clarity travel hand in hand, much as beautiful typography clarifies the printed word. The sweeping designation of scribal practices as "calligraphy" occludes their operational and communicative role.[1] Ottoman scribes certainly created beautiful artistic imagery. But they also designed beautifully functional texts. Stylistic variety played a useful communicative function. Recasting "Arabic calligraphy" as a practice of textual and graphic design downplays qualitative considerations of artistic value. As calligraphic associations of classicism, beauty, and propriety recede, design concepts of utility, arrangement, and effective communication move to the fore. Design analysis asks how the visual appearance of a text serves its message. How and why was a text designed? How does its appearance and design reflect its role? How do styles of script employ script grammar for communicative effect? Stylistic variety, visual composition, and aesthetic balance shape content. The diverse styles of Arabic script are not simply calligraphic drawings of art for art's sake; they are beautiful and well-designed examples of textual content.

The Arabic word *khatt* carries little connection to qualitative judgments of art and classical beauty.[2] Rather, the word indicates the process of tracing a line, marking out, and outlining. The semantic field of *khatt* encompasses ideas of sketching, measurement (as in the lines of a classroom ruler), spaces (as in boundary lines), and precise description (as in delineation). *Khatt* merges linguistic practice, in which speech takes visual form (that is, "writing"), with aesthetic practice, in which the hand traces lines and shapes (that is, "drawing"). The hand-drawn lines of *khatt,* the gestural traces of writing, produce the concrete visual form of Arabic language. *Khatt* organizes the visual, linear, and textual space of writing. Both reading and writing follow a line of *khatt.* Laura

Marks usefully describes *khatt* as a regulated vector: "a line of writing and a line of communication, as in airline, telephone line, and railroad line."[3] *Khatt* is not simply the line of written characters; it is also a line of communication and language. Much like railway and telephone lines, *khatt* traces networks of connection, communication, and practice. Vectors of *khatt* draw both words and boundaries.

The lines of *khatt* standardized Arabic writing across time and space. Ibn Muqlah's proportional system connected the increasingly large territory of Abbasid administration. And the regulated consistency of Ibn al-Bawwab's tenth-century *khatt* remains legible more than a thousand years later. *Al-khatt al-mansub* fuels a powerful and enduring system of scribal design. It formalizes styles in the proportional relation of point, line, and plane—three of the foundational elements of contemporary graphic design.[4] Modern design often begins with the placement of discrete forms in a predetermined space (for example, the arrangement of movable type in a preexisting grid). Points create lines in a plane, and space is filled with written characters and forms. *Khatt,* in contrast, begins with tracing a line. The point *(nuqta)* grows into a line *(alif),* and space emerges via the act of writing. Practices of *khatt* are both aesthetic and linguistic, technical and expressive: "For writers of the past, a feeling or observation would be described in the movement of a gesture and inscribed in the trace it yields. What mattered was not the choice of semantic content of the words themselves but the quality of the line itself."[5] Scribes draw linguistic expression as a visual form. Expression arises from the shapes being drawn and the way in which they are drawn: the style, movement, and appearance of the line. *Khatt* is this way, this line. The regulated vectors of *khatt* outline language, image, and meaning.

The tradition of Ottoman *khatt* begins in Amasya, the shared hometown of Yaqut al-Musta'simi and Şeyh Hamdullah (1436–1520 C.E.). The vector of *khatt* that runs from the triad of Ibn Muqlah, Ibn al-Bawwab, and Yaqut, to Şeyh Hamdullah, his disciples, and beyond passes through Amasya. Yaqut continued to practice his *naskh* even as Abbasid Baghdad fell around him. Two hundred and fifty years later, Yaqut's line of communication was received by a young scribe in his hometown. Hamdullah takes up the pen, refines *naskh,* and outlines the foundation of Ottoman scribal tradition. Amasya provides a geographic linchpin that sutures Ottoman and Abbasid tradition. During his formative years, Sultan Bayezid II studied *khatt* under Şeyh Hamdullah in Amasya. Bayezid so loved his teacher that he would hold the master's inkwell, watching in admiration as Hamdullah traced his lines. One day, the sultan-to-be humbly inquired about the perfection of Yaqut's handwriting. He innocently asked if Yaqut's styles could be improved. Hamdullah responded by secluding himself for forty days.[6] He collected every available sample of Yaqut's work, and he immersed himself in studying their design. Hamdullah pored over the details: the weight of the line, the depth of the curves, the inclination of verticals, the size of the counters, the placement of *nuqta,* the dance of *tashkil,* and the variety of forms. He analyzed letters in isolation and letters in combination. He found the edge of every shape and practiced every possible cursive connect. He drew parts of letters and letters in full. As Hamdullah became familiar with the styles and forms, he began to subtly refine them: a twist of the pen to polish a letter, a horizontal extension to balance a word.[7] Through iterative experimentation and incremental improvement, Hamdullah redesigned the lines of *khatt.* When he emerged from his study, he brought a new harmony to styles of *naskh.*

Figure 2.1 displays a *basmala* drawn in Hamdullah's style. The tall verticals pitch slightly toward the left, which guides the eye in the direction of reading. Extended horizontals and sweeping bowls emphasize the effect. *Tashkil* markings, which also angle from top left to bottom right, frame the primary line of *rasm.* The austere extension of the opening word *bism* draws the viewer into the text. The letters *bā'* and *sīn* ripple on the far right, flowing like a wave and breaking into a spray of letters on the left. The final *nūn* of *al-rahman* sweeps below the line and cradles the final word *al-rahim.* The *nūn* of *al-rahman* points to the final *mīm* of *al-rahim,* uniting the two adjectives as a visual gestalt. The line does not march along a straight and narrow path; it dances among the layers and shapes of Arabic script, from letter block to *tashkil* and into the next letter block.

Hamdullah's primary refinements addressed the complementary styles of *thuluth* and *naskh* (referring here to a specific proportional style rather than a general category). These proportional styles, which visually balance each other, became the dominant styles of Ottoman practice. The prevalence of *naskh,* in particular, displaced other styles. Balancing legibility and compactness, it became the de facto style for works of science, knowledge, and education, as well as the primary style for copying the Qur'an. *Naskh* operated as the Times New Roman of the Ottoman era. *Naskh*'s sister style, *thuluth,* which is larger and more ornate, provided decoration and display. Titles written in decorative

46

Figure 2.1. Şeyh Hamdullah, *Basmala*

The Islamic invocation *basmala* (In the name of God, whose mercy is comprehensive, whose mercy is specific) drawn in the style of Şeyh Hamdullah (1436–1520). Note how the layers of Arabic script interweave vertically. This is particularly apparent on the left side of the phrase, where the *rasm* (layer 1) of the final *nūn* in *al-rahman* sweeps below the *tashkil* and *muhmal* (layers 3–5) of the final word *al-rahim*. (Illustration courtesy of Mohamed Zakariya.)

thuluth organize bodies of text written in workmanlike *naskh*. Hamdullah demonstrated this interaction in Qur'anic *masahif*. His example, which pairs *thuluth* headings with *naskh* text, served as a design template for subsequent scribes. Later Ottoman *masahif* copied Hamdullah's scripts, his method of illumination, and even his bindings.[8]

Şeyh Hamdullah's *khatt* was celebrated, fêted, and praised. He obtained a level of fame comparable to that of modern celebrities, and he inspired generations of scribes. As his fame rose, Hamdullah's legendary exploits grew larger than life, both on and off the page. He excelled in archery, falconry, and swimming, and he impressively swam the width of the Bosphorus while holding his reed writing pens between his teeth.[9] Hamdullah became known as the *qibla,* or direction, of *khatt*.[10] He provided the model and example to which Ottoman scribes should turn their attention. By the seventeenth century, Hamdullah's influence had all but erased competing schools of *khatt*.[11] Later scribes meticulously studied, emulated, and redrew Hamdullah's examples— much as the master himself had immersed himself in the style of Yaqut. Ottoman scribal tradition therefore re-created both the *khatt* of Hamdullah's practice (the vector of his study) and the *khatt* of his letters (the vector of his visual lines).

Two hundred years later, Hafiz Osman (1642–1698 C.E.) followed this vector to comparable fame. Osman diligently studied, copied, and recreated Hamdullah's examples. His mastery of *khatt* and his prodigious output eventually earned him the epithet "second Şeyh."[12] Osman celebrated Hamdullah's styles in beautiful compositions, and he penned more than twenty-five complete

Qur'ans, most of which replicate Hamdullah's template. If Hamdullah was a master "font" designer who refined the proportions of canonical styles, Osman was a layout artist. He beautifully arranged predesigned styles and raised their application to new heights of design.[13] Near the end of the seventeenth century, Osman designed a layout masterpiece in the form of the Ottoman *hilye*. (See Figure 2.2.) The *hilye* template is both a wonderful example of textual design and a beautiful form of calligraphic art. It gracefully juxtaposes a variety of classical scripts to celebrate the moral and spiritual character of the Prophet Muhammad. When asked how he wished to be remembered, Muhammad responded: "Write my *hilye* so the ones who will see it will be as if they saw me after I pass away."[14] Decorative *hilye* answer the call. The proportional layout and beautifully written words convey a calligraphic portrait of the Prophet's qualities.[15]

Osman's design organizes a variety of classical styles in harmony, grandeur, and aesthetic balance. The textual content presents Qur'anic passages and *hadith* that describe the Prophet and his mission. Although the writing is meticulously produced and easily legible, the text does not need to be read in order to be appreciated. Viewing a *hilye* provides various successive experiences, one of which *may* have included the experience of reading.[16] Alongside reading and comprehension, *hilye* inspire aesthetic viewing and spiritual contemplation. The eye navigates visual and textual elements as if they were a chessboard: jumping from text block to text block, comparing shapes, considering their relative movement, finding connections, and, occasionally, capturing words. The character of the Prophet can be read in the text, but it can also be discovered between the lines. The constituent components of the *hilye* template are shown in Figure 2.3.

1. *Başmakan* (Prelude): A rectangular block on top of the composition presents the *basmala* in stately *muhaqqaq* style.
2. *Göbek* (Navel / belly): A circular block is centered below the *başmakan*. The circle typically holds nine lines written in the dominant style of Ottoman *naskh*. These lines begin the *hadith* that describe the appearance and character of Muhammad.[17]
3. *Hilal* (Crescent): An ornamental crescent holds the *göbek*. Often gilded and heavily decorated, the visual symbol of Islam cradles the textual description of the Prophet.

4. *Köşeler* (Corners): Four roundels display the large style of *jali-thuluth*. The roundels hold the names of the four righteous caliphs of Ottoman Sunni orthodoxy: Abu Bakr, Umar, Uthman, and Ali. They are positioned around the large circular *göbek*.

5. *Ayat* (Verse): The rectangular block below the *göbek* contains a single line written in the celebrated style of *thuluth*. The *ayat* presents a Qur'anic verse related to the Prophet and his mission.

6. *Etek* (Foot): A rectangular text box containing additional lines of *naskh*, which are identical with the style used for the *göbek*. The text continues the *hadith* of the *göbek* and, sometimes, the *ayat*. The width of the *etek* is slightly narrower than the box of the *ayat*.

7. *Koltuklar* (Alleys): Two ornamental rectangles, free of text, bracket the indented *etek*. These boxes, like other non-textual spaces, are filled with floral, geometric, and decorative motifs.

8. *Pervaz* (Frame): An illuminated frame borders the entire composition. The design often contains both an inner frame and a larger outer frame.

The result is an aesthetic construction, balanced both visually and textually, with a devotional quality arising through the designed interplay of decoration, wording, and penmanship. The organization and styles of script champion the classical proportions of *al-khatt al-mansub* and metaphorically extend that balance to the ethical, spiritual, and mental poise of the Prophet Muhammad. Practices of *khatt* demarcate lines of text, as well as the larger meaningful space that the text inhabits. Two lines of *khatt*—one in *muhaqqaq* style and another in *thuluth* style—are balanced by two blocks of *khatt* in the smaller *naskh* style. The roundels display the decorative style of *jali-thuluth*, which further extend the range of stylistic sizes and variations. And the illuminated borders and alleys hold the component texts in colorful and spatial relation. The *hilye* template exemplifies the multiple meanings of *khatt:* the visual expression of language, the linear organization of script, the drawing of forms, and the design of meaningful space. The lines of *khatt* trace textual content, stylistic variety, and spatial arrangement.

Hafiz Osman, like Hamdullah before him, was a master craftsman, master artist, master calligrapher, and master designer. Both scribes beautified the textual content on which they operated. Both practiced *khatt*. When placed side

Figure 2.2.   Hafiz Osman's *hilye* template

The *hilye* template beautifully combines multiple styles of script as an aesthetic composition and visual gestalt. The content of *hilye* celebrates the moral and spiritual qualities of the Prophet Muhammad. Hafiz Osman (1642–1698) formalized the template in the seventeenth century. The displayed scripts include *muhaqqaq, thuluth,* and *naskh.* (Image courtesy of Mohamed Zakariya.)

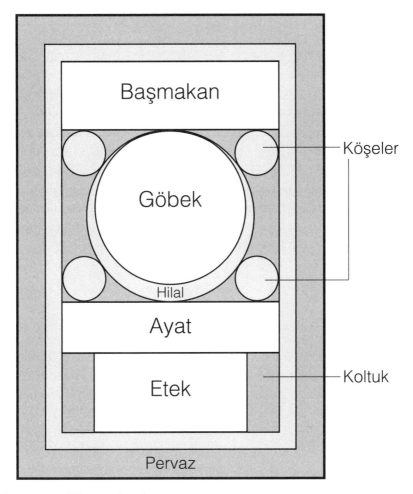

Figure 2.3. *Hilye* template diagram

This diagram labels the constituent components of Hafiz Osman's *hilye* template. (Image produced in Adobe Creative Suite, based on a design by M. Şinasi Acar; see Acar 1999, 154.)

by side, moreover, they illustrate complementary aspects of graphic design. Şeyh Hamdullah parallels a type designer and classical typesetter. He perfected classical fonts and demonstrated their proper use. Today, type designers recover classic metal typefaces and reconstruct their proportions in digital environments. The digital toolbox is filled with fonts that emulate the examples, and hold the names, of past masters: Bodoni, Didot, Baskerville, Garamond, Granjon. Hamdullah similarly "modernized" the classical designs of Yaqut. He redesigned the proportions of *naskh* for a new era. Hafiz Osman, in contrast, applied Hamdullah's "fonts" to design a lasting layout. He created a style sheet, which was repeated, utilized, and performed by a host of subsequent designers. After Osman formalized the template, Ottoman scribes produced a wide variety of *hilye,* from small versions to large wall hangings. The layout and content remain consistent from piece to piece, and beauty arose in the artistic execution of a recognizable form. *Hilye* artists were performers, rather than font or layout creators. Şeyh Hamdullah designed the styles with which they wrote, and Hafiz Osman designed the form. If *al-khatt al-mansub* established musical keys for the composition and enjoyment of harmonious *naskh,* Şeyh Hamdullah perfectly tuned the instruments, and Hafiz Osman composed a musical standard.

The Ottoman System of Scripts

Designers work with a toolbox of instruments, standards, styles, and forms. In modern practices, the toolbox includes a wide variety of fonts as well as predesigned templates and style sheets. Most designers do not construct fonts and letters from scratch; they utilize existing tools to effectively shape written messages. Most Ottoman scribes worked similarly. They rarely designed new styles of script or new templates. They too had a toolbox of styles and templates from which to choose. And they applied styles appropriate to the message at hand. Religious, literary, scientific, and administrative documents are not the same. They request visual differences of style and formal differences of layout. Aesthetic variations—in contemporary and scribal design—are neither idiosyncratic nor simply subjective expressions. They are repeatable "types" (as in the movable type of typography). Ottoman styles of script were visually identifiable and recognizably distinct.

The following entries describe the styles available to Ottoman designers. If Ottoman scribes could access a drop-down menu of "fonts," these are the choices that would appear. The list begins with the classic styles of *al-aqlam al-sittah* (the six pens). These six classical styles of *naskh* were formalized during Yaqut's era and reinvigorated by the school of Şeyh Hamdullah. *Al-aqlam al-sittah* subdivided into three pairs, each of which partnered a larger display script with a smaller body script of complementary proportions. (See Figure 2.4.) The most popular pairing linked *thuluth,* the predominant Ottoman display style, and *naskh,* the canonical style of general textual copy. The other pairings, *muhaqqaq-rayhan* and *tawqi'-riqa',* were expected of trained scribes (and familiar to learned readers), but less common in practice. Their connotations were more specific and limited. The scribal toolbox was further bolstered by a variety of non-*naskh* styles, such as the Persian-derived style of *ta'liq* and the Ottoman chancery style of *diwani,* both of which connoted particular types of content. The list ends with notes on the Ottoman *tughra* signature, a typographic form reminiscent of modern logotypes. Ottoman scribal variety was incredibly vast, and the following list is far from exhaustive. It contains only the most common styles, with descriptions of their recognizable features and proper usage.[18] Stylistic differences are demonstrated in figures for visual comparison. The illustrations were written and drawn by master calligrapher Mohamed Zakariya, and they all transcribe the same passage from the Egyptian Sufi ethicist Ibn Ata'Allah al-Sikandari (d. 1309 C.E.): "Thought is the movement of the heart in the arena of all that is other than it."[19]

Al-Aqlam al-Sittah (The Six Classical Pens)

Thuluth (Turkish: *sülüs*)

Thuluth, which means "one-third," is the most famous of the Ottoman styles. The name derives from its relationship to *tumar,* the grand signature script of the Umayyad. Early versions of *thuluth* measured one-third the height of *tumar.* Ottoman scribes utilized *thuluth* as a display script for headings, titles, and grand statements. It was rarely used for copying the body of text. *Thuluth* is the sister script of *naskh,* and Qur'anic *masahif* in the style of Şeyh Hamdullah pair *thuluth* headings with *naskh* text. Elsewhere, Ottoman artists celebrated *thuluth*'s compositional possibilities in display panels *(lewha)* and architectural inscriptions. *Thuluth* inscriptions decorate mosques, monuments, gates, wall hangings, and tombstones. The style's association with decorative headings and display conveys artistic and regal connotations.

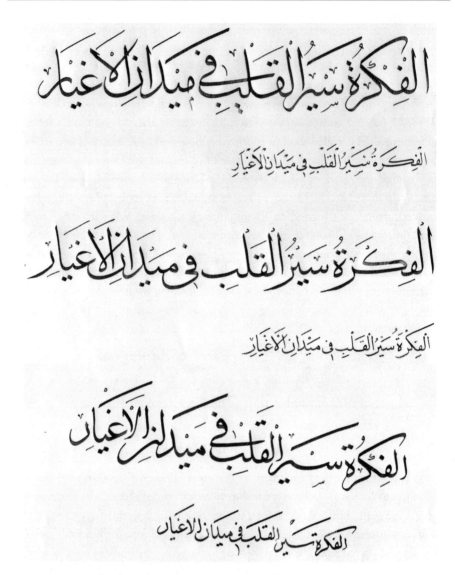

Figure 2.4.   Al-aqlam al-sittah

This figure shows all six styles of *al-aqlam al-sittah* and their relative proportions. The styles are divided into three pairings of larger and smaller styles. From the top: *thuluth* and *naskh, muhaqqaq* and *rayhan*, and *tawqi'* and *riqa'*. All the styles transcribe the same line of text. (Illustration courtesy of Mohamed Zakariya.)

Figure 2.5.   Thuluth and naskh
This pairing of styles consists of the larger *thuluth* (Turkish: *sülüs*) and the smaller *naskh* (Turkish: *nesih*). These are the most common styles of Ottoman practice. Both styles transcribe the same line of text. (Illustration courtesy of Mohamed Zakariya.)

Visually, *thuluth* appears highly fluid, with a balance of straight verticals and curved horizontals. (See Figure 2.5.) The *alif* measures seven *nuqta* tall. It sports a top serif that points down and toward the right, and its bottom curves slightly to the left. Ottoman scribes described the shape of the *thuluth alif* as "a man looking at his feet."[20] Bowls and final curves display a wide degree of visual bounce, and letter blocks frequently stack above one another. Occasionally, letter terminals sweep up in fine hairlines to touch the bottom of subsequent blocks. These finial connections guide the eye in the direction of reading and bring separate letter blocks into visual harmony. Since *thuluth* is a large display style, *tashkil* markings are drawn with a finer pen. This establishes a formal hierarchy of script layers. *Rasm* and *i'jaam* (script layers 1 and 2) are distinguished by bolder strokes, while *tashkil* and higher layers (layers 3–7) appear much lighter. The higher layers assist legibility, fill spatial gaps, and aesthetically balance the composition. This contrasts with *naskh,* in which all layers are drawn with the same-size pen.

Naskh (Turkish: *nesih*)

Naskh is the preferred bookhand for running text and the most common of all the Ottoman styles. It emphasizes legibility and operates as the Times New Roman of Ottoman practice. *Naskh* transcribes a wide range of educational, scientific, legal, popular, devotional, and literary content. Şeyh Hamdullah established *naskh* as the preferred style for copying the Qur'an, and its durable popularity earned it the epithet *khadim al-Qur'an* (servant of the Qur'an). *Naskh* also lends its name as the general term for all rounded, or cursive, styles of Arabic script (in contrast to the geometric, or *Kufic*, styles). Some commentators note that the name is a synonym of "cancel" and thereby suggest that *naskh*'s popularity abolished other styles.[21] *Naskh*'s presentation champions clarity, and it later provided the visual model for printed Ottoman typefaces.

The *naskh alif* measures five *nuqta* tall and displays very little curvature. (See Figure 2.5.) Although the *alif* has no serif, the *naskh lām* is distinguished by a small serif on the top right. *Naskh*'s small size reduces horizontal sweep, and a consistent baseline is rigidly enforced. Final flourishes rarely extend below subsequent letter blocks. The horizontal compactness and reduced curvature accentuate clarity, even at small sizes. And Ottoman *naskh* inclines slightly to the left, a stylistic variation introduced by Şeyh Hamdullah.[22] Compared to *thuluth*, *naskh*'s vertical strokes are shorter, its horizontals are straighter, and its counters appear larger. *Naskh* plays the straight man to the dancing curves of the larger display style. Its bowls appear flatter than the bowls of *thuluth*, and blocks of text display more regular vertical arrangement. *Tashkil* are written with a similar-size pen as those used with *rasm* and *i'jaam*. But the layers of *tashkil* display more separation from the letters they modify. This guides the reading eye, much like the serifs of printed Latin.

Muhaqqaq (Turkish: *muhakkak*)

Muhaqqaq, which means "meticulously produced," is the most hieratic style of *al-aqlam al-sittah*.[23] It was one of the first proportional styles employed for Qur'anic *masahif*, and it has very strong religious and sacred connotations. Ottoman scribes employed *muhaqqaq* for displays of religious significance and as a framing device for grand *masahif* and Qur'anic passages. It was rarely, if ever, used as a copyist style for nonreligious material.[24] *Muhaqqaq* is the sister style of the smaller *rayhan*, but it also operates in counterpoint to the flowing curves of *thuluth*. This can be seen in Osman's *hilye* template, where the sharpness of *muhaqqaq* contrasts with the more fluid pairing of *thuluth* and *naskh*. The *muhaqqaq basmala* frames the *hilye* with an aura of sacredness, stateliness, and deeply classical religiosity.

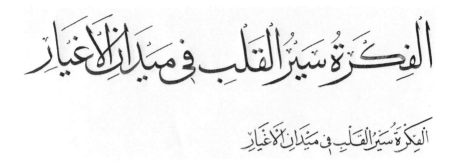

Figure 2.6. Muhaqqaq and rayhan
This pairing of styles consists of the larger *muhaqqaq* (Turkish: *muhakkak*) and the smaller *rayhan* (Turkish: *reyhani*). Distinctive features include the straight verticals and the sharp points of the terminals. Both styles transcribe the same line of text. (Illustration courtesy of Mohamed Zakariya.)

Muhaqqaq's defining features are its grandness, the straightness of its lines, the flatness of its bowls, the openness of its counters, and the sharpness of its terminals. (See Figure 2.6.) It is the tallest of *al-aqlam al-sittah,* with an *alif* measuring nine *nuqta* tall.[25] It is also the most angular, with letters tapering to knifelike points. The *muhaqqaq alif* is tall and straight, with a rightward-facing barbed serif and a pointed base, and the *rā'* class of letters ends in sharp leftward-facing terminals. These arrowlike forms direct the eye along the baseline axis of reading. The stark contrasts of tall verticals, flat horizontals, and open counters invoke a sense of exactitude and clarity. The *tashkil* of *muhaqqaq*—like those of *thuluth*—are drawn with a finer pen. This further emphasizes the sharpness of the primary *rasm,* contrasting bold and stately letters with more delicate *tashkil.*

Rayhan (Turkish: *reyhani*)

Rayhan appears as a smaller, more delicate version of *muhaqqaq. Rayhan* letters resemble those of its larger, statelier cousin, but they are traced in a finer pen. (See Figure 2.6.) As a result, terminals appear less sharp and display less contrast between thick and thin. Despite its small size, and unlike *naskh,* the *rayhan alif* retains a small serif on the top right.[26] Due to a linguistic similarity with the Arabic word for "basil," *rayhan* is sometimes described as the visual and written equivalent of finely pointed basil leaves.[27] *Tashkil* and the primary text are traced with the same pen, and *rayhan* may therefore be described as *muhaqqaq* lines drawn with a *tashkil* pen. Ottoman scribes employed *rayhan* infrequently, and usage declined noticeably alongside the rising popularity of *naskh*. It occasionally appears as a decorative style for small passages or in contrast with the sister style of *muhaqqaq*. In the later Ottoman period, the term sometimes referred to a larger variant, which more closely resembles *muhaqqaq*.[28]

Tawqi' (Turkish: *tevki*)

Tawqi' is the rarest of *al-aqlam al-sittah* in Ottoman practice. It began as an Abbasid chancery style, and its name relates to the Arabic word for "signature." In Abbasid decrees, a *tawqi'* signature authenticated texts written in the smaller sister style of *riqa'*. The fluidity of *tawqi'* and its occasional unorthodox connections served to distinguish these decrees from earlier Umayyad protocols, which were penned in the grand style of *tumar*. *Tawqi'* is slightly smaller than *thuluth,* and the line of writing rises to the left. (See Figure 2.7.) The style exaggerates curvature, and the *tawqi'-riqa'* pair is the most rounded of all *al-aqlam al-sittah*. Ottoman scribes employed *tawqi'* as a display style where its exaggerated roundness stood opposite *muhaqqaq*'s rigid straightness. In relation to *thuluth*, *muhaqqaq* is taller and straighter while *tawqi'* is shorter and smoother. Identifying traits also include overlapping and vertically stacked letter blocks. A distinctive feature of *tawqi'* is the occasional unorthodox connection.[29] In later Ottoman *tawqi',* for example, the combination of *alif* followed by *lām* may resemble a strong horizontal crossbar.[30] In proper Arabic script grammar, *alif* does not connect with the letter that follows it.

Riqa' (Turkish: *rika*)

Riqa' is the smaller sister style of *tawqi'*. Its vertical shortness emphasizes curvature, and the writing displays a wide degree of visual bounce in relation to the thickness of the pen. (See Figure 2.7.) Like *tawqi',* the line of letters rises as it moves to the left. The Ottomans also referred to *riqa'* as the *ijazah* (Turkish: *icaza*) style. It played a particular role in the drafting of *ijazah,* a diploma or certificate of transmission.[31] An *ijazah* certified a scribe's ability to write in a particular style of script. The process of obtaining an *ijazah* was time intensive, and apprentice scribes would devote years to studying and copying historical

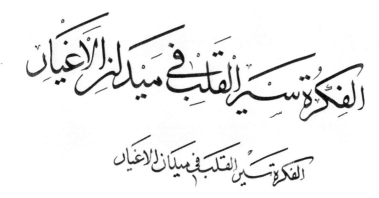

Figure 2.7. *Tawqi'* and *riqa'*

This pairing of styles consists of the larger *tawqi'* (Turkish: *tevki*) and the smaller *riqa'* (Turkish: *rika*). Note how the baseline of these styles rises slightly to the left. Both styles transcribe the same line of text. (Illustration courtesy of Mohamed Zakariya.)

examples. Once ready, the student would copy an exemplar in the chosen style (for example, *thuluth, muhaqqaq, tawqi'*, etc.). The copy should accurately represent the style and proportions of the original. If an authorized teacher approved the student copy, that is, the teacher perceived the *khatt* and form of the student's work as identical to the exemplar, the student received an *ijazah*. The formal certificate would display the student's passage in the chosen style, followed by the teacher's acceptance written in *riqa'*. With certificate in hand, the student could practice the style, copy texts that required it, teach it to others, and sign her or his name on decorative pieces.[32] The dedication and precision required to obtain an *ijazah* preserved the various scribal styles as visually distinct and recognizable types.

Other Scripts and Forms

Ta'liq (Turkish: *talik*)

The Ottoman script of *ta'liq* is known in Persia as *nasta'liq,* which is itself a combination of *naskh* and *ta'liq*.[33] It developed as a Persian chancery style, and the name refers to its distinctive "hanging" appearance.[34] *Ta'liq* has particularly strong connotations of Persian influence, and it is occasionally referred to as *al-khatt al-Farisi* (Persian script) in the Arab world. The hanging structure and sweeping curves align with Persian orthography, and *nasta'liq* remains the dominant handwritten style of Iran, Pakistan, and much of Central Asia.[35] In Ottoman circles, the popularity of *ta'liq* grew over time. By the end of the Ottoman era, *ta'liq* even rivaled *thuluth* as the dominant style of decorative panels. Usage spread from the copying of Persian poetry to prose works, popular religious materials, and educational texts. In the religious realm, *ta'liq* presented devotional and mystical commentaries, and it eventually came to represent official pronouncements of the grand mufti, the *Şeyhülislam*.[36] But *ta'liq*'s religious role was supportive and devotional rather than hieratic. It was rarely, if ever, utilized for the transcription of Ottoman *masahif*.[37] *Ta'liq* was used for interlinear Persian translations of Qur'anic Arabic passages, but it was never applied to the primary Arabic text.

The line of *ta'liq* slopes from top right to bottom left, and letter blocks descend as if hanging from a clothesline. (See Figure 2.8.) Blocks often stack vertically with the first letter of a block located directly above the final letter of the previous block. The *alif* is very short relative to the *nuqta,* and it does not sport a serif. Vertical motion arises from the angled line rather than the height of individual letters. A number of visual differences distinguish *ta'liq/nasta'liq* from *naskh*.[38] These include the pronounced slant of the line, the comparative shortness of the verticals, the elongation of horizontal letters, and the stacking of final forms. The counters of the *mīm,* medial *'ayn,* and *fā'* are often filled solid, or blind, and the vertical teeth of the *bā'*-class letters appear minimal. The teeth of the *sīn* class may disappear altogether, transforming the *rasm* into a long, sweeping horizontal. The overall effect conveys a sense of fluid, almost dancelike diagonal movement. This contrasts sharply with the solidity of *naskh* in particular, and *al-aqlam al-sittah* more generally, in which the perpendicular interplay of horizontal and vertical remains dominant.

Diwani (Turkish: *divani*)

Diwani served as the official style of the Ottoman chancery and takes its name from the imperial council. It recorded Ottoman *fermans* (permissions), *vakifs* (endowments), *berat* (title grants), statements of honor, appointments, and patents.[39] The imperial court maintained proprietary control, and the style was not to be used for unsanctioned communications. It was never used for Qur'anic

Figure 2.8.   Ta'liq

The display style of *ta'liq* (Turkish: *talik*). Note how the baseline sweeps down from the right. The *ta'liq* style originated in Persia and signified texts of Persian origin or influence. The example transcribes the same line of text as the other examples. (Illustration courtesy of Mohamed Zakariya.)

masahif, nor was it used for quotidian texts. In contrast to *al-aqlam al-sittah,* which represent classical Arabic—and the particular trio of *thuluth, naskh,* and *muhaqqaq* that transcribed the eternal Qur'an—*diwani* signified the temporal order of the Ottoman state. Umayyad decrees employed the early *tumar* style, Abbasid decrees employed the signature *tawqi'* style, and Ottoman decrees employed *diwani*. In each case, secular authority was encoded and enforced through a distinctive style of script.

Diwani resembles an excessively cursive and super-structured version of *ta'liq*. (See Figure 2.9.) Its bowls are deep and rounded with exaggerated final loops. Both *alif* and *lām* display a distinctive half-moon shape and sport a pronounced left-hand serif. Like *ta'liq,* the *mīm* is blind, and the teeth of *bā'* and *sīn* are underplayed. And the *nūn* may adopt a near-circular shape with its *nuqta* in the center. The earliest *diwani* styles were written without *tashkil,* but complexity developed over time.[40] The addition of *tashkil* and the higher layers of Arabic script evolved into a dense pattern of decorative elements. The density of forms approximates solid shapes when viewed from a distance, and the line rises on the left to resemble the prow of a ship. The excessive curvature and density sharply contrasted with the horizontal emphasis of more prosaic *naskh* texts.

The style's visual complexity reinforced its functional role. *Diwani* preserved precise legal wording as drawn and linear structure. Excessive decoration and intense curves distinguished *diwani* from other Ottoman styles, especially *al-aqlam al-sittah.* And *diwani*'s distinctive shape protected content from forgery and fraudulent additions. *Diwani* was difficult to write, and it was drawn only by specifically trained scribes of the Ottoman chancery. It was difficult to read,

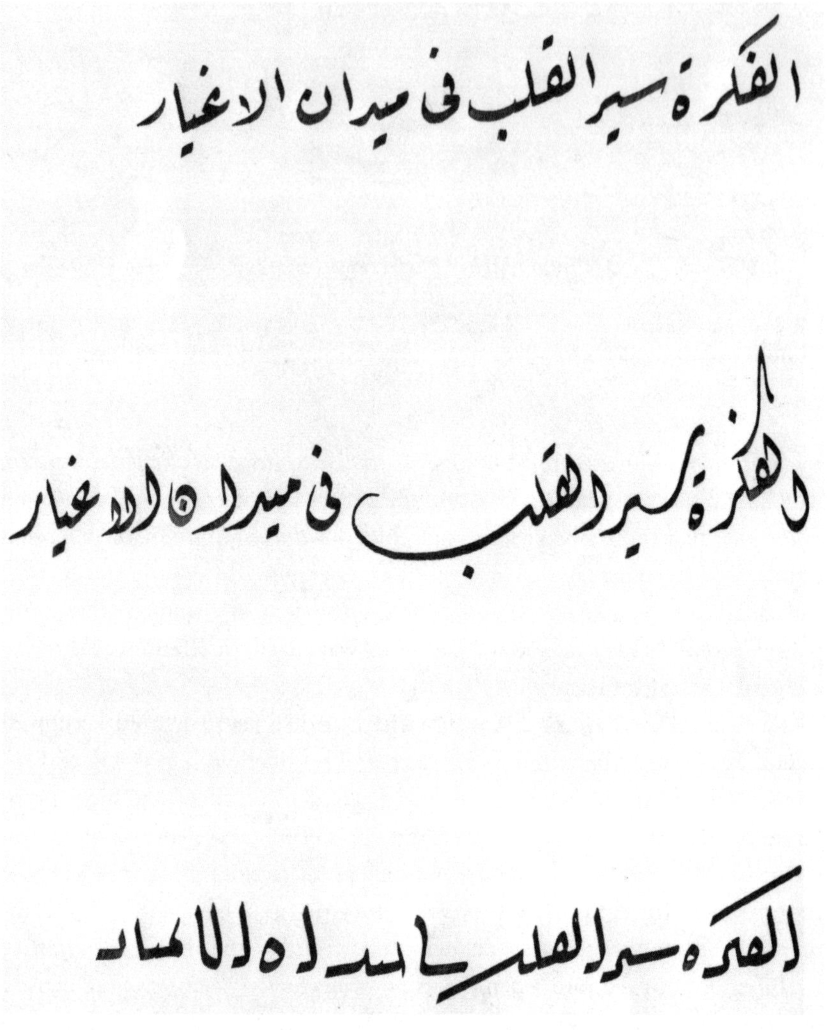

الفكرة سير القلب في ميدان الاغيار

الفكرة يسير القلب في ميدان الاغيار

الفكرة سر القلب اسد اه لا ساب

Figure 2.9.   Ruq'ah, diwani, and *siyaqah*

The styles of *ruq'ah* (Turkish: *rik'a*), *diwani* (Turkish: *divani*), and *siyaqah* (Turkish: *siyakat*). *Ruq'ah* was the style of everyday penmanship. *Diwani* was the exclusive style of the Ottoman royal chancery. And *siyaqah* recorded financial transactions. All the styles transcribe the same line of text. (Illustration courtesy of Mohamed Zakariya.)

and it was typically deciphered only by official bureaucrats. The requisite precision, combined with expensive materials such as gold-flecked inks and an illuminated *tughra* signature, visually certified a document of royal origin. Extended sheets of paper recorded the entirety of the proclamation without page breaks, and *diwani* scrolls were often displayed as vibrant visual markers of royal permission.

Siyaqah (Turkish: *siyakat*)

Siyaqah recorded Ottoman financial documents and land registers.[41] Although the textual content of such registers strove for directness and clarity, the visual presentation is highly ambiguous and difficult to decipher.[42] *Siyaqah* is also known by the name *qirmah* (broken), which adequately describes its appearance.[43] (See Figure 2.9.) The style deliberately breaks common rules of orthography and script grammar. It consists only of *rasm* (script layer 1), without any *nuqta* or *tashkil*, and words were written with a great deal of alphabetic abbreviation. *Siyaqah*'s purposeful ambiguity protected financial documents from false additions and limited readership to certified officials with the requisite literacy. When a trained reader recited a *siyaqah* text, the clearly worded legal content was shared with listening audiences. The style played a purely bureaucratic role, and it was never used for artistic, decorative, or religious purposes.[44]

Ruq'ah (Turkish: *rik'a*)

Ruq'ah labels the style of daily memos and personal correspondence, and it continues to be used for everyday handwriting across much of the Arabic world. The name is often confused with *riqa'* due to lexical similarity. The names of both styles derive from the common root word for a sheet of paper. Visually, however, the styles are quite distinct. *Riqa'* is a smaller version of the highly curved *tawqi'*. *Ruq'ah*, in contrast, resembles a flatter version of *ta'liq*. As the style of daily penmanship, *ruq'ah* aids quick transcription and conveys an aura of informality. This distinguishes *ruq'ah* texts from formal publications copied in *al-aqlam al-sittah, diwani,* and other styles. The distinction continued into the era of print. Most Arabic typefaces mimicked the publishable and clearly formed style of *naskh*, while unpublished handwriting remains *ruq'ah*.

Ruqʿah letters are vertically short with thick strokes relative to their height. (See Figure 2.9.) The *alif* has no serif. As with *taʿliq* and *diwani,* letter blocks begin above the baseline and slope downward to the left. The final letter of each block rests on a common baseline. Despite its informality, *ruqʿah* follows clearly delineated rules of penmanship that minimize the number of required strokes.[45] This facilitates quick transcription. *Nuqta,* for example, are marked in short-hand: dual *nuqta* merge as a horizontal dash, and triple *nuqta* take the form of a carat (with the right-side ascent noticeably thicker than the left-side descent). *Tashkil* typically remains unmarked but may appear sporadically in order to clarify an ambiguous term, highlight a particular vocalization, or specify a foreign name.

Jali (Turkish: *celi*)

The term *jali* identifies larger and more decorative versions of other styles. It is not a unique style in its own right. As a style becomes larger, its character is emphasized and its proportional relations become more noticeable. *Jali* transformations adapt stylistic proportions for larger-size pens and larger displays. They preserve the proportions of smaller scripts at larger sizes. The most common *jali* varieties are *thuluth jali, taʿliq jali,* and *diwani jali. Thuluth jali* was used for architectural inscriptions, wall hangings, and decorative display pieces. *Taʿliq jali* was used for decorative display of Persianate poetry and religious aphorisms. And *diwani jali,* although not necessarily larger than other *diwani* writings, appears excessively decorated.

Jali-thuluth affords artists and designers great flexibility. *Jali* designs are composed as spatial constructions rather than singular lines of writing. Principles of balance, rhythm, unity, and architecture guide the placement of forms. Letter blocks arrange vertically and horizontally, with phrases beginning on the bottom right. Completed compositions adopt a wide range of shapes and forms, from medallions to cones to fruit and birds. (See Figure 2.10.) The *alif* of *jali-thuluth* pitches slightly to the left and displays a prominent wedge-shaped serif, which points downward and to the right. The terminals of final letters often end in thin curves that point upward. All seven layers of script are common, with *tashkil* and decorative marks standing in aesthetic and compositional counterpoint to the dominant *rasm* forms. The *tashkil* marks are drawn with a smaller pen, often one-third or one-fourth the size of the *rasm* pen.[46] They aesthetically balance the composition by filling spatial holes between letters.

Figure 2.10. Jali thuluth composition

This calligraphic composition is composed in *jali thuluth* (Turkish: *celi sülüs*) style. The highly structured image displays all seven layers of Arabic script. The transcribed text is the same passage that appears in the examples of the various styles. (Illustration courtesy of Mohamed Zakariya.)

As letters increase or decrease in size, the relational system governing positive and negative space must adjust accordingly. In typographic design, larger point sizes require typesetters to minimize and alter the kerning (spacing) between characters. Similar problems plagued *jali thuluth* until Mustafa Rakim Efendi (1757–1826 C.E.) proposed a solution in the eighteenth century. Rakim applied a system of squares that geometrically enlarged small-scale compositions for large-scale applications. Using this method, Kazasker Mustafa Izzet Efendi (1801–1877 C.E.) designed the large *thuluth* roundels in Hagia Sophia. The roundels accurately recreate the relationships of *thuluth,* and although they appear handwritten, they were geometrically enlarged. Drafting them by hand would have required a pen measuring thirty-five centimeters in diameter.

Ghubar

Ghubar labels diminutive varieties, and the name derives from the Arabic word for a speck of dust. As a measure of size, *ghubar* stands opposite the large decorative varieties of *jali.* The name often references a diminutive form of *naskh,* but, as a descriptor of size, it can apply to any style.[47] *Ghubar* versions of other styles, such as *ghubar muhaqqaq* and *ghubar ta'liq,* also exist. Despite their minuscule nature, *ghubar* varieties preserve legibility. As functional styles, they recorded messages sent by pigeon post. Ottoman scribes also applied the small size to a variety of aesthetic, talismanic, and spiritual practices. *Ghubar* copies of Qur'anic *masahif* measure less than five centimeters across. They take the form of small codices or octagon-shaped amulets and were often worn on cords or hung from battle standards.

Tughra

The *tughra* is a calligraphic form that serves as the royal signature of Ottoman sultans. (See Figure 2.11.) Although it is composed of writing, it is not a style per se, and it therefore differs from other entries in this list. Instead, the closest modern analogy of the *tughra* is the logotype. Logos communicate a visual synthesis of an idea or entity. They remain recognizable as unique marks, regardless of familiarity with the referent or an immediate ability to decipher textual content. *Tughra* operate along similar principles: they serve as the logo of the Ottoman state. *Tughra* incorporate a stylized version of the sultan's name as an official seal and signature. Although the written name changed with each new sultan, the *tughra* shape did not. The logo form remained a consistent visual marker of Ottoman authority, even as its specific linguistic content shifted with the times.[48]

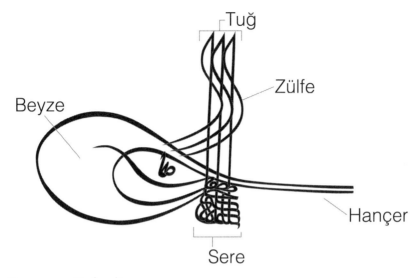

Figure 2.11.   *Tughra* diagram

The *tughra* logotype was the official signature of Ottoman sultans. It often topped and authorized chancery pronouncements written in the royal *diwani* style. This diagram labels the constituent components of the *tughra,* which remained consistent over time. The displayed signature is that of Sultan Süleyman the Magnificent (reigned 1520–1566). (Image produced in Adobe Creative Suite, based on a design by M. Şinasi Acar; see Acar 1999, 163.)

Tughra were drawn by specialized artist-designers, and their presence certified official documents penned in the *diwani* style. Key components of the *tughra* logo include (1) the *sere,* a stacked base of compressed letters that indicate the name and genealogy of the sultan, as well as honorifics such as "khan" and *al-muzaffar da'im* (the eternally victorious); (2) the *tuğ,* three tall shafts that vertically extend the *alifs* of said honorifics; (3) *zülfe,* S-shaped serifs that fall from the left-hand side of the *tuğ* into semblance of battle standards; (4) ovular *beyze* that expand the letter *nun* as a large loop to the left of the *tuğ;* and (5) the *hançer,* which draws the lines of the *beyze* in a fine pincerlike dagger on the right.[49] Like any good logo, the shape translates concept into visual form. It communicates a sense of "gathering." The expansiveness of the ovular *beyze* are threaded, needlelike, through the shafts of the *tuğ* and into the point of the *hançer.* The sultan's name provides a solid foundation on which lines march through vertical battle standards.

Ottoman Scribes as Typographers and Designers

In 1930, Beatrice Warde famously described typography as a crystal goblet.[50] A crystal goblet presents wine in optimal fashion: its clear glass highlights the wine's color, its shape channels the wine's aroma, and its delicate stem allows one to hold the content up to the light before directing the wine to the lips. The wine is the message, and the goblet delivers the message without interference. The taster should notice the wine, not the glass. Warde suggested that type holds content in similar fashion. It reveals the color and flavor of a text, and it should step aside when delivering its message. Both vessels—goblet and type—direct attention away from themselves and toward their content. Typography should not interfere with presentation of text; readers should feast on the meaning and message of the words. Stanley Morison seconds Warde's analogy in his *First Principles of Typography:* "any disposition of printing material which, whatever the intention, has the effect of coming between the author and the reader is wrong."[51] Classical typography is an invisible and infrastructural art. It strives for clarity and transparency. It is ever-present and necessary but unobtrusive and unnoticed.[52] Type holds text like a goblet holds wine.

To craft the proper goblet, a typographer considers the textual copy. A designer has a toolbox of fonts and styles, and she or he determines which of the available options best honors the requested task. Some contents appear best in Helvetica, others in Times New Roman, Palatino, Garamond, or Edwardian Script. Font variations of regular, **bold,** *italic,* and SMALL CAPS further dress the text, as does the sizing, justification, and alignment. Legal documents do not employ Comic Sans, and children's books do not condense stories into eleven-point Times New Roman. Long-form printed texts are more likely to employ serif typefaces; small text displayed on screens works better with sans serifs.[53] Professional typographers, like scribes, certainly beautify texts, but their craft acts in service to the intended message. Successful typography conveys necessary information to necessary audiences, all the while remaining faithful to content, source, and sponsor. Type clothes the message in an outfit suitable to its role.

The same principles apply to scribal design. Ottoman scribes dressed written messages in the proper garment of display.[54] They copied, clarified, honored, and occasionally disguised written content in the selection and application of appropriate styles. *Khatt* was the typography of the Ottoman era, and Ottoman scribes drew the goblets that held textual wine. In some cases, the goblet clearly indicated genre, origin, and authority: the *diwani* style signified official pronouncements of the imperial court, and the *siyaqah* style recorded financial statements. Other goblets operated through connotation: the *muhaqqaq* style conveyed a stately divinity, and the *ta'liq* style implied Persian influence. The vectors of *khatt* directed texts into appropriate channels.

Robert Bringhurst defines typography as "a craft by which meanings of a text can be clarified, honored and shared, or knowingly disguised."[55] A more apt description of Ottoman scribal practice is hard to find. Scribal design strives for the same ideals as Bringhurst's vision of typography: (1) invite the reader into the text, (2) reveal the tenor and meaning of the text, (3) clarify the structure and order of the text, (4) harmonize the text with supporting elements (such as illustrations, citations, and notes), and (5) induce a state of energetic repose.[56] The following section demonstrates this parallelism by applying Bringhurst's *Elements of Typographic Style* to Ottoman scribal design.[57]

First, our hypothetical Ottoman designer "chooses a [style] or a group of [styles] that will elucidate the character of the text."[58] This begins with technical considerations of material and medium: "consider the medium for which the [style] was originally designed."[59] Modern typographers distinguish between natively digital fonts and those adapted from metal type.[60] Styles of Arabic script were similarly designed for different technologies and tools. Texts carved or printed in stone look and feel different than texts written on papyrus, parchment, or paper. The bold forms of archaic *Kufic* work well when scratched onto parchment and papyrus. And geometric *Kufic* lends itself to mosaic tiling. *Kufic* styles pair well with hard mediums, and they remained popular in architectural inscription long after being replaced on paper. The *naskh* styles, in contrast, were designed for paper. The adoption of paper nudged Arabic script toward a more delicate line. But not all paper is created equal: "Choose [styles] that suit the paper you intend to [write] on, or paper that suits the [styles] you wish to use."[61] As early as Umayyad times, the size of the paper sheet informed the size of the Arabic pen. The base measure of *tumar* refers to both a sheet of paper and the size of its corresponding pen.[62] Similarly, the large pens of *muhaqqaq* do not serve the delicate line of *diwani,* and the reed pen for *thuluth* is larger than the pen for *naskh.* The larger styles of *thuluth* and *muhaqqaq* utilize a smaller pen to mark *tashkil,* whereas the *tashkil* of *naskh* and *rayhan* are drawn with the same pen used for the base letters.

Next, the designer, "chooses [styles] that suit the task as well as the subject."[63] The proper style has "historical echoes and associations that are in harmony with the text."[64] Thus, the classical Arabic styles of *al-aqlam al-sittah* were employed for Qur'anic *masahif*. Classical styles visually and scribally linked Ottoman *masahif* with the Arabic source and Arabic language of the Qur'an. *Al-aqlam al-sittah* reference Yaqut al-Musta'simi and Abbasid scribal tradition. The call was answered by Şeyh Hamdullah and echoed in his association with Yaqut's hometown. The stylistic connection subtly underscored Ottoman claims to the caliphate and Sunni orthodoxy. The historically Persian associations of *ta'liq*, in contrast, echo romantic Persian poetry and spiritual reflection. The *ta'liq* style transcribed Persian texts and Ottoman writings in Persian style. Although *ta'liq* became an incredibly popular style, Ottoman scribes never employed it for copying the Qur'an.[65] The Arabic language of the Qur'an and the visual language of *ta'liq* spoke different idioms. Persian translations and commentary were occasionally inserted between lines of Qur'anic text. When this occurred, the interlinear insertions used *ta'liq*, while the primary text preserved classic Arabic style. The cultural connotations of the two styles differentiated Arabic source from Persian interpretation. The *diwani* style, in contrast, suited the task and subject of Ottoman power. It echoed the royal court and recorded texts in Ottoman Turkish. *Al-aqlam al-sittah*, *ta'liq*, and *diwani* all display letters and forms of Arabic script. But they communicate in different cultural, linguistic, and connotative registers.

The styles of *al-aqlam al-sittah* operate like a font family. Their shared history and classical connotations provide "variety and homogeneity at the same time: many shapes and sizes but a single [scribal] culture."[66] The sister-script pairings of *al-aqlam al-sittah* provided complementary styles at different sizes. This afforded both consistency of idiom and visual contrast. Scribes seeking the classical connotations of the scribal family could still choose a particular style "whose individual spirit and character [are] in keeping with the text."[67] In the unique case of the Qur'an, the visual varieties of *al-aqlam al-sittah* explored the depth and multiple messages of the text. *Muhaqqaq*, the most preeminently hieratic of *al-aqlam al-sittah*, exclusively recorded Qur'anic passages and quotations. The meticulous and stately appearance of *muhaqqaq* exhibits the eternal spirit and character of the Qur'an. *Thuluth* characterizes the Qur'an's fluidity, adaptability, and compositional perfection. And the spirit of *naskh* communicated the

Qur'an's clarity and accessibility. These three Qur'anic scripts share a common idiom of classical Arabic, but they convey the idiom with distinct character.

Elsewhere, stylistic variety conveys textual hierarchy. The Ottoman pairing of *thuluth* and *naskh* parallels the typographic distinction of display type and text type.[68] *Thuluth* titles and headings mark textual divisions and modulate the body of *naskh* text. Display types are typically larger and more expressive. They present titles and headings and seek to capture reader attention. Text types are typically smaller and more consistent. They present the body of written content, emphasize legibility, and seek to hold reader attention. As a display style, the flexibility and decorative fluidity of *thuluth* captures attention. As a text, or body, style, the clarity of *naskh* presents content in an easily legible register. *Naskh's* clearly distinguished letterforms, consistent baseline, open counters, and track-like *tashkil* stress legibility. Its spirit and character benefit the presentation and reading of long-form texts. Not surprisingly, therefore, *naskh* became the model for Ottoman and Arabic movable type. Within the wide spectrum of Ottoman scribal styles, *naskh* already recorded texts of wide distribution and shared legibility.

Finally, our Ottoman designer aligns the chosen styles with other visual elements and the page as a whole.[69] Designers strive to articulate the conceptual relationships of visual elements: "Shape the page and frame the text block so that it honors and reveals every element, every relationship between elements, and every logical nuance of the text."[70] The nuanced design of logical relations occurs in the layers of Arabic script itself. The higher layers of *tashkil* and *i'jaam* inform the logical priority of *rasm*. Styles such as *muhaqqaq* and *thuluth* reveal and honor this relationship by using a larger pen for *rasm* and a smaller-tipped pen for *tashkil*. *Tughra*-topped *diwani* scrolls provide another wonderful example of coordinated design. *Diwani* texts functioned as official slips of permission, and they were often displayed as such. Thus, the text was drafted as a single block on an extended scroll. The scroll format allowed the entire text to be displayed at once. The *tughra* logotype confirmed the sultan's authority, and the text that followed, written in *diwani,* conveyed the idiom of Ottoman power. *Diwani* flaunts ornateness, complexity, and a highly aestheticized presentation.[71] Its unorthodox ligatures and the density of its forms made the content difficult to decipher, while protecting the pronouncement from forgery and unsanctioned interpolations. Although the textual content was highly significant, that significance did not translate into efficient legibility. The coordinated design of a *diwani* scroll both protected and authorized its contents. The recognizable *tughra* logotype, the stylistic complexity, the textual content, the extended sheet, and the suitability for display all convey a logically consistent message: a precisely worded grant of royal permission.[72]

Hafiz Osman's *hilye* template raised the visual arrangement of textual and visual elements to a new plateau. (See Figures 2.2 and 2.3.) A variety of elements—both linguistic and otherwise—bolster and reinforce a shared message. *Hilye* transform stylistic variety into a richly layered symbolic architecture. They operate within, between, and among recognizable conventions. Communicative depth arises in the perception of multiplicity: multiple styles, multiple textual passages, and multiple forms. As scribal depictions of the Prophet, *hilye* encapsulate the varieties of Ottoman style and the importance of reading between the lines. Stylistic variety entices viewers through a contrast of linear rhythms: "The flowing movement produced by writing can be compared to the lapping of waves produced by water. Effect and counter effect form both the water's wave and that of script. [A script] is a rhythmic shape with a succession of similar shapes. Its chief rhythmic elements are: straight-curved, vertical-horizontal, arch shaped-garlanded, slanted-back slanted, circular-straight, pressure-resistance, tension-counter tension, upwards-downwards, start-end."[73]

Emil Ruder wrote these comments about typographic rhythm. They equally express the beauty of *hilye.* By organizing scribal tensions, Osman's template invokes a new language of design. The text flows from the pinnacles of *muhaqqaq,* through the regulated pacing of *naskh,* to the deep valleys of *thuluth,* and back again. The effect is emphasized by the eddies of *thuluth jali* that surround the deep central pool (the *göbek*) of *naskh. Hilye* traverse a series of stylistic comparisons and tensions: big and small, *thuluth* and *naskh, thuluth* and *muhaqqaq,* circular and rectangular, text and decoration, writing and image. *Thuluth* rose to supremacy as the predominant Ottoman display script, and it occupies the design's commanding central position. *Muhaqqaq* is strongly hieratic. It implicates the divine and opens the *hilye* as a pious and spiritual remembrance. *Naskh* presents longer lines of content clearly and consistently without challenging the primacy of the larger styles. To borrow from Bringhurst: The interaction evokes a style beyond style. Viewers learn to appreciate differences of style, each in its proper place and each with a distinct aesthetic calling. Scribal style, in this broad and communicative sense of the word, does not refer to any one particular Ottoman style, but the power to move freely through the whole domain of scribal practice with grace and vitality.[74]

Considering Scribal Design

Ottoman scribes were textual designers. They certainly beautified text, and their products more than deserve aesthetic appreciation as calligraphic art. But Ottoman scribal texts were also functional and operational. Visual style and textual copy are two sides of the same coin. Styles of script communicate alongside, and in support of, written content. Ottoman scribes dressed written messages in appropriate outfits. They designed texts to connect content and audience. Visual distinctions began with notational differences. Arabic, Hebrew, Greek, Armenian, and Latin characters all targeted distinct communities. Stylistic variety internal to a script further specified the direction of the text. That direction, the vector of communication, was visualized through *khatt*. The lines of *khatt* draw letters, outline text boxes, direct messages, target audiences, and connect readers across time and space. *Al-khatt al-mansub* provided a powerful system for the construction of formalized proportions and recognizable types. These types, or styles, were systemized, practiced, and taught. They were repeated by multiple scribes in multiple scriptoria across multiple centuries. Ottoman scribal tradition was incredibly durable, with a deep understanding of visual, graphic, and textual design.

The rich vocabulary of Ottoman design can be mined for contemporary considerations as analytic concepts. Some terms, such as *al-aqlam al-sittah,* delineate specific proportions and identify specific styles of script. Others, such *jali* or *ghubar,* refer to the size or scale of a particular variation. And yet others, such as *tughra* and *hilye,* refer to particular forms and the spatial organization of textual content. The range of *khatt,* understood as design, unites a vast range of textual and visual activity. Designs can be formal or informal, rounded or stately, traditional or experimental; style of script can be large or small, red or black, bold or fluid; the regulated vector of textual content can unfold as a single line or splinter into a collection of frames and boxes. Despite drastic differences in content, technology, and practice, the considerations of contemporary graphic design and scribal practice overlap. Digital designers weigh choices of hardware, software, and fonts. Ottoman designers weighed choices of paper, pen, and style. Different sizes and finishes of paper, different widths and cuts of the reed pen, and different styles of script all carried cultural, practical and regional connotations.

Ottoman design applied suitable styles and suitable tools to the copy at hand. If form follows function, the diversity of Ottoman styles attests to a diversity of functional solutions. Reframing scribal practice—and calligraphy more broadly—as textual design allows us to recover these earlier processes as models of current practice. It repositions products of Ottoman design as communicative objects with form, function, and practical insight. As we now digitize and remediate the Ottoman scribal legacy, how do we retain, remember, and reinvigorate these practices? And how might similar practices inform contemporary communication? Is there a place for conventionalized styles in a digital, global, and networked world? Scribal models encourage us to examine our communicative dilemmas from new and pertinent angles. The wealth and quantity of textual material have certainly increased since Ottoman times, but Ottoman society was no less design literate than our own. Approaching Ottoman *khatt* as a practice of communicative design reinvigorates it. The lines of *khatt* once again become functional templates and models of design solutions.

Chapter Three

European Printing and Arabic

Movable type printing certainly altered the production, as well as the appearance, of written communication. The spread of print standardized, democratized, and disseminated mass quantities of identical texts. These changes, in turn, heralded the mass production of material goods, rising rates of literacy, and new channels of textual authority. Movable type was one of Europe's first steps toward modernity, and Europe modernized hand in hand with the press. As the tide of printed material rose, the new technology interfaced with broad changes in European society. Print spurred the Protestant Reformation, the Italian Renaissance, and the Scientific Revolution. It challenged religious, political, and scientific authority. It spread new ideas, new genres, and new forms of text. Capitalism, secularism, and democracy followed in its wake. Although none of these changes were determined by the new medium, the printing press was undoubtedly an agent of change.[1] However, as much as printing's influence cannot be understated, it also cannot be generalized across the globe. In regions where Arabic script was dominant, printing spread much more slowly. Scribal production remained the norm across the Middle East until the nineteenth century.

Printing's benefits were neither instantly apparent nor universally embraced. In Europe, both religious and state hierarchies initially resisted print. But printers easily evaded restrictions thanks to political and religious fractures.

75

No central authority administered the new technology due to the decentralized and disparate political organization of fifteenth- and sixteenth-century Europe. During the same centuries, the Ottomans consolidated their hold on Asia Minor, the Levant, North Africa, and the Balkan Peninsula. As print spread across Europe, Ottomans scribes propagated proportional Arabic script (*al-khatt al-mansub*). Ottoman civilization developed hand in hand with the refinement of *naskh*. While Europe grappled with political disunity and an unregulated new technology, the rising tide of Ottoman dominance invested in time-tested scribal practices. Although print spread to Ottoman lands by the end of the fifteenth century, Ottoman Muslims did not adopt or utilize the technology until the early eighteenth century.

Chapter 2 explores the Ottoman practices of scribal design. Scribal and stylistic variety informed Ottoman written messages: diverse styles of script designed content according to function, genre, and audience. Chapter 4 examines how print operated alongside, and eventually infiltrated, scribal variety. This chapter steps to the side of that trajectory. It addresses European printing and the assumptions that informed the design of Arabic type. Arabic movable type was first designed and employed by European printers, who were less familiar with stylistic variety and the subtleties of handwritten Arabic. Instead, they applied Latinate models of print and type to a foreign script. These models shaped the appearance of Arabic type, as well as the expected relationship between print distribution and textual copy. Visually, Arabic script was segmented into reusable letterforms that could be cast as typographic sorts, much like the discrete letters of printed Latin script. On a more abstract level, European printing emphasized a specific aspect of textuality: the extension and distribution of written content. Print produced identical copies of typeset content, which it shared far and wide. In doing so, it redesigned content for movable type; it translated handwriting into a new medium. Aesthetic designs were relegated to the separate, supportive channel of illustration. European print mechanically reproduced the content of Arabic text, but it failed to reproduce the design of Arabic scribal form.

Printed Bibles and Hand-Copied Qur'ans

Gutenberg famously set the Bible as one of the first printed texts, and print culture was subsequently and intimately tied to the printed Bible. In the history of Christian Europe, the printed Bible symbolizes an opening of sacred knowledge to wider audiences. Prior to print, the Bible was monitored, controlled, and locked away by the Christian clergy. The press unchained biblical text from monastery desks. But biblical content was far from an obvious choice for the first printed work. Other early products of Gutenberg's print shop, such as calendars and indulgences, were less conventional.[2] Calendars point toward new forms of standardized texts, and printed indulgences emphasize mass production. These texts foreshadow textual changes beyond the opening of sacred knowledge. Yet they recede into the shadow of the printed Gutenberg Bible. As the canonical text of Christian Europe, the Bible models relations of religion, community, knowledge, and script.[3] The printed Bible merges these notions, and the religious changes of Reformation Europe, with the adoption of new technology. The printed Bible greatly influenced Christian perspectives on the intersections of reading, religion, and authority.

Martin Luther, in particular, deployed the new technology to challenge Catholic authority. Before printing the Bible, Gutenberg printed an indulgence. The indulgence recruited soldiers willing to protect Christian Cyprus from the advancing Ottoman Turks.[4] Via print, more indulgences could be distributed than ever before. Luther attacked the practice of indulgences, and, in doing so, he may have observed the power of printed repeatability. But he saw the power directed toward the wrong ends. If the repeatable powers of print could reinforce Catholic authority, it could also challenge that authority. Luther recruited and employed "printing as a Protestant weapon."[5] He proposed that lay readers should access the Bible directly without intermediaries.[6] Print was the vehicle that made this possible: "Printing is the latest and greatest gift of God. With it he wanted the cause of true faith to be spread to the ends of the earth and translated into every language."[7] Luther establishes a divinely inspired publication strategy. The Bible, which holds the "cause of true faith," should be both translated and printed. Translation opens the text to "every language," and print gifts biblical translation to "the ends of the earth."

Luther pursued this strategy in translating and quickly printing a German edition of the New Testament. His changes altered both the look and the language of biblical text. In translating from the original Greek, he replaced Greek letters with Latin letters. The two scripts look very different, and they dress the text differently. Luther claimed that he impartially translated "sense for sense."[8] But all translations are necessarily interpretative, and translating from one script to another alters the look and feel of a text. Luther argued that the biblical message shines forth, regardless of language or script. He prioritizes content over form, suggesting that the spirit of the text dwells in its content rather than its appearance and design.[9] This occludes his role in redesigning the Bible. Luther reorganized and reformatted content for a new audience of German readers. He added a variety of new elements, including prefaces, marginal glosses, and polemical illustrations.[10] The prefaces summarize biblical stories and identify prominent issues, the marginal commentaries play a similar role for individual passages, and illustrations reinforce the text with parallel imagery. This is design: the visual and textual arrangement of content in order to connect a particular message with a particular audience. Luther's design highlighted certain biblical themes and quieted others. He even opened the book with a list clarifying "Which are the True and Most Noble Books of the New Testament." Biblical books were hierarchically organized into tiers of importance, and some chapters did not even receive chapter numbers. By rearranging the text, prioritizing elements, and adding new components, Luther ensured that his *printed translation* clarified the meaning of "true religion."[11]

Luther's New Testament affirms design relationships of script, content, and form. He cast the books of the Bible into a new shape, a new script, a new language, and a new organization. He then utilized God's gift of printing to distribute and share his Bible with a wider German audience. Many of Luther's readers may have never seen or held a Bible. Elizabeth Eisenstein has commented that the printed Bible replaced cathedral windows, rather than the manuscript or scribal Bible, for popular audiences.[12] During the Middle Ages, most Christians visually encountered biblical content through stories depicted in stained glass. Very few knew what a written Bible looked like. This changed with print. Biblical content was now encountered as typographic words on a page: "Bible stories presented by stone portals and stained glass went out of favor even while Bible stories conveyed by printed chapter and verse were being translated into vernaculars and published far and wide."[13] Printed vernacular translations were often the first written image of the Bible that audiences encountered. Mechanical reproduction of identical copies magnified the effect. Since one copy appeared the same as the next, printed design conveyed an air of universality. Identical copies of the printed Bible, held in numerous hands, became the de facto model. Luther printed his German translation of the New Testament in 1522 C.E., and he issued a complete Bible in 1534. Within three years, more than

77 percent of German biblical citations employed Luther's wording, regardless of whether the citing author supported or opposed his religious views.[14] Luther's Bible confirmed the power of standardization via mass reproduction and print distribution. Even those who criticized and denounced Luther reproduced his wording and language.

Print emphasizes the extension, standardization, and distribution of written content. The "latest and greatest gift" of print spreads numerous identical copies to "the ends of the earth." Numerous technical advances came together to make this possible. One was movable type, which abstracted textual content into a series of interchangeable and repeatable letters. Another was paper, the substrate on which letters were printed. Paper plays the silent partner in the story of Europe's print revolution. Without paper, there would have been very little material on which to print. Papermaking spread across Europe during the fourteenth century, just over a hundred years before Gutenberg's innovations in movable type. Prior to paper, Europe's primary substrate was parchment, which is both and time- and labor-intensive. Made from cured animal hide, parchment operated within a competitive economy of resources. Hides were also outfitted for clothing, armor, storage, binding materials, and a variety of utilitarian purposes. By the late fifteenth century, the demands of printers would far exceed the available supply of animal skins. The Gutenberg Bible alone would have required as many as 170 calfskins per copy, or approximately five thousand hides for an edition of only thirty-five copies.[15] Paper nipped this problem in the bud. Paper was made from linen scrap and did not compete with leather goods for hides. And new techniques of paper milling supported cheap, abundant production. The flood of newly blank pages was quickly filled with printed copy.

In the Islamic Middle East, paper adoption had similar dramatic effects. It drastically altered the scale of written production and distribution. But Islamic papermaking began in the tenth century, five centuries before wide-scale adoption in Europe.[16] The quickly expanding Abbasid state suffered from a dearth of writing surface. As in Europe years later, paper answered the call. But the flood of newly blank pages was filled with the handwritten styles of *al-khatt al-mansub* rather than movable type. In both Europe and the Middle East, paper increased textual production while standardizing the appearance of scripts and type. *Al-khatt al-mansub* standardized the cursive line of handwritten Arabic, while metal type standardized the blocklike printed letters of Latin script. One adoption interfaced with scribal production and proportional handwriting; the other interfaced with mechanical printing and movable type. In the fifteenth and sixteenth centuries, paper shared printed letters with new European readers. Half a millennium earlier, paper shared proportional script with Muslim readers. Muslim intellectual tradition built on the relative abundance of paper paired with wide-scale scribal production. When movable type arrived in Muslim lands, it encountered a reading connoisseurship already familiar with, and celebratory of, hand-written cursive.

Muslim presses did not begin printing until the eighteenth century, nearly three hundred years after print spread rapidly through Europe. Unraveling the interaction of paper and scribal production in the Middle East, and paper and print in Europe, elucidates the perceived delay of Islamic printing. Muslim readers accessed script on paper long before the development of movable type. The Qur'an, moreover, was even slower to come to print. Whereas the Bible was the first book printed with movable type in Europe, the Qur'an was one of the last books printed in the Middle East. The first disastrous European attempt to print the Qur'an occurred in 1537 C.E., but the first Muslim typesetting of the Qur'anic text did not occur until 1787. And even that edition was produced in Kazan, Russia, at the request of the Christian empress Catherine the Great.[17] The Ottomans did not print copies of the Qur'an until the nineteenth century, nearly half a millennium after Gutenberg's Bible, and almost two centuries after they adopted printing for secular content. Qur'anic *masahif* were not widely printed in Muslim societies until movable type was challenged by lithographic printing, which supported the mass reproduction of scribal and handwritten style.[18] Unlike the Bible, the Qur'an did not quickly *translate* into the medium of movable type.

The Bible and the Qur'an model very different types of textual content and design. The Bible is a curated collection of diverse texts: "the sheer number of dissimilar materials drawn from different places, eras, and linguistic groups is particularly striking."[19] In biblical reading, multiple books are compared, related, and cross-referenced.[20] The Prophetic books interrogate the Torah, the Gospels reference the Old Testament, and the Epistles interpret the Gospels. The various elements unite to convey a message that the elements lack in isolation. This structure benefited Luther when he wished to further segment and reorganize biblical content through the addition of prefaces, glosses, and illustrations. Biblical structure—one text arising from multiple discrete elements—

acquired a technological parallel in movable type. Movable type printing not only shared biblical content; it reflects its composition. Letters of movable type are arranged and typeset to form blocks of texts, text blocks are collected and laid out in printers' grids, and the resulting pages are bound as a unified whole. The printed book conveys a message, which the individual components of type cannot. With movable type printing, segmentation informs the entire work. Various books segment into verses, verses segment into words, and words segment into distinct letters.

The conceptual and textual model of the Qur'an differs significantly. The Qur'anic text is much shorter and much more unified than that of the Bible. Although it contains 114 distinct *surahs,* they were all revealed to the Prophet Muhammad over a short period of twenty-three years. The Qur'an is certainly multifaceted; it encompasses an incredible range of topics, stories, and rhetorical styles. But unlike the Christian Bible, it does not collect disparate writings in different genres by different authors from different eras. The Bible consists of textual elements collected across time; Qur'anic *surahs* were revealed in time. The Qur'an, moreover, does not relate a story of divinity (for example, the life of Christ). The Qur'an is itself *divine:* the structure, the language, the wording, and content cannot be altered or translated:

> Only when one gets a clear understanding of the Muslim's attitude to the Qur'an as revelation primarily and not simply literature, can one sympathize with or explain the historical decisions made. Only then can one understand why the Bible and the Qur'an played such radically different roles in the history of printing in Europe and the Muslim world respectively. And finally, only then could one understand why there was no Qur'an . . . in the vernacular. Even at the risk of precarious simplification we could say that whereas for the Christian the primary access to the Divine Presence is not through the words since the "Word became flesh," for the Muslim the primary access is through the sacrament of the "written," revealed Arabic scripture.[21]

The Qur'an was, is, and will always remain necessarily Arabic. The Qur'an cannot be translated because the medium is the message. Form and content are divinely linked. Whereas Luther translated biblical content for new German readers, Muslims align themselves with (or "translate" themselves into) the specific Arabic patterns of the Qur'an.[22]

In a semantic analysis of the self-image of the Qur'an, Daniel Madigan interrogates Qur'anic usage of the term *kitab,* an Arabic word commonly translated as "book." Madigan distinguishes four aspects of the word—composition, display, storage, and redisplay—and discovers that the majority of Qur'anic references to *kitab* signify composition.[23] When referring to itself as a book, the Qur'an draws on the authority of its divine composition. Virtually none of the Qur'an's usage of *kitab* has to do with storage. Print emphasizes the far other end of the spectrum: redisplay. Print displays and distributes identical copies of a book for a widely dispersed audience. The Qur'an is also redisplayed, but Islamic tradition emphasizes redisplay of the mode in which the book was composed: oral recitation. If print places the Bible before the eyes of multiple readers, Qur'anic recitation envelops audiences in the sound and patterns of divine composition. Practices of scribal copying record, preserve, and protect the compositional moment. The earliest hand-copied *masahif* served as mnemonic devices. They supported recitational performance by readers who committed the text to memory. Changes in appearance and design were slow and conservative.[24] Religious scribes took great care to prevent the slightest alteration or abrogation. The adoption of paper and the redisplay of Qur'anic *masahif* for a broader audience necessitated a series of scriptural changes. Additional layers of script specified recitational precision, without altering the primary line of *rasm.* The addition of *tashkil* guided proper vocalization while semantically redundant *muhmal* letters protected against erroneous copying.

Early printing offered a poor substitute for scribal accuracy.[25] If a word was overlooked while copying the Qur'an, the scribe would insert a paratextual mark that directed readers to the margin, where the missing word could be found.[26] If a word was missed or letters were confused during the setting of type, the resulting error was mass-produced and identically duplicated across an entire edition. The new technology multiplied the circulation of faulty copies, and instances of textual corruption actually increased with print.[27] As late as 1631, English proofreaders failed to catch the egregious typesetting error contained in what became known as the "Wicked Bible." Printed copies of that edition erroneously list the Sixth Commandment as "Thou shalt commit adultery."[28] Problematic errors were even more common with Arabic, especially when typeset by printers unfamiliar with the language and script. The first European attempt to print the Qur'an contained an incredible amount of unforgivable mistakes on the opening pages alone. From an Islamic perspective in which emphasis fell on the protection of divine composition rather than the redisplay of content, "it seemed unacceptable that the holy text should be subjected to error-strewn duplication through the printing press."[29] European printers addressed these issues with errata pages. Errata might be added to the end of a text to identify known mistakes, or they might circulate after the fact to address issues of a particular edition. For European readers, errata corrected content in lieu of earlier mistakes. For Muslim audiences, however, the circulation of errata underscored the fallibility of print and the available typography.[30]

Arabic Script Printed in Europe

Print transformed the design of the book. Both the look and the contents of printed works differed from their handwritten scribal predecessors. The translation of texts into a variety of printed vernaculars was a significant change. Another was the abstraction of both letters and content into the "homogenous segmentation" of typographic elements.[31] On the technical level, letters of movable type were arranged and rearranged in printers' grids. On the textual level, texts were reedited, reorganized, and reissued. Vernacular Bibles lent themselves to these practices. Both the discrete characters of Latin alphabets and the disparate books of the collected Bible reinforce ideals of homogeneous segmentation. As print expanded, it applied a similar model to other texts and other traditions. Movable type was quickly adapted to Greek and Hebrew, which appeased European readers' interests in classical texts. Both these scripts, like Latin, easily segmented into a limited number of discrete characters. The cursive line of Arabic was more problematic. Not only do Arabic letters connect; they change shape according to position. To tackle these challenges, European type cutters analyzed and parceled Arabic manuscript samples, but the resulting characters were equally influenced by the printer's notion of how Arabic letters should interface with the new technology.[32] Printed Arabic teased a potentially vast market, if only the script could be set in type. And in order to be cut as movable type, the cursive line of Arabic script required homogeneous segmentation.

The isolation of Arabic letters as discrete elements began with the first printings of Arabic script in Europe. But the isolated forms did not begin as movable type. Printed Arabic began as an illustrated image opposite Latin movable type. Wood-block printing, and later copper engraving, operated alongside the new method of typographic printing. The technical division reinforced yet another ideal of segmentation: a separation of text and image. For scribal writing, "the hand that writes does not cease to draw."[33] This was not the case in print production. Typesetters handled written content, while engravers provided illustrations. Letters of type composed text; engravings displayed images. A similar divide informs the digital separation of text and image files, hence the need for optical character recognition on scanned pieces of text. Images must be analyzed, parceled, and recognized in order to be processed as text.

Printed analysis of Arabic as segmentable forms began in 1486 C.E. That year, Erhard Reuwich printed Bernhard von Breydenbach's *Peregrinatio in Terram Sanctam*. The travelogue describes Breydenbach's journeys in the Middle East, during which Reuwich accompanied him as an illustrator. Alongside Breydenbach's Latin text are Reuwich's reproductions of woodcut illustrations and drawings. These included an impressive meter-long panoramic foldout of the Venetian skyline, illustrated panoramas of other notable cities, representations of local fauna, and a map of Palestine and Egypt.[34] In addition to representative drawings, Reuwich illustrated letter tables for seven foreign alphabets encountered during the journey: Arabic, Hebrew, Greek, Syriac (Chaldean), Jacobite (Coptic), Ethiopic (Amharic), and Armenian. The wood-block Arabic alphabet is the first printed appearance of Arabic script in Europe. (See Figure 3.1.) As an illustration, it separates from the primary text, which was printed with movable Latin type. Latin type operated on one technical register, while non-Latin scripts were allocated to the technical registry of image.

At the time of printing, this was a practical concern. Non-Latin typefaces were not yet in circulation. Interestingly, however, Reuwich's woodcut alphabets imply that such typefaces *could be* cast. The illustrated alphabets are presented as tables of isolated and distinct forms. Each letter is assigned to an individual box. As such, the illustrations resemble primitive drawers of type. The Arabic illustration, for example, displays thirty-one forms: twenty-nine Arabic letters (including two versions of the letter *lām*), the essential *lām-alif* ligature, and a crude representation of the cursive word *walsulam (pax)*. Only the final box demonstrates Arabic script's necessary cursive grammar. The other forms suggest that Arabic letters can be strung together as individual shapes, much like the movable type of printed Latin. Reuwich's Arabic letters display sharp angles and are perhaps closest to the *Kufic* style of Arabic script. They certainly

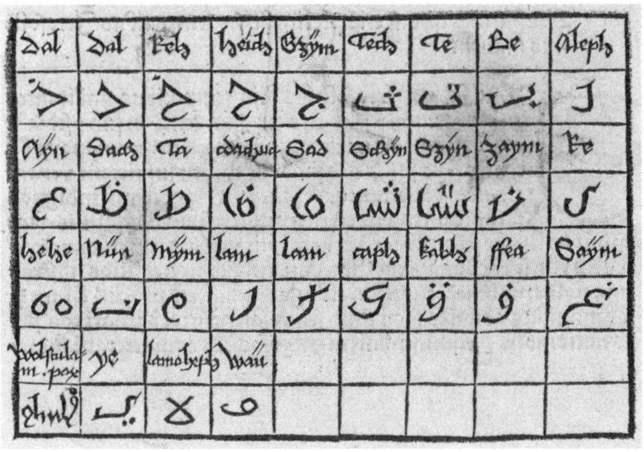

Figure 3.1.   Erhard Reuwich's woodcut alphabet

This wood-block alphabet was the first printed appearance of Arabic script in Europe. The isolated letters appear strongly geometric, and the organizing grid that holds them is reminiscent of a case for the storage of movable type. (Image courtesy of the Newberry Library.)

do not conform to any of the proportional *naskh* styles used for most Arabic manuscripts in circulation. Since the table isolates Arabic letters and isolated letters rarely appear in written Arabic, a reader would be hard pressed to locate the displayed forms in any piece of handwritten cursive. Reuwich's illustration presents an abstracted Arabic alphabet consisting of distinct letterforms; it does not replicate the cursive line of handwritten Arabic script.

Another woodcut Arabic alphabet was printed in 1505 C.E. The 1492 capture of Granada transferred Spain to Christian rule, and the new rulers wrestled with the conversion of local Arabic speakers. Pedro de Alcalá wrote *Arte para ligeramente saber la lengua araviga* in order to assist local missionaries. The work presents a useful and focused study of Arabic language, and Pedro de Alcalá's woodcut alphabet supports the primary focus of the text; it is not simply one example among many foreign scripts. The illustrated Arabic letters reflect the *maghribi* style of orthography used in parts of northern Africa and Andalusia.[35] The letters *qāf* and *fā'*, for example, are distinguished with a *nuqta* above the letter *qāf* and the *nuqta* below the letter *fā'*. In the *naskh* styles, both letters receive *nuqta* above their primary form: two *nuqta* for *qāf*, one *nuqta* for *fā'*. Pedro de Alcalá's letter table also includes the medial forms of certain letters as well as their isolated appearance, thereby increasing the total number of forms from thirty-one to fifty-eight. And the opposite page intersperses Arabic characters with Latin text, in order to specify how Latinate transliteration operates throughout the rest of the work. The book rode a wave of philological and orthographic scholarship that accompanied early European printing. And movable type implied that identifying distinct letters and characters could break linguistic codes. Once identified, foreign letters could be arranged, printed, transliterated, translated, and understood.

The segmentation of foreign scripts was a powerful key that opened them to receiving the gifts of print. Languages without movable type were excluded from the new exchange. In the 1520s, Robert Wakefield published a treatise on Semitic languages titled *Oratio de laudibus & utilitate trium linguarum Arabicæ Chaldicæ & Hebraicæ*. The printed version omitted an entire section of Wakefield's handwritten copy due to the lack of adequate type.[36] Throughout the sixteenth century, Arabic alphabets continued to appear as illustrations in Latinate texts.[37] One of the most famous appeared in 1529 in Geoffrey Tory's *Champ Fleury*. Tory's widely influential text on the "Art and Science of Proportion" examines each of the Latin letters in isolation. He presents the ideal geometric construction of distinct Latin forms. Although the project certainly overlapped with the proportional rules of *al-khatt al-mansub,* Tory was either unaware of the Arabic system or chose not to address it. In 1583, Protestant printer Jacob Mylius produced a readable Arabic version of Saint Paul's Letter to the Galatians via a technical work-around. The text is printed from whole-page wood blocks carved with running Arabic script.[38]

The first attempt to print Arabic script with movable type occurred in 1514. Pope Julius II sponsored the printing of an Arabic Book of Hours, *Kitab Salat al-Sawai*. Although the imprint identifies Fano as the city of production, printing likely occurred in Venice. The Fano imprint was likely a convenient work-around for local restrictions.[39] The book was set entirely in Arabic and targeted Arabic-speaking Christians in the Levant.[40] It was produced by Gregorio de Gregari with woodcut type. The type sits on a consistent baseline, with noticeable gaps between letters and erratic vocalization. The letters are strongly geometric and more closely resemble Syriac forms than the flowing lines of Arabic *naskh*. A polyglot psalter followed in 1516 C.E. It was printed in Genoa and set with wooden Arabic type alongside characters of Hebrew, Greek, and Chaldean. The psalter's Arabic type resembles the *maghribi* style, likely due to manuscript examples acquired from Spain.[41] Neither set of type appears again.

In both cases, the wooden type was likely unusable after the initial run. This is common for wooden type, as repeated pressings cause the fragile forms to chip around the edges.[42] Nevertheless, textual copy was now being typeset in Arabic; Arabic script was no longer a woodcut illustration. Arabic script moved from the realm of printed image into the realm of printed text.

The appearance of *naskh* was a casualty of the process. The formal proportional relationships of *al-khatt al-mansub,* which had preserved script grammar and ensured a consistent recognizable form, were not respected. *Naskh*'s flowing cursive line was simplified, broken, and forced into the square cells of movable type. The results, although recognizable, were not pleasing to native Arabic readers. And the problematic results were amplified in the earliest European attempt to print the Qur'an. The Venetian brothers Paganino and Alessandro Paganini printed the book, which is certainly one of the strangest and most mysterious artifacts of early Arabic printing. Shortly after production in 1537, the book disappeared. No copies were known to exist until Angela Nuovo rediscovered one in a Franciscan monastery during the 1980s.[43] A number of characteristics indicate that the book was intended for export and sale in Arabic or Ottoman markets. First, the text is entirely Arabic; it contains no translation or front matter that would prove useful to European scholars. Second, the book preceded any printed translation of the Qur'an into any European language. A complete Latin translation was not printed in 1543.[44] Prior to that, the potential European clientele for an Arabic edition would have been extremely small. Finally, very few copies ever circulated in Europe, which is confirmed by their absence in European archives. Instead, the printers likely targeted a lucrative export market. The plan, however, did not pan out. No copies have been found in Ottoman or Arabic archives either. The book's mysterious disappearance is attributed to intentional destruction. Rumors include burning by papal order and confiscation upon arrival at Ottoman ports. In any case, the Paganini brothers failed to reap financial rewards and soon went bankrupt.

The singular unearthed copy of the Paganini "Qur'an" contains extensive textual and orthographic errors. If it had indeed been intended for an Islamic market, the book would have shocked Muslim audiences. In a weighted examination of the benefits and dangers of printing, Mushin Mahdi proclaimed that pious readers would assume that "only the Devil himself could have produced such an ugly and faulty version of the holy book."[45] When compared to Ottoman Qur'anic *masahif,* the Paganini version appears dark, dirty, and disorganized.

Egregious orthographic mistakes include faulty letter connections, improper spelling, improper vocalization, a lock of rosettes between verses, and a confusion of similar, but significantly different, letters: *tā'* replaces *thā'*, *dhāl* replaces *dāl,* and so on. The orthographic layer of *i'jaam* (that is, the placement of *nuqta*) is particularly flawed. Letters of a particular class (for example, the *bā'* class, the *dāl* class, the *'ayn* class, etc.) are frequently confused. This sharply undermines legibility. Both the visual design and the phonetic representation of the text are compromised. The opening pages alone display innumerable mistakes. In *Surah al-Fatihah,* the words *al-din* and *alladhinna* appear exactly the same.[46] The letter *dhal* appears in both words, when the first should contain the letter *dal* instead. On the facing pages, the verse count of *Surah al-Baqarah* transcribes part of the verse count as *tamanun* (with initial letter *tā'*) rather than the correct word *thamanun* (with initial letter *thā'*). *Fathah* is the only represented *tashkil,* and it often appears alongside letters that properly receive *kesrah* or *dammah.*[47] Simply put, the reproduced text is not Qur'anic text. It is an orthographic aberration of the original.

Such blatant mistakes undermine centuries of careful Qur'anic preservation. The Paganinis may have assumed that few Ottoman readers had seen a Qur'anic copy and that their printed version would be the first on the scene. They wagered that the first print edition, much like Luther's German Bible, would become the de facto standard. Even a glimmer of market research would have shown the opposite to be true. Unlike Europe, where most readers never saw a manuscript Bible, Qur'anic *masahif* were in circulation. They were not hidden away and chained to desks in monasteries.[48] Ottoman readers, if they owned any book, would likely have an accurately copied Qur'anic *mushaf.* Even those without the book may have read or studied passages in local mosques. And they certainly would have viewed passages of Arabic text on public display in architectural inscriptions. Ottoman clients assessed written text, and Qur'anic *masahif,* in particular, with highly discerning eyes. The Paganinis' obvious dismissal of proper orthography, not to mention their complete disregard for proper proportional relations, appeared unreadable and offensive to an intended Muslim audience. The obvious faults appear even more glaring in a printed book arriving from Christian Europe, especially since the Qur'an itself stipulates that only purified readers should handle the text. The Paganini "Qur'an" visually argues for its own impurity and therefore calls for destruction. Nor was it alone in such mistakes. In 1539, the noted Orientalist Guillaume Postel (1510–1581) published his *Grammatica Arabica*. To print the book, Postel attempted to obtain the Paganinis' Arabic type, but the fonts likely had been melted down as a result of the book's financial failure. Postel settled on wooden type, and despite inclusion of the word "grammatica" in the title, the script grammar remains highly errant. The sample Arabic texts display wide spaces between individual letters, which parcels the fluidity of the cursive line. Postel presents *Surah al-Fatihah* as one example, and he repeats many of the same errors as the Paganinis. Once again the words *al-din* and *alladhinna* appear identical. But whereas the Paganini version used *dhāl* in both words, Postel uses *dāl* for both letters.

The European travails with movable Arabic type ease slightly near the end of the sixteenth century. Master type designer Robert Granjon (1513–1589) cut five Arabic typefaces, which display marked improvement over preceding attempts. Granjon's type appears highly cursive. Characters connect in consistent fashion, and the space between forms is minimized. From 1545 to 1588, Granjon carved type on commission in Paris, Antwerp, Lyons, and Rome. He designed well over forty different typefaces and cut approximately six thousand punches. His reputation was built on the precise lines of his typographic flowers and italic designs. This established him as a specialist in complex scribal forms.[49] In 1557, Granjon designed the *civilité* typeface, which he modeled on the handwritten French style known as *cursiva*.[50] Granjon offered *civilité* as a uniquely French alternative to the triumvirate of Roman type, italic, and black letter. Latin and Italian printers typically employed humanist Roman forms and their supportive italics, whereas Germanic language printers were more likely to employ the style of black letter. Granjon suggested that *civilité* was similarly suited to the idiosyncrasies of written French. The typeface demonstrates flowing shapes and delicate lines, which appealed to Giambattista Raimondi. Raimondi had recently been appointed scholarly director of the Tipographia Medicea (Medici Oriental Press) in Rome, and he enticed Granjon to join the operation and recut its cursive Arabic type.

When Granjon arrived, he inherited a set of type cut by Giambattista Eliano in 1564. Eliano cast the type by papal request for the Tipographia del Collegio Romano, where it was used to print a dual-language exposition of Catholic faith in Arabic and Latin. Tipographia del Collegio Romano operated within a Maronite college established by Pope Gregory XIII. The pope wished to rebuild ties with Eastern Christianity in the wake of the Reformation by launching a series of diplomatic and educational projects.[51] And the college included technical instruction in printing as part of its college curriculum. Press operations were later placed under the supervision of Cardinal Ferdinando Medici and renamed Tipographia Medicea. Cardinal Medici personally appointed Raimondi as director. During his extensive travels in the Middle East, Raimondi studied Arabic, Persian, and Turkish, translated classic Islamic works into Latin, and collected a wide range of manuscript samples, grammars, and dictionaries. Raimondi's expertise would guide the press with Medici's financial backing. The partners located a building near Rome's Piazza del Monte d'Oro and set up shop. In addition to Granjon, Raimondi's team included Domenico Basa, who assisted with type punching and final casting, the Armenian printer Marc Antonio (formerly Sultanshah Dpir), whose father ran a successful press in Constantinople, and Giacomo Luna (formerly Yaqub ibn Hilal), a graduate of the Maronite college, who would go on to manage the daily operations after Granjon's passing.

The first specimens of Granjon's Arabic type appeared in 1580, and the Medici press employed them for more than twenty publications. Notable books include Arabic versions of the Gospels, Euclid's *Elements* (complete with geometric diagrams and al-Tusi's commentary), Ibn Sina's medical treatise *Al-Qanun,* and an abridged version of al-Idrisi's geographic treatise *Nuzhat al-Mushtaq.* The press's showcase piece, *Alphabetum Arabicum,* beautifully displays Granjon's Arabic type alongside a Latin essay on Arabic script and language. The text begins with a list of Arabic letters, which provides the letter name in both Arabic and Latin along with a Latin letter of sound equivalency.[52] The list is followed by the now common table of four forms, in which the Arabic letters are displayed with isolated, initial *(in principio),* medial *(in medio),* and final *(in fine)* forms.[53] The presentation of forms demonstrates the homogeneous segmentation of Arabic script. The discrete shapes can be strung together to create cursive letter blocks: all letter blocks begin with an initial form, end in a final form, and contain one or more medial forms as necessary. The accompanying Latin essay explains how Arabic script connects cursively, discusses the use of alternate variants for certain letters (such as *hā'* and final *yā'*), and identifies the unique *lām-alif* ligature. Additional ligatures, which greatly expanded the type set beyond the number of Arabic letters, are displayed in a thirty-page syllabary, which presents a variety of possible letter combinations. The syllabary is fully vocalized with *tashkil,* which are set around the letters from separate metal sorts. The book ends with sample texts set with Granjon's Arabic typefaces.

The table of four forms, the syllabary, and the sample passages beautifully demonstrate movable Arabic type in all its variations: as a collection of distinctly shaped letterforms, in connected syllabic letter blocks, and as running text. The samples include the Lord's Prayer, the "Ave Maria," Psalm 116, and the opening of the Gospel of John. Lines of text display a wide range of visual bounce. They are fully vocalized with *tashkil,* ligatures are common (allowing letters to connect both vertically and horizontally), and final forms vary from block to block. The four-form table presents the letters' "isolated" forms as an alternate "final" form, and they are used as such. The letter *nūn,* for example, displays a smaller semi-circular shape with a central *nuqta* and a larger sweeping shape, both of which are presented as discrete "final" forms. Granjon's Arabic typefaces maintain a consistent horizontal structure despite their vertical motion, which is reminiscent of *civilité.* The upper line of *tashkil* is evenly spaced above the letters they modify, and the lower level of *tashkil* (that is, *kasrah*) occupies the same line as the sublinear *nuqta.* Most of the *tashkil,* and some of the *nuqta,* were individually cast and set as distinct sorts. Other, more complex relations, such as *shaddah* plus *fathah,* were cut as a combined sort. Granjon's designs mimicked the handwritten line and elevated Arabic type to a new level.

Tipographia Medicea publications were widely circulated, across both Europe and the Middle East.[54] Of those exported to Ottoman lands, the most famous is a 1594 edition of Euclid's *Elements.* The book is fully printed with Arabic type and notably contains the copy of a decree by Sultan Murad III. The decree, which transcribes text of Ottoman Turkish, states that the Bandini Brothers are free to import books without fear of seizure. Like the Paganinis before them, the Bandinis may have sought to corner a potentially vast market. If the threat of seizure could be minimized, the size of the Ottoman market promised large financial returns. The wording of the decree implies that seizures of other works had already occurred. If Ottoman authorities were indeed confiscating printed imports, receiving official permission was a wise tactic.[55] Including a printed copy of the decree was an astute preventative measure.

Formal pronouncements of the Ottoman sultan communicated through textual content and visual design. They were penned in the complicated *diwani* chancery style, drafted on extended scrolls, and topped with a majestic *tughra* signature. The *diwani* style of script in particular distinguished royally issued Ottoman Turkish from Arabic scientific texts, such as Euclid, which were written in the common *naskh* style. These classificatory design distinctions disappear in the Bandini reprint. The print copy conflates content with royal authority, and as such, it may not have been understood as the Bandinis intended. In print, the Turkish content of the decree and the Arabic text of Euclid employ the same typefaces. Visually, the printed decree distinguishes neither the linguistic difference (Arabic / Turkish) nor their different provenance. The royal Turkish text and the Arabic scientific text appear as if they originated from the same hand, which they indeed did if we replace "hand" with "mechanical press." Even the sultan's name is standardized. Murad's name and title appear as a large, legible piece of centrally justified text, which is a far cry from the complex logotype of an official *tughra*. Although the printed page copies the textual content of a royal decree, it contains none of the visual and stylistic markers that convey the channels of Ottoman authority: the style is *naskh* rather than *diwani,* and the *tughra* shape is completely absent.

Printed Words and Scribal Forms

By isolating individual Arabic letters, European movable type reproduced the content, but not the design, of Arabic and Ottoman writings. Printed reproduction offers a distinctly different communicative performance than handwritten text. An Ottoman *ferman,* for example, performs as a visual gestalt. The content is only one of many communicative aspects. Indeed, the content may not even be the most important aspect.[56] Since a *ferman,* like other pieces of textual design, contains language, the linguistic aspect rises to prominence. But other aspects of the design are equally significant: the style of script, the format, the length of paper, the surrounding illustration, the presence (or absence) of a royal signature, and so on. Emphasizing content over form implies translatability: the ability to translate words from one appearance to another. But the style of an Ottoman *ferman* cannot be translated. The visually complex style of *diwani,* which holds the content of a *ferman,* is intentionally difficult to decipher. Visually translating that content into a legible typeface alters its communicative channel.

One model of writing—a model that informed the printing of vernacular Bibles—privileges the display of content. Content translates across scripts, languages, forms, and media. Even the term "copy," as in "printer's copy," refers to basic textual content that is typeset and printed. Copies are mechanically reproduced and visually identical. An alternative model of writing—a model that resonates with practices of scribal design and Qur'anic preservation—privileges the recitation of compositional authority. Both the original language of composition and the visual traits of a document represent that authority. Altering either rewrites the text. In this model, a copy is not the same as the original simply because it "looks like the original in the photo-identity sense accomplished by mechanical reproduction but because it has passed through an authoritative process of human reproduction and collation."[57] Copies are defined by practices of composition—including the practice of handwriting—rather than similarities of redisplay. A handwritten copy unfolds in time, much like a recitation. Movable type, in contrast, composes writing from pre-provided "copy" and preformed letters. Typesetters arrange characters in static grids, and the press transfers them to the page all at once. The process is repeated again and again, producing multiple copies of the same page. The printing of movable type confounds textual and compositional order. Books are constructed from disparate elements—letters, words, and pages—which are reorganized, rearranged, and bound in proper order to display content.

Like other scribal traditions, European handwriting evolved a range of formal variants and compositional styles.[58] Print translated these variations into a limited number of recognizable, discrete, and reusable forms. The dual alphabet of uppercase and lowercase Latin letters, with which we are now familiar, solidified in response to print technology. The terms "uppercase" and "lowercase" reference printer cases in which the movable type was stored.[59] The number of forms was reduced over time, finally settling into a nadir limited by the number of keys on a keyboard.[60] Printers, unlike typewriters, retained a range of ligatures and complex forms. And early printers employed an even wider array of sorts. Gutenberg took great pains to replicate the manuscript style in his earliest printings. His forty-two-line Bible displays almost three hundred sorts, most of which represent letters, ligatures, and variants that were later segmented and simplified or simply fell out of use.[61] With print, these differences were standardized into a formal set of twenty to thirty letters, along with standardized accents, and punctuation.

Reducing written form to a consistent set of letters and punctuation aided efficient typesetting. Individual pieces of type resulted from a three-step process: punch, matrix, mold. First, the shape of a character was cut in hard metal. This is known as the punch. Second, the punch was struck into softer metal, leaving an impression of the character known as a matrix. Finally, the matrix was placed in a mold to cast the type. Liquid metal was poured into the mold, filled the matrix, and hardened into the shape of the character. The matrix assured that multiple pieces of a single character, or sort, looked identical. Rarely used ligatures required their own punches and matrices. Working on tight budgets and schedules, printers and type cutters were loath to produce forms that would be set only once in a blue moon. Breaking a ligature into individual letters reduced the number of punches and matrices while increasing the number of reusable sorts. If one could disentangle a complex ligature into three discrete forms, each of those forms could be used in a variety of settings. This increased the speed and efficiency of typesetting, as printers became familiar with the location of commonly used letters in the case.

Applying a similar logic to the fluid lines of *naskh* proved problematic. Arabic letters display multiple variations, many of which require tweaking, bending, and occasional breaking in order to fit within a printing grid. Letter shapes change according to context, and certain letters connect with other letters in unique ways. Cursive connection itself was not the issue. The Arabic typefaces of Robert Granjon and others successfully imitated cursivity through careful alignment of sorts. For native readers, larger issues arose from the appearance of those connections and the letters they connected. Literacy not only teaches readers to recognize shapes; it leads readers to expect patterns of similarities and contrast. And movable Arabic type failed to mimic the expected movement of the line. Early Arabic types are frequently described as "unsatisfactory," "unrefined," and "inelegant."[62] Even Giambattista Eliano's typefaces, which Granjon inherited, remained "insufficiently cursive and calligraphic, and lacking adequate sorts for some letters, especially in their medial forms."[63]

To Ottoman and Arabic readers accustomed to scribal variation, the "inelegant" regularity of movable type was glaring. Foreign typefaces appeared "decidedly unlovely" to discerning eyes.[64] In 1652, Jesuits stationed in Constantinople noted a predilection for handwritten texts. They claimed that even Ottoman Christians dismissed printed matter as unreliable, foreign, and "Frankish."[65] Such commentary highlights persistent local resistance to typographic style. Some of this criticism can be attributed to egregious orthographic errors, such as those in the printings of the Paganinis and Postel. Elsewhere, it targets the structural and aesthetic reform of Arabic script in the name of typographic convenience: "In manuscripts and elegantly printed books many of the letters are interwoven with one another, and form ligatures. . . . These ligatures, in which one letter stands above another, are very inconvenient to printers . . . and most founts have some device to bring the letters into line. . . . [S]implicity and convenience have caused [this] to be largely adopted in modern founts. But in writing Arabic the student ought to use the old ligatures as they are shown in [manuscripts]."[66] As late as 1792, Carsten Niebuhr attributed the low number of printed books in the Middle East to the value placed upon "a species of elegance, which consists in their manner of joining their letters, the want of which makes themselves dislike the style in which Arabic books are printed in Europe."[67] The "value" placed on "elegance," which Niebuhr identifies, is much more than simple "dislike." The "manner of joining" the letters is the crux of the issue. Altering letter connections alters the script and deviates from expected norms. The "want of" familiar connections challenges legibility.

Neibuhr's commentary reduces a structural criticism of Muslim readers to aesthetic, or local, preference.[68] Ottoman readers not only expected a certain manner of joining letters; they celebrated the elegance of those connections. Display panels of *meshk* (Turkish: *meşk*) exercises, such as those penned by the nineteenth-century scribe Kazasker Mustafa Izzet Efendi (1801–1876), demonstrate every possible letter connection. (See Figure 3.2.) Such panels clearly display the "species of elegance" that defines Ottoman *naskh*. Scribal letters do not mechanically repeat throughout a text. They respond to the letters that precede and follow them. The *bā'* class letters, for example, do not always connect with subsequent forms in similar fashion. The *bā'* class displays a range of connections (sometimes vertical, sometimes horizontal, sometimes brief, sometimes extended) that modulate the line.[69] *Meshk* panels demonstrate every possible cursive iteration. Rather than transforming letters into a series of movable (and interchangeable) sorts, they perform letters as flexible forms that respond to the surrounding environment. By reducing the number of complex ligatures, the "simplicity and convenience" of *naskh* typefaces deviated from expected visual rhythm. Current readers of Latin script often find PRESENTATIONS OF TEXT IN ALL CAPS DIFFICULT TO READ. Running text in capital letters disrupts the expected rise and fall of lowercase Latin letters. Readers find such texts "decidedly unlovely" and favor "a species of [lowercase] elegance," the want of which tires the eyes. Ottoman readers accustomed to scribal texts may

Figure 3.2. Mustafa Izzet Efendi's *meshk* exercises

Meshk (Turkish: *meşk*) panels such as these by Kazasker Mustafa Izzet Efendi (1801–1876) demonstrate every possible cursive letter connection. The center frame displays the connections of initial *bā'* to other classes of letters in *naskh* style, and the bottom frame displays the connections of initial *bā'* to other classes of letters in *thuluth* style. The top frame displays the isolated forms of *thuluth* letters.

have similarly shirked the uniformity of printed matter, which disrupted the rise and fall of the cursive line. Movable Arabic type appears overly static when compared to the rhythm and fluidity of scribal *naskh*.

The meeting of European movable type and Arabic script produced a hybrid form of type-script that Thomas Milo labels "Eurabic."[70] Eurabic imposes preconceived notions of homogeneous segmentation on the heterogeneous connections of scribal form. It replaces the fluid line of Arabic script grammar with static models of European typography. Arabic letters become exchangeable forms, which resemble the shapes of Latin letters. In particular, Milo highlights three Eurabic shapes that impose Latinate forms on Arabic letters.[71] The first is the inverted v, or carat (^), which was often used for the medial form of *bā'* class letters. A series of *bā'* class letters comes to resemble a mountain range, with *nuqta* placed above and below the peaks. Alternatively, the *bā'* class may

96

be represented by a backward L, sometimes set at a slight angle. In both these Eurabic adaptations, every instance of the *bāʾ* class displays a consistent height (which resembles the x-height of Latin typography). In scribal writing, letters of the *bāʾ* class were differentiated—from one another and from letters of the *sīn* class—by subtle changes in the height of their stem. The contrasting heights modulate linear rhythm and assist legibility. *Bāʾ* class letters remain recognizable even when *nuqta* are obscured or absent. The reinforcement of varied height and *nuqta* bolsters legibility. Both variations differentiate letters. Only one of these differentiations (viz., *nuqta*) transitioned into movable type. The expected height variation disappears in sets of movable type in which all instances of the *bāʾ* class display an identical medial form. A third Eurabic feature is the backward Z, which was used as medial form for letters of the *jīm* class. The ends of the backward Z cursively connect with the typographic letters that precede and follow it. In scribal models, however, the preceding letters connect to medial *jīm* from the top rather than the right side. None of these features—inverted v, backward L, or backward Z—operate as primary forms in handwritten Arabic script. European printers invented them by recycling familiar forms of Latin script.

Historically, the European simplification of movable type corresponds with the pinnacle of Ottoman proportioned script. Ottoman calligraphy and handwriting manuals proliferated during the fifteenth and sixteenth centuries, the same centuries during which print swept across Europe.[72] Illustrated devotional works were another popular genre. Many of these contained calligraphic pages depicting the names of Muhammad and the early caliphs in the decorative style of *jali thuluth.* The large ornate script is paired with a caption that repeats the name in more legible *naskh.* A calligraphic roundel displaying the name of Abu Bakr, for instance, might have the following caption: "This is the name of his excellency Abu Bakr, may God be pleased with him."[73] Jamal Elias suggest that the framing and artistic presentation of the roundels are "not the *textual* rendition of the name but its *image.*"[74] The communicative channels separate: the legible *naskh,* like movable type, is text; the ornate *jali thuluth,* like engraving, is image. But unlike typesetting and engraving, in which the channels separate technologically, both the *jali thuluth* name and the *naskh* caption are handwritten by pen. The hand that writes does not cease to draw.[75] And rather than diverging, the two styles may synthesize relations of text and image. The caption reinforces the decorative name as *text.*[76] It reaffirms the written content of the decorative script while teaching readers to appreciate the aestheticized "manner of joining" the letters.

In 2002, the British Museum published *Arabic Calligraphy: Naskh Script for Beginners* by Mustafa Ja'far.[77] It provides a simplified and popular introduction to Arabic script grammar and the proportional rules of *naskh.* Ja'far wrote the book to accompany introductory Arabic calligraphy workshops. The target audiences were English museumgoers and workshop participants with very little knowledge of either the Arabic language or Arabic script. Ja'far's book is therefore a far cry from the writing manuals and illustrated volumes that circulated in the Ottoman Middle East. Those texts targeted specialist scribes and an elite reading public intimately familiar with the script and a variety of languages that employ it. *Arabic Calligraphy* operates on a much simpler level. Yet the introductory nature of the work makes it particularly revealing. The book does not purport to teach the Arabic language; it does not concern itself with the need to translate linguistic content. Instead, the presentation teaches the basics of *naskh* script. It emphasizes visual design and script grammar: the manner of joining the letters and the species of elegance that define this popular style.

Ja'far's textbook outlines three stages of practice followed by a gallery of contemporary and historical examples. The practice schedule begins with "Stage One: *Mūfradat* single letters." Each letter is defined as a series of ordered pen strokes. Letters of the same class (for example, the *bā'* class) are grouped together by common *rasm,* and the proportions of all *rasm* are measured in *nuqta.* Significantly, Ja'far does not present a four-form table of Arabic letters and their positional variants. The opening page notes, "Arabic letters vary according to their position in the word (initial, medial, or final) and whether they are joined or unjoined."[78] But Ja'far quickly undermines any assumption that initial, medial, and final forms are universally consistent. His sole example exhibits five widely different appearances of the letter *hā',* and he indicates that further variations will be demonstrated in the second stage. "Stage Two: *Murakkabāt* joined letters" presents three pages of densely packed sample sheets illustrating a wide variety of letter connections. The section begins with a caveat stating that the displayed connections are not exhaustive: "To illustrate all forms of joined letters is beyond the scope of this manual."[79] Still, Ja'far provides more than two hundred heavily annotated samples. The annotations compare various means of connection and describe the conditions under which letter shapes and proportions alter in response to particular contexts. The following examples are noted on one of Jafar's sample pages (see Figure 3.3):

- "Initial *hā'* has two different forms: (a) closed if it is followed by an ascending letter; (b) open if it is followed by a descending letter."
- "The proportions of initial *'ayn* are dictated by whether it is followed by a descending or an ascending letter."
- "Final joined *kāf* has a different form and proportions from the unjoined one." (Ja'far's joined *kāf* measures four *nuqta* wide compared to three *nuqta* for the unjoined letter.)
- The initial *kāf* can be either swordlike *(kāf sayfī)* or armlike *(kāf zannādī)*.

Ja'far's collection of letter connections removes any doubt that *naskh* letters have a single form per position. Among other variations, he demonstrates two sets of proportions for initial *'ayn*, two forms of initial *kāf*, two forms of initial *mīm*, two forms of medial *mīm*, two forms of initial *hā'*, three forms of medial *hā'*, two specialized forms of final *hā'* (which connect to a preceding *dāl*, a letter that does not normally connect with the following letter), and three forms of final *yā'*. These examples are followed by "Stage Three: *Kalimāt* words," in which sixty-nine sample words and phrases "demonstrate not only all the single unjoined letters of the alphabet, but also many of the variations of joined initial, medial, and final letters."[80] Ja'far's book does not simply teach students how to write. It teaches them to recognize, read, and expect the visual variation of *naskh* script.[81] The simple course bears witness to the complex linear rhythm and formal variety that disappeared with movable type.

The spread of movable type in Europe and the refinement of scribal *naskh* unfolded contemporaneously. As the first rough Arabic alphabets were being printed in Mainz and Spain, Şeyh Hamdullah was polishing letter designs that would become the exemplary Ottoman style. As European printers recycled Latin forms and altered linear rhythm, Ottoman scribes received *ijaza* certificates for perfectly reproducing scribal exemplars. As Eurabic shortcuts repeated the inverted v and backward Z, *meshk* panels illustrated the subtle and varied connections of the cursive line.[82] The resonances of these divergent trajectories still linger. During the early twenty-first century, Mustafa Ja'far taught novices to appreciate the linear variability of *naskh*. Digital type, meanwhile, continued

99

Stage Two: *Murakkabāt* **joined letters**

This section is designed to show as many joined letters as a beginner should need to practise at this stage. To illustrate all forms of joined letters is beyond the scope of this manual.

1 Initial *ḥā'* has two different forms:
(a) closed if it is followed by an ascending letter (1).
(b) open if it is followed by a descending letter (1a, 1b).

1 Notice how *dāl* is written above the base line by one dot.

6 Final joined *kāf* has a different form and proportions from the unjoined one. Compare this joined *kāf* with the large unjoined version on page 15.

2 The gradual narrowing of this stroke is achieved by twisting the pen very slightly clockwise.

3, 4 The proportions of initial *'ayn* are dictated by whether it is followed by a descending (3) or an ascending (4) letter.

5 Initial *kāf*, known as *kāf sayfī* (sword like), followed by different letters.

7 Another initial *kāf*, known as *kāf zannādī* (arm like).

Figure 3.3. Mustafa Ja'far's *meshk* page

This page from a contemporary introduction to *naskh* script by Mustafa Ja'far demonstrates how letterforms and cursive connections can adopt a variety of shapes. Ja'far's annotations describe two forms of initial *ḥā'* (annotation 1) and two forms of initial *kāf* (annotations 5 and 7), among other variations. (Image courtesy of Mustafa Ja'far.)

to segment Arabic script into a collection of repeatable characters and four-form tables. Such persistent distinction of aesthetic script and movable type betrays a deeper conceptual model, in which print reproduces textual copy rather than aesthetic form. European printers translated scribal form into textual content. The reproduction of content was shared to "the ends of the earth and translated into every language."[83] In the same move, the content of movable type separated from aesthetic practices of illustration and design. When applied to Arabic text, movable type was unable to replicate the expected form of literate and scribal *naskh*.

Chapter Four

Print in Ottoman Lands

*W*hen Sultan Mehmet Fatih marched into Constantinople, Gutenberg was still wrestling with movable type. The Ottomans took Constantinople on May 29, 1453 C.E., and Gutenberg completed his forty-two-line Bible a year later. The two events mark distinctly different historical trajectories. By the time of Mehmet's death in 1481, presses were located in well over a hundred European cities. Ottoman Muslims, however, would not beginning printing until the eighteenth century. During the early centuries of European printing, the Ottomans were a rising power. They captured the jewel of the Byzantine world, and their territorial gains would continue to increase throughout the sixteenth and seventeenth centuries. The new Ottoman capital exerted cultural and political influence over a vast geographic area. Europe, in contrast, was in the midst of tumultuous changes. The continent consisted of numerous principalities and competing courts of influence. And the Protestant Reformation would soon splinter the cultural unity of the Catholic Church. Newly printed works ignited contentious religious and ideological debates. Many European powers initially resisted print and sought to control the new technology. But they lacked the territorial and political influence to halt print's spread.

While this occurred, the Ottoman realm consolidated its gains. In seventy short years, Ottoman armies would conquer the Balkans and knock on the gates of Vienna. The Ottoman advance welcomed, absorbed, and benefited from the incorporation of foreign knowledge and expertise. The royal library held Islamic and European works—both recent and classic—side by side. Ottoman textual production was booming, and Şeyh Hamdullah would soon revitalize and perfect the proportional *naskh* of *al-khatt al-mansub*. Diverse scribal styles produced a range of texts, from Qur'anic *masahif* and administrative decrees to scientific classics, educational manuals, and Persian poetry. Useful European knowledge, from art to science and technology, was embraced. Sultan Mehmet personally commissioned a wide range of translations from Greek and Latin sources,[1] he retained Christian Greek architects for the design of his grand mosque,[2] he commissioned the Venetian painter Gentile Bellini to produce a royal portrait,[3] and he received European engravings, as well as incunabula with Latin type, as gifts.[4] Movable type printing also entered Ottoman lands. The autonomous Ottoman *millet*s, officially recognized religious communities, adopted print technology to meet their own textual needs. Ottoman Jewish, Armenian, and Greek Orthodox communities all established presses. Ottoman Muslims, however, neither acquired a printing press nor did they aspire to.[5] A large scribal class adequately addressed the textual needs of state and popular consumption. Ottoman society felt no pressing urge to alter the textual and scribal practice that underwrote its rising dominance.

Histories of media technologies must weigh these opposing trajectories side by side. In hindsight, we appreciate the dramatic effects of a "printing revolution." Print drastically altered scholarly and textual exchange, reshaping Europe and the world in its wake. But print's success does not imply historical inevitability. The contribution of the press—the foundational need that the technology addressed—was the mass production and distribution of written content. This same need can be answered with alternative technical means, such as the vibrant scribal communities that preceded it and the digital practices that eventually replaced it. Ottoman society was familiar with print, both in foreign lands and within its own borders. But print was not officially adopted by the Ottoman state, nor was it applied to Arabic script by local printers, until the eighteenth century. By that time, the geopolitical tables had turned: Ottoman power was on the wane, and Europe was ascendant. As Ottoman reformers looked to European models to revitalize and extend Ottoman glory, they found a useful tool in the printing press. The benefits of print for strategic advantage and scholarly exchange had become apparent during the intervening centuries. Ottoman perceptions of the press began to shift. It was no longer simply a means of technical reproduction. It was also a tool of state modernization. When Ibrahim Müteferrika opened the first official Ottoman print shop in 1727, he targeted an elite audience of state bureaucrats, administrators, and military commanders. The results would alter the trajectory and appearance of *naskh* as both a handwritten and a printed style.

Printing and the Ottoman *Millet* System

Upon winning Constantinople, Sultan Mehmet turned to the task of rebuilding and consolidating the realm. Political and cultural reforms preceded the flourishing of art and architecture. Mehmet instituted the Ottoman *millet* system, in which approved religious communities retained administrative and juridical rights.[6] The Orthodox Christian, Armenian Christian, and Jewish communities all became semiautonomous. The new system repopulated the city with Muslims and non-Muslims alike. The population grew steadily, as Greeks, Jews, Armenians, Slavs, and others immigrated to Istanbul in light of the new protections. Each of the *millets* operated with its own language and script: Orthodox Christians employed Greek script, Armenian Christians employed Armenian script, and the Jewish community employed Hebrew script.[7] Arabic script, which identified Islam, served the Ottoman Muslim population. These linguistic and notational divisions played an important role in the diffusion of print in Ottoman lands. Scripts identified communities of practice, and multiple scripts often transcribed the same language depending on the intended audience.[8] Each *millet* independently administered the printing of its recognized language and script.

The Ottoman Jews were the first *millet* to produce printed works. When Spain expelled the Jews in 1492 C.E., Sultan Bayezid II invited them to settle in Ottoman lands. Immigrant Jews arrived with presses in tow, and Bayezid quipped that the new Spanish king Ferdinand was impoverishing his own kingdom while enriching Ottoman lands.[9] The first printing in Ottoman lands occurred less than fifty years after Gutenberg's Bible and merely a year after the Jewish expulsion from Andalusia. The earliest Hebrew printing from Constantinople is dated 1493, and Don Yehuda Gedalya, a refugee from Lisbon, produced an edition of the Torah in 1504.[10] Constantinople quickly rivaled Venice and Amsterdam as a center of Hebrew printing. The pioneering Soncino family, which began printing in Venice in 1483, relocated to the Ottoman cities of Constantinople and Salonika in 1527, and one member later expanded operations to Ottoman Cairo in 1557.[11] In 1556, the Soncino press produced a multilingual Pentateuch. The book included texts in Hebrew, Aramaic, Arabic, and Persian, with all four languages printed phonetically in Hebrew characters.[12] The Ottoman Jewish printing community was incredibly robust. Printers often traveled to and traded with Europe. In the sixteenth century, traveler Nicolas de Nicolay recorded that Ottoman Jews were known for printing books in numerous languages, including "Greek, Latin, Italian, Spanish, and Hebrew."[13] When Arabic script was finally printed in Ottoman Istanbul, the Jewish printer Jonah ben Jacob Ashkenazi would cut the type.

The next *millet* to adopt printing was the Armenian Christian *millet*. And it too printed in a variety of languages. Hakob Meghapart first printed Armenian characters in Venice in 1512.[14] Fifty years later, Abgar Dpir acquired both Meghapart's machinery and his original typefaces. Dpir moved the press to Constantinople in 1567, where there was a much larger Armenian community. He printed six works, including a short Armenian grammar and devotional manual. Dpir's son Sultanshah, who later adopted the name Marc Antonio, studied printing in Rome. While there, he worked alongside Robert Granjon at the Tipographia Medicea. The two produced an Armenian typeface that rivals Granjon's Arabic types in its beauty and clarity. Other notable Ottoman Armenian printers include Grigor of Merzifon, who began printing in 1698. Grigor was the first Armenian to make printing his sole profession, and he trained a generation of Armenian printers. Grigor's student Astvatsatur opened a printing shop that operated for more than 150 years. By the eighteenth century, Ottoman Constantinople had become a vibrant center of Armenian printing. Beginning in 1700, Constantinople-based printers produced at least one Armenian title per year, and Constantinople's annual production of Armenian books frequently topped that of all other cities.[15]

For the Christian Orthodox *millet,* a significant turning point occurred in 1627. That year, Cyril Lucaris, the Orthodox patriarch of Constantinople, opened a Greek language press. Lucaris was a highly politicizing figure, and his eighteen-year tenure as patriarch was rife with intrigue.[16] He was particularly averse to Roman Catholicism, and he steered the Orthodox Church closer to Reformist and Calvinist theology. Lucaris enticed the successful London-based printer Nicodemus Metaxas to Constantinople to run the press. Metaxas arrived with a large surplus of Orthodox texts, two sizes of Greek type, and all the necessary machinery to set up shop.[17] But he was unaware that by stepping off the docks, he was stepping into a political firestorm. Unknown to Metaxas, Lucaris had neither obtained nor sought import permission from Ottoman authorities. Instead, he secretly turned to Thomas Roe, the British ambassador, for help in passing the equipment "unsearched" through customs.[18] The ambassador agreed, but he refused to house the press on his premises and advised that all parties should "proceed warily" in putting it to use.[19] Given Lucaris's strong anti-Catholic stance, local Jesuits perceived the newly arrived press as a direct threat. After the first book was printed locally, they highlighted potentially inflammatory passages and brought them to the attention of the grand vizier. Janissaries stormed Metaxas's workshop, halted printing operations, and destroyed the press machinery.[20] In a legal review, Ottoman judges later chastised the Janissaries for acting too brashly and awarded reparations for the lost machinery. The judicious ruling stated that the Orthodox Christian *millet* was entitled to debate its beliefs in whatever format it wished—including print—even if those statements were contrary to Islam.[21]

By the mid-seventeenth century, printing presses were operating in all non-Muslim Ottoman *millets*. Some of the Hebrew presses had been continuously printing for almost two centuries. Armenian presses had similar track records, and they too were operating without problem. Expertise, techniques, and machinery were shared among local printers.[22] *Millet* printers traded with European partners and trained in European cities. And visiting emissaries patronized local presses. None of this appears to have greatly bothered the Ottoman administration. The only notable exception is the Lucaris press, which deliberately stoked religious factionalism. And even that fiasco ended with a retroactive ruling that the press should not have been shut down in the first place. When Nicodemus Metaxas retired to the island of Cephalonia after his unwitting role in the Lucaris scandal, he donated his remaining machinery and typefaces to an Armenian press.[23] The Armenian printers acquired them without incident and employed them to publish less-controversial Greek texts.

Ottoman Muslims were certainly aware of printing. Multiple presses operated in the Ottoman capital, they printed in multiple languages, and Ottoman libraries held printed works. Yet the Ottoman Turks did not adopt printing for their own purposes, nor did any of the local presses print with Arabic type.[24] Numerous studies frame Sultan Bayezid II—the same sultan who elevated and admired Şeyh Hamdullah's *naskh*—as the primary culprit. Sultan Bayezid II allegedly banned print, and André Thevet publicized the bans in *Histoire des plus illustres et scavans hommes de leurs siècles* (1671). Thevet's book, which notably appeared shortly after the troubles surrounding the Lucaris press, mentions a 1483 edict. Thevet reports that Bayezid stipulated the death penalty for anyone attempting to print in Arabic. He goes on to say that Bayezid's successor, Selim I, reaffirmed the ban in 1515. But Thevet had a reputation for exaggerating his claims about foreign lands.[25] These doubts are further bolstered by a lack of records indicating any such punishment.[26] Yet, there are also no records of Turks wishing to print. In 1855, the French typographer Ambroise Firmin-Didot reaffirmed the bans in his *Essai sur la typographie*. Firmin-Didot hailed from a respected family of French printers and worked as a French envoy in Istanbul. But like Thevet, his reliability is questionable. Firmin-Didot was a staunch supporter of Greek independence, and the Athens printing museum contains a bust celebrating his efforts. Among other contributions, he smuggled press machinery into Greece for the anti-Ottoman resistance. Firmin-Didot's political affiliations may have therefore influenced his claims of Ottoman despotism.[27]

The veracity of the descriptions—and even the existence—of the bans remain unverified.[28] If Bayezid II did indeed issue such a harsh decree, he did so while welcoming immigrant Jews who quickly established Hebrew presses. These concurrent policies are perplexing at best. Bayezid's interaction with European powers also included the exchange of visual works and artifacts, including printed gifts.[29] In 1482, he received a print copy of Francesco Berlingheri's *Geographia*.[30] Berlingheri originally wished to dedicate the *Geographia* to Sultan Mehmet, who was an avid collector of maps, but the sultan died shortly before Berlingheri completed his work. The geographer hastily added a new dedication extolling Mehmed's successor, Bayezid II. Berlingheri gifted another copy of his masterpiece to Prince Cem, Bayezid's brother, who also staked a claim to the throne. Cem's copy was dedicated to him, rather than Bayezid, and it praised the errant prince in nearly identical terms.[31] Berlingheri may have wanted a copy ready at hand, inscribed to whoever ultimately won the throne. But Cem's challenge failed. He fled first to Rhodes and later to Rome, where Pope Innocent I placed him under protection. The exiled brother was living in Savoy when he received his copy of Berlingheri's work. If Bayezid II had seen his brother's dedication, he would have almost certainly frowned upon it as a challenge to his throne.

Cem's travails were popularized in 1494 by Guillaume Carousin, who published *Obsidionis Rhodie Urbis Descriptio (Description of the Siege of Rhodes)*.[32]

The 1496 print edition includes a series of woodcuts that paint Cem in a favorable light and present Bayezid as a usurper. Accusations circulated that the new sultan may have had an active hand in his father's poisoning, and the woodcut imagery strongly condemns Ottoman idolatry.[33] The prints likely offended Ottoman officials. Given his well-known iconoclastic leanings, Bayezid II himself would have taken particular offense at the use of figurative imagery. The seditious prints insulted his father, challenged his rule, and propagandized on behalf for his traitorous brother. Bayezid's severe condemnations of print—if he did pronounce them—may have targeted these prints in particular. Even if Bayezid's bans were as strict as later sources insist, their sting is reduced when situated as responses to specific texts that challenged his rule. He may have sought to prevent Ottoman subjects from acquiring seditious material, rather than the technology writ large.

European rulers also tried to control print within their borders. But early printers benefited from religious and political disunity on the European continent.[34] Rival presses cultivated and promoted competing ideologies for economic profit, and a lack of central authority allowed enterprising printers to easily circumvent bans and censorship edicts. Books banned in one locale were easily printed elsewhere and smuggled across porous borders: "free-wheeling merchant publishers had good reasons to avoid well-ordered consolidated dynastic realms and to fear the extension of central control."[35] Ottoman rule was a paragon of a well-ordered consolidated dynastic realm. The Ottomans secured a much larger area than any of the European states, and the arm of centralized control reached much farther. If printing restrictions were indeed active, the Ottoman state was in a much stronger position to enforce them than its European counterparts. The Ottoman realm was a rising political star with extensive reach. Print, which may have been tacitly accepted as a useful tool for weaker *millets*, may not have offered immediate benefits for an already dominant state.

Print as a Vehicle of Reform

By the early eighteenth century, tides had shifted. Ottoman power was in decline, and Europe was on the rise. The printing press, which was previously viewed with skepticism, became a useful tool. The first Ottoman press to print in Arabic script would open in 1727 C.E., at the tail end of the Tulip Period

(1718–1730), which shifted the dynamics of court and political life. Dutch tulip bulbs, which gave their name to the period, became particularly popular. Tulip cultivation signified the pleasures of leisure and nobility, and the tulip motif spread as a decorative motif from gardens to walls to books and clothing. The young Sultan Ahmet III epitomized the leisurely turn of the royal court. As he pursued gardening, calligraphy, painting, and poetry, administrative power shifted to the position of grand vizier. The reform-minded Nevşehirli Damat Ibrahim Pasha obtained the post in 1718. While the sultan dallied in his garden, Ibrahim Pasha pushed an agenda of military modernization, political change, and bureaucratic reform. Support for the first Ottoman printing press is one of his lasting legacies.

As a young man, Ibrahim Pasha negotiated the 1699 Treaty of Karlowitz. The treaty resulted in the first significant loss of Ottoman territory in Europe, and it marks a shift from Ottoman expansion to a much more defensive stance. Two decades later, the Treaty of Passarowitz ceded additional territory to the newly expanding Habsburgs. The golden era of Ottoman growth was in decline. In 1529, Ottoman troops were knocking on the gates of Vienna. A century and a half later, the realm was in retreat. The rising tide of defeat weighed heavily on the new vizier. Ibrahim Pasha sought to learn from Europe's rise in order to regain Ottoman glory. And information control was a key component of the envisioned resurgence. The vizier sponsored a wide range of translations and founded numerous public libraries.[36] A 1718 decree prevented the export of manuscript copies. Well-funded European collectors were purchasing mass quantities of Ottoman manuscripts, and the loss of information was adversely affecting Ottoman scholarship.[37] The vizier's export restrictions slowed the tide of economic and textual loss, in hopes of reviving and protecting local education. Particularly important subjects included geography, history, and military tactics.

Less than a year after becoming grand vizier, Ibrahim Pasha received a printed map of the Sea of Marmara. The map was printed in 1719, and it was the first map—indeed the first text—printed locally by Ottoman Muslims. The map, which measures 19.5 by 43.5 centimeters, displays few place-names. Ephemera of boats and mountains dot the landscape, and an imposing Ottoman seal dominates the upper left corner.[38] The boxwood printing plate was engraved locally and printed by Ottoman bureaucrat Ibrahim Müteferrika. The printer included a short dedication addressed to the vizier: "If my Excellency so wishes, larger works can be produced."[39] Recognizing the utility of modern maps,

Ibrahim Pasha enthusiastically requested more. Charts of the Black Sea, Ottoman Asia, Persia, and Egypt followed over years, each demonstrating significant technical improvement. The map of the Black Sea, printed in 1724 C.E., was engraved on four copper plates. Engraved text clearly labels a wide variety of places by name, a map key defines prominent symbols, a measurement scale calculates distance, and a fully boxed compass rose indicates thirty-two navigable directions.

As much as the grand vizier championed the maps, other factions were less enthusiastic. A note accompanying the Black Sea map states that it was produced "despite objections."[40] Ibrahim Müteferrika decided to formally counter the objections. He drafted "Vesiletü-t Tibaa" (The Utility of Print), an explanatory essay outlining the benefits that print offers Ottoman society.[41] Müteferrika analyzed European printing, weighed the consequences, and carefully presented his plan to both the royal court and the religious hierarchy. Müteferrika would later operate the first official Ottoman press. But ten years passed between the printing of his first map in 1719 and the first book in 1729. The interstitial period entailed a series of negotiations, and the revolutionary potential of print was enacted through a series of calculated political reforms. The questions of print adoption required answers, even if the questioning was restricted to an elite cohort of military officials, religious judges, and imperial counselors. The official decision was handed down in 1727, when Sultan Ahmet III issued a *ferman* authorizing the establishment of an Ottoman press. The *ferman* is certainly a watershed moment in Ottoman history, but it represents the end point of negotiation, rather than the opening salvo.[42] Ottoman print began with administrative reform rather than technological revolution.

Bureaucratic support arrived with the return of Ottoman statesmen Yirmisekiz Mehmed Çelebi and his son Said.[43] While Ibrahim was circulating his maps, the Çelebis were touring France. Yirmisekiz Mehmed led a diplomatic delegation that awarded France permission to repair the Church of the Holy Sepulcher in Jerusalem. The prestigious architectural bid signaled a lessening of religious tensions and increasing openness to foreign investment in Ottoman lands. France was quickly becoming a primary Ottoman trading partner, and the delegation was also tasked with studying modern French methods of organization and knowledge. For eleven months, the entourage toured the country, recording their observations. Mehmed Çelebi's *sefaretname,* a record of diplomatic travel, became the most famous example of the eponymous Ottoman genre. The account balances Ottoman interest in France with the equally awed wonderment of French society for its Ottoman visitors. Çelebi recorded particular delight in the interest that Parisian women displayed during his Ramadan fast. He also comments on a wide variety of sights, including botanical gardens, hospitals, military fortifications, and the Paris observatory. In a meeting with Comte Henri de Saint-Simon, the visiting dignitary even confided his plans to establish a press in Istanbul.[44]

The 1720s were an exciting time for French printing, and the Çelebis' enthusiasm resonated with local French interest. In 1723, Martin-Dominique Fertel published France's first manual on the "science of print."[45] More than twenty years earlier, in 1699, Louis XIV had commissioned the design of Romain du Roi.[46] These "Roman letters of the King" were the exclusive typeface of the Imprimerie nationale. As printed materials became increasingly important for matters of state, European powers established state presses under their direct control. The royal French government directly administered the Imprimerie nationale, and the use of Romain du Roi for anything other than officially sanctioned texts was a criminal offense. Among other idiosyncrasies, Romain du Roi added a small nob halfway up the stalk of the capital letter I. Such formal eccentricities identified the royal typeface and protected against forgery. Romain du Roi visually and typographically distinguished royal publications from the products of other presses. The proprietary typefaces were first used in 1702, and the full set of royal fonts was completed in 1745. The casting and design of the royal letters therefore coincided with the Çelebi's visit. The ambassador may even have encountered the royal typefaces during his travels. In Ottoman circles, the complex chancery style of handwritten *diwani* signified official pronouncements of state. The style's complexity protected royal documents from forgery and duplication. State control of the Imprimerie nationale and the visual idiosyncrasies of Romain du Roi may have convinced the delegation that similar safeguards could occur in print.

Upon returning to Istanbul, Mehmed Çelebi presented his discoveries before the imperial council. He celebrated the wonders of France and may even have introduced the idea of the Imprimerie nationale and its specialty typefaces. His gifts to the sultan included a series of printed engravings that displayed the grounds of Versailles and astronomical tables from the Paris Observatory.[47] The latter advanced the work of the famous Persian astronomer Uluğ Bey, and

Mehmed sadly noted that they remained unprinted. But it was Mehmed's son Said Çelebi who enacted his father's hope of opening an Ottoman press. Said partnered with Ibrahim Müteferrika, and the two drafted a formal agreement in 1726. The contract stipulated that Ibrahim would handle press operations while Said would assure financial backing.[48] The grand vizier, the patron Çelebis, and Ibrahim Müteferrika all agreed that printing offered great benefits to Ottoman circles. The next steps entailed collecting the requisite documents. They requested a religious opinion *(fatwa)* from the Şeyhülislam (the top religious judge) and a royal permission *(ferman)* from Sultan Ahmet III. They also gathered supportive blurbs from respected scholars and jurists. When the first book rolled off the presses in 1729, it included endorsements from sixteen eminent scholars. Şeyhülislam Abdullah Efendi likened the book to a beautiful pearl, and his judgment was supported by eight military judges and seven local luminaries.

Ibrahim Müteferrika: Ottoman Printer

In his autobiographical work *Risale-i Islamiye,* Ibrahim Müteferrika (1674–1745 c.e.) records his early Unitarian leanings and subsequent conversion to Islam.[49] His hometown of Koloszvár was a center of debate among competing Christian factions in Transylvania. The region was staunchly Unitarian and strongly critical of the Catholic hierarchy. Unitarians challenged the Church's centralization in Rome and its allegiance to the holy Trinity. Competing Calvinists, in turn, seized upon the region's anti-Catholic rhetoric as an opening for Reformist ideals. The ideological and textual debates among Unitarians, Catholics, and Calvinists likely influenced young Ibrahim's decision to justify his personal beliefs in writing. More significantly, the medium was the message. The religious debates in Ibrahim's hometown were conducted, and occasionally enflamed, through the medium of print. The famed Hungarian printer Miklós Kis (1650–1702 c.e.) opened a Calvinist print shop in Koloszvár in 1689.[50] The young Ibrahim Müteferrika almost certainly encountered Kis's publications, and he may even have trained at the press.[51] The technical means and mode of debate shaped the young scholar, who never forgot the utility of print for disseminating information.

Müteferrika was not the first Ottoman to advocate or analyze print. In the mid-seventeenth century, historian Ibrahim Peçevi recorded the first mention of Gutenberg in Ottoman sources. Peçevi, like Müteferrika, was of Hungarian descent. His history draws heavily on European sources, and he was familiar with the same matter of the printed exchange of ideas that influenced Müteferrika during his youth.[52] Peçevi's short comment on print argues that printed works expand the historical and intellectual archive. Peçevi interestingly focuses on the circulation of recent writings by independent and currently active writers. He does not promote the printing of classic works. He then describes the printing circuit, with particular emphasis on the transmission of work from scholar to audience. The process balances a high initial investment with the possibility of great returns: "At first, putting all the separate letters in place takes as much time as hand-copying but then a thousand copies can be printed easily, with less trouble than making a single copy by hand."[53] According to Peçevi, European scholars seek patronage in order to cover the large initial costs of printing. Müteferrika would later follow this model in establishing his own print shop: Said Çelebi provided financial patronage, and Müteferrika operated the press.

In *Vesiletü-t Tibaa,* Müteferrika presents the case for administrative Ottoman printing. Since the mid-1400s, the long revolution of print had ushered in new modes of European scholarship. Print distributed recent works of science and geography to the scholarly community. And Ibrahim Müteferrika displays familiarity with these developments. Many of Müteferrika's arguments for print could not have been made during the early centuries of European printing. He synthesizes lessons learned in the two hundred years since Gutenberg, and he mirrors observations written (and shared via print) by European scholars.[54] The essay begins with a *basmala* and a benediction seeking God's aid in presenting the text. Ibrahim relates his "sudden, clear inspiration that there are means and instruments that societies and groups of people might use for benefitting the organization of important human matters and for the glory and power of the empire and state."[55] From the outset, print is framed as a benefit to the state. Books are a primary means of "perfecting the nation and state" and creating "solidarity in the community."[56] The production of books benefits the preservation of law, the sharing of knowledge, and the "good order" of the community. Ibrahim tempers his praise with the admission that distributed books must be "sound and accurate." He repeatedly balances recourse to tradition with forward thinking. Printing will not disrupt the established order but extend it. And it therefore offers "a noble profession and a beautiful calling." In proper bureaucratic fashion, he ends with a request for royal permission in order to silence potential critics.

Vesiletü-t Tibaa then shifts into more formal argument. Ibrahim notes a series of historical incidences in which valuable written knowledge was lost, sometimes through the vagaries of time or warfare, sometimes because divergent versions of a text created intellectual confusion. Ibrahim commends the Jews ("Beni Israel") for preserving the Torah, although conquest and dispersal had diluted the text. In Christianity, the hasty collation and competing accounts of the Gospels resulted in misunderstandings and quarrels over religious dogma (for example, the contentious debates among Unitarians, Catholics, and Calvinists that unfolded in Hungary during Ibrahim's youth). Learning from these mistakes, Islam carefully protected the orthographic integrity of the Qur'an. In doing so, Muslims transcribed and disseminated knowledge "without defect." Müteferrika then pivots away from religious texts. He never suggests printing the Qur'an, nor does he assume that the Qur'an is unavailable to Muslim readers. Instead, he focuses on lost scholarship. During the Mongol invasion of Baghdad, the Tigris "washed away" numerous tomes of Abbasid knowledge. During the Spanish conquest of Andalusia, Umayyad science was "torn from the arms of Islam." And yet more books are lost to material decay, natural disasters, and fires. Ibrahim does not specifically mention recent Ottoman military losses, but the listing of earlier Muslim defeats would have resonated with his readers.[57] To stem the tide, Ibrahim introduces print. Print offers a means of replenishing the books that have become "scarce and rare" in Ottoman lands.

Ibrahim's primary argument revolves around ten benefits. Before introducing them, he insightfully situates print within technical practices already employed by Ottoman craftsmen: "printing is a type of inscribing analogous to the action of engraving and writing by pressing words and lines on a page. It is like coining money or inscribing walls, or like the impression from a signet ring when pressed upon a document." Ottoman craftsmen practiced all of these methods. Illuminators pressed stencils and patterns on paper. Architectural decorators carved letters into wood, metal, and stone. Ottoman coinage was minted for circulation. And letters were sealed with signet rings. By linking printing to accepted technologies, Müteferrika deflects the possible challenge that printing is foreign to Muslim practice.[58] Print does not challenge tradition; it benefits and extends Muslim glory. He specifies the following ten benefits:

1. Print answers "the needs of the people for books," especially dictionaries and scientific texts. These will "create tremendous educational benefit."

2. The reprinting of classic works will reinvigorate scholarship: "newly printed books, both numerous and accurate, being restored and invigorated, as if they had been recently authored, will publish and present" the collected history of Islamic knowledge.[59]

3. Printing can produce and distribute books of beautiful design without "mistakes, flaws, or errors." These accurate editions facilitate learning, and the printer's ink is more durable than the ink of manuscripts.

4. Printed works strengthen the economy as "items of commerce." Inexpensive books support the education of rich and poor alike.

5. Printed books are more user-friendly: they contain tables of contents, indexes, and summaries. "If it is necessary to refer to the book, its contents and organization are immediately accessible."

6. The price of books will decrease. More readers will be able to afford them, and the "widespread dissemination" of printed material will "reduce ignorance."

7. Libraries will "become full of books," even in rural areas. Outlying regions will develop on account of more books and better education.

8. Books exalt the Ottoman state and "enliven" the Muslim community. The printing of books will benefit those who dwell in "the shadow of [Ottoman] royal happiness."

9. Christian countries already print works in Arabic, Persian, and Turkish. But these works are "full of misspellings and mistakes, and the letters and lines are not easily read." Moreover, the financial benefits of selling these books flow to foreign rather than local merchants.

10. Printed books "increase and augment the glory and majesty of the Ottoman state." Ottoman printed books will benefit the global Muslim community, both within and beyond Ottoman borders.

Overall, the ten benefits construct a field in which better education, the continued glory of the Ottoman legacy, and economic benefits provide the big takeaways. Müteferrika completes the list with a final appeal to Ottoman glory. Printing offers the Ottoman state yet another chance to mark its place in history: "it will be remembered with goodness by the tongues of the world and will bring forth the good prayers of all believers."

Ibrahim sought to work and reform the Ottoman state rather than attack it from the outside. He was a government bureaucrat, rather than a religious reformer or a political radical. His intended audience was similarly administrative and legalistic, and the memo reads much like a governmental white paper. Ibrahim's petition advances the Ottoman state through new modes of print scholarship. The mention of indexing and textual reorganization (point 5) is particularly noteworthy. The index developed alongside the spread of print. Its textual and cognitive benefits became apparent only over time.[60] But Ibrahim writes as if the benefits of indexes are self-apparent, which suggests that Ottoman civil servants already accessed and appreciated these novel textual tools.

Ibrahim concludes his essay by specifying the types of books to be printed: "dictionaries, histories, medical texts, science books, philosophy, astronomy, and information about nature, geography and travelogues." He specifically excludes books of "law *(fiqh)*, [Qur'anic] exegesis *(tafsir)*, traditions [of the Prophet] *(hadith)*, and theology *(kalam)*." These specialty fields are the province of religious scholars and are therefore the most likely to draw pushback from conservative voices.[61] Since Ibrahim was not trained in any of these religious fields, he does not ask to print them. He directs debate toward more general concerns of education, science, and government. Claims that the Ottoman religious or royal establishment banned Müteferrika from printing religious texts are inaccurate. Ibrahim never requested permission to print religious works. Ibrahim's focus is secular and administrative. He does not ask, nor does he wish to ask, religious questions. He simply wishes to strengthen the state, its educational system, and its military. In order to make this clear, Ibrahim reiterates his request for a royal permission *(ferman)*, and he adds a further request for a religious opinion *(fatwa)* from the Şeyhülislam. He asks for these documents as confirmation that "printing conforms with Holy Law."[62] And he states that including the permissions in printed books will ease "the doubts" of potential critics.

In proper bureaucratic fashion, the precise contents of the requested permissions may have been less important than their separate issue from the requisite sources. Both the religious *fatwa* and the royal *ferman* were received, and both were favorable toward the endeavor. The wording of the decrees closely follows

Ibrahim's original petition. The authorizing *ferman* from Sultan Ahmet III summarizes and restates Ibrahim's main arguments. It excludes the same religious topics listed in *Vesiletü-t Tibaa,* but only as a preface to permitting the printing of geographic, scientific, and reference works. The *ferman*'s listing of permitted and excluded topics repeats Ibrahim's wording verbatim, and it bases the permission on the "pearl pen of wisdom" presented in the religious *fatwa,* which was issued by Şeyhülislam Abdullah Efendi. Consistent with its legalistic form, the *fatwa* presents a deliberately worded answer to a carefully chosen question. The question inquires about the printing of dictionaries, works of logic, philosophy, and astronomy; it *does not* inquire about print in general or the printing of religious texts.

> ***Question:*** If a man undertakes to imitate the characters of hand-written books, such as dictionaries, works of logic, philosophy, astronomy, and other scientific works, by forging letters [of metal], making type and printing books conforming absolutely to handwritten models, is he entitled to legal authorization?
>
> ***Answer:*** God knows best. When a person who understands the art of the press has the talent to cast letters and make type correctly and exactly, then the operation offers great advantages, such as clarity of work, the ability to pull a great number of copies, and the low price at which anyone may acquire them. If one [the sultan] can propose persons learned in literature to correct the proofs, the printer cannot but find favor in this enterprise, which is most beautiful and praiseworthy.[63]

The *fatwa*'s glowing admiration approves Ibrahim's request, and the suggestion of proofreaders reiterates—rather than limits—Ibrahim's proposal. Ibrahim's essay *Vesiletü-t Tibaa* requests three or four scholars who will ensure that the printed works are "accurate and free of any defect or mistake in respect to the perfection of [their] composition and language."[64] Once again, Müteferrika demonstrates informed familiarity with the techniques and practices of print. Printing's reproductive powers not only multiply texts; they also magnify textual errors. A printed mistake, once distributed, cannot easily be undone. But printed works, unlike manuscripts, can be corrected in proof.[65] The royal *ferman* responded to the *fatwa*'s stipulation and Müteferrika's request by naming four prominent scholars: Khadi Mevlana Ishak of Istanbul, Khadi Mevlana Sahib of Salonika, Khadi Mevlana Asad of Galata, and Şeyh Mevlana

Musa of the Kasım Paşa Mevlihane (a religious order). The appointed proof-readers committed themselves to the task with rigor and precision. When they noticed that the manuscript models used for the press's first publication contained multiple mistakes, they halted all typesetting until the contents of the original could be corrected and verified.[66]

The appearance and accuracy of the Arabic *naskh* typeface were also prime concerns. Ibrahim's essay specifically refers to the *maghribi* (western) style of European type. Elsewhere in the essay, Ibrahim uses the word *ferengi,* or "Frankish," to discuss products of Western or European origin. He uses *maghribi* only when specifically referencing the type itself. In choosing the word *maghribi,* Ibrahim was likely identifying the stylistic appearance of European typefaces as much as he was indicating their European origin. The term refers to both the Western (European) origin of the type, as well as the particular style of handwriting that prevailed in the western Islamic lands of Morocco and Andalusia. *Maghribi* styles of Arabic script do not adhere to the proportional rules of *al-khatt al-mansub* and therefore appear odd to Ottoman readers. To rectify the situation, Müteferrika hired one Jonah, apparently Jonah (Yonah) ben Jakob Ashkenazi, a local Jewish type cutter and printer who founded a Hebrew printing dynasty in Istanbul during the eighteenth century. Ibrahim and Jonah attempted to approximate as closely as possible the look and feel of Ottoman *naskh.*[67] The resulting typeface contains well over five hundred sorts.[68] Although European types often included variants for select letters, the Müteferrika typeface displays contextual and variant forms unlike any Arabic types previously cast in Europe or elsewhere. The type emphasizes a strong horizontal baseline but also displays a wide range of linear and vertical bounce. For example, preceding letters often lead into medial forms of the *jīm* class or into a final *mīm* from the top rather than the side. These connections are consistent with handwritten Ottoman *naskh.*

Once the type was ready, typesetting began for the initial publication. The press operated out of Ibrahim's home, which was located near the community mosque of Mismari Suca in the Sultan Selim quarter of Istanbul.[69] Swedish diplomat Edvard Carleson, who observed the press during one of his visits, recorded that "indispensable workers from Germany" provided much of the technical expertise.[70] These "German" workers were likely Jonah, his sons, and others in his circle who spoke German and could have been identified by outsiders as "German."[71] Jonah was a successful and influential businessman in his own right. He was born in the Polish-Ukrainian city of Zaliztsi and immigrated to Istanbul in the early eighteenth century. He began cutting type and engraving printing plates as early as 1710, and he trained in Amsterdam during the early 1720s.[72] Jonah employed more than fifty workers at two Hebrew presses: one in the Istanbul suburb of Ortaköy and another in Izmir. He printed over 125 books during his lifetime, and he sold his wares in both Europe and Palestine. In a letter dated 1726, Müteferrika informs the grand vizier that he had already been working with Jonah for eight years. The two colleagues were close friends and collaborators. Jonah may even have helped engrave Müteferrika's early maps, and he taught Ibrahim's five sons how to operate press machinery.[73] In a later letter, Müteferrika requests that Jonah be spared from paying taxes on wages earned while working for the Turkish-language press.[74] The close partnership continued throughout their lives. Jonah and Ibrahim both died in 1746.

Books of the Müteferrika Press

Three years after receiving royal authorization, the Müteferrika press released its first book in 1729.[75] The book, as advertised, was a reference work: the celebrated *Vankulu* Arabic-Turkish dictionary. *Kitab-ı Lügat-ı Vankulu (Sihah El-Cevheri)* took its name from Mehmed of Van, who translated the Arabic *Sihah* of Jawhari into Turkish. The massive tome consists of two volumes in folio: the first with 666 pages, the second with 756 pages. It includes more than twenty-two thousand words, all of which are illustrated in proper Arabic usage and translated into Ottoman Turkish. The primary text is printed within a ruled box measuring 15 by 26 centimeters, and three letter roots are printed in the margin for easy reference. Ibrahim stuck to his claim that indexes and marginal notes can help readers navigate printed work. The initial volume also contains extensive front matter. As promised, Ibrahim reproduces the bureaucratic documents that helped establish the press. He includes a new introduction (which claims that knowledge of Arabic language is the key to the sciences—another nod to possible conservative criticism), a copy of the royal *ferman* of Sultan Ahmet III, a copy of the religious *fatwa* by Şeyhülislam Abdullah Efendi, the sixteen statements of support from respected scholars, the *Vesiletü-t*

Tibaa essay on the benefits of print, the qualities *(manaqib)* of Jawhari, the qualities *(manaqib)* of Vankulu (Mehmed of Van), and a table of contents. Sultan Ahmet III was duly impressed, and he controlled cost to encourage sales. The price of an unbound copy was set at thirty-five *kurush*. Although the price was not insignificant, it was a bargain for a useful reference work of this size.

Overall, the press issued seventeen works in twenty-three volumes over thirteen years, and subsequent works continue the argument for print in support of education. Ibrahim Müteferrika was more than just a printer; he was an editor and publisher who continually championed printed books and print technology as vehicles of change. His publishing program targeted leaders of the elite *askeri,* or soldier class. Geographic and military knowledge played a prominent role, and many of the books emphasize recent knowledge rather than classical scholarship.[76] Interestingly, none of the publications address medicine or logic, both of which are listed among the specific requests in Ibrahim's petition. In one of the final printings, *Tarih-i Naima,* Ibrahim appends a list of print runs. One work ran 1,200 copies, two other works ran 1,000 copies, and the rest numbered 500. These numbers compare favorably with the run size of European printings during the incunabula period.[77] Ibrahim consistently added tables of contents, indexes, and book summaries to assist readers. The introductions summarize the contents of the works and reiterate printing's benefits. Ibrahim was a tireless promoter of print; his additions and emendations serve as advertisements for and arguments on behalf of the press, which—much more than simply producing printed works—demonstrated a new model of state-oriented scholarship and publishing.

Three of the published works were written by Katip Çelebi, a respected Ottoman geographer who promoted the printing of accurate maps and nautical charts.[78] Çelebi was a personal favorite of Ibrahim Müteferrika. Müteferrika's early printed maps answered Çelebi's call, and his second printed book was *Tuhfet-ül Kibar fi Esfar el-Bihar* (1729), Çelebi's fundamental work on Ottoman naval history and tactics. Ibrahim supplemented the text with four regional maps, a detailed illustration of a mariner's compass, and his own calculations of distances, quantities of landmasses, and bodies of water.[79] Çelebi's *Cihannüma* (Mirror of the World) followed in 1732. This grand geographic survey is the jewel of the Müteferrika press. Ibrahim's introduction reiterates the need for accurately printed maps, and the book contains some of Müteferrika's and

Jonah's most beautiful engravings. It is wonderfully illustrated with thirty-nine images depicting the cross section of an astrolabe, diagrams of lunar and solar eclipses, star charts, astronomical figures, and terrestrial maps. Ibrahim's print edition was heavily edited: 325 of the 698 pages contain additions or amendments. The new material brought Çelebi's work into agreement with the latest astronomical and geographic studies. Ibrahim translated passages and discussed the theories of Copernicus, Tycho Brahe, Galileo, Descartes, and others.[80] His additions mark the first time that these thinkers were presented to Muslim scholars. The third book of Müteferrika's Çelebi trilogy, *Takvim üt-Tevarih,* was printed in 1733. The book contains a series of chronological and historical tables, which can be usefully cross-referenced. The tables provide a means for converting dates recorded in various calendars and denominations,[81] and Ibrahim's introduction stresses the importance of Çelebi's contributions to modern science.

Another focus addresses military and regional history, with particular emphasis on recent events. The printed corpus includes studies of Persia, Afghanistan, Egypt, Iraq, Bosnia, and the Americas. The press's third printing, *Tarih-i Seyyah* (1729), details the Afghan invasion of Persia. Jesuit missionary Tadeusz Juda Krusinski wrote a Latin journal while witnessing the events in 1722. At the request of the grand vizier, Müteferrika translated Krusinski's journal into Turkish along with another short work on Persia.[82] The two works were typeset and printed in a single volume in 1729, less than eight years after the events they describe. The following book, *Tarih-i Hind-i Garbi* (1730), informed Ottoman readers of the world's oceans and the American continents. It describes the explorations of Columbus, Balboa, Magellan, Cortés, and Pizarro. The book is heavily illustrated with images of tapirs, manatees, armadillos, pelicans, and other American oddities.[83] Two later works circulated the recent writings of Turkish historian Nazmizade Murtaza bin Ali (d. ca. 1722). In *Tarih-i Timur Gürgan* (1730), Nazmizade translates Ibn Arabshah's history of Timur (Tamerlane) into Turkish. The translator clearly disapproved of Timur's harsh methods, and the text serves as an apologia for the comparative openness of Ottoman rule. Ibrahim's introduction urges readers to compare Timur with current Ottoman leadership and to be thankful for the differences.[84] Nazmizade's other work, *Gülşen-i Hülefa* (1730), chronicles the Ottoman conquest of Iraq alongside eyewitness accounts of Baghdad. The press's penultimate printing, *Ahval-i*

Gazavat der Diyar-ı Bosna (1741), reports on the Bosnian war of 1736–1739 between the Ottomans and the Habsburgs. The author, Ömer Efendi, drew on eyewitness accounts, and the report was printed in 1741 C.E., less than two years after the events it describes. Ibrahim's introduction affirms the importance of well-organized armies and modern military tactics.[85]

Near the end of his life, Müteferrika printed the official historical record of the Ottoman court. Grand Vizier Hekmioğlu Ali Pasha (d. 1758 C.E.) requested the set, which consists of three works in six volumes. All six volumes were written by court-appointed historians during the periods described. Ibrahim provided introductory summaries of all the chronicles, and he split the larger works into multiple, more manageable volumes. A consistent format of thirty-three lines per page, a printed area of 13 by 25 centimeters, and similar opening illustrations unified the volumes both visually and textually. The complete set covers Ottoman history from the turn of the Islamic millennium (1000 A.H., sixteenth century C.E.) onward. It includes two volumes of Na'ima's history (*Tarih-i Naima;* volume 1 covers 1001–1050 A.H. / 1592–1640 C.E., volume 2 covers 1051–1070 A.H. / 1641–1659 C.E.), three volumes of Raşid's history (*Tarih-i Raşid;* volume 1 covers 1071–1115 A.H. / 1660–1703 C.E., volume 2 covers 1115–1130 A.H. / 1704–1717 C.E., volume 3 covers 1130–1134 A.H. / 1718–1721 C.E.), and one volume of Çelebizade Isma'il 'Aşim's history (*Tarih-i Çelebizade;* covering 1135–1141 A.H. / 1722–1728 C.E.). The set was printed between 1734 and 1741, and special emphasis was placed on the most current histories. The third volume of Raşid and the single volume by Çelebizade were often bound together. Per Ibrahim's request, the court set an affordable price of forty *kurush* for bound copies and thirty *kurush* for unbound copies of these two volumes. Once again, emphasis falls on the educational and strategic importance of recent events.

Ibrahim played an active editorial role in almost all of the press's output. He wrote, translated, or added significant content to eight works, and he added introductions, appendixes, summaries, and indexes to every one of his printings. The ninth and tenth publications were Ibrahim's own writings. The second of these, *Fuyuzat-ı miknatisiye,* a brief work on applied magnetism, was published in 1732. Ibrahim compiled the book from personal translations and original studies of European sources.[86] The preceding book, printed the same year, was Ibrahim's magnum opus: *Usül ul-hikem fi nizam il-umem* (The Ordering of Nations).[87] This political treatise discusses the various means of government and national organization. Ibrahim published the book shortly after the Patrona

Halil Revolt. During the revolt, conservative Ottoman factions killed the reform-minded Grand Vizier Ibrahim Pasha, forced the abdication of Sultan Ahmet III, and elevated the conservative-leaning Sultan Mahmud I to the throne. Ibrahim likely wrote the book for his close friend, the late Grand Vizier, who died in the uprising. He dedicated the printed version, however, to the newly appointed sultan. Although Ibrahim does not mention the revolt or directly criticize Ottoman rule, he presents a strong argument for political and military reform along European lines: "it has become an evident and urgent need to collect information about European affairs in order to prevent their harm and repel their malice. Let Muslims cease to be unaware and ignorant of the state of affairs and awaken from their slumber of heedlessness. . . . Let them act with foresight and become intimately acquainted with European methods, organization, strategy, tactics and warfare."[88]

Whereas historical works standardized the Islamic and Ottoman past, Ibrahim's political treatise looked to the future. In the first section, Ibrahim explores monarchy, aristocracy, and democracy as three distinct forms of government. This is the earliest presentation of modern democratic ideals within Ottoman scholarship. The book then discusses the importance of sound geographic knowledge, a common theme of both Müteferrika's writings and the works he chose to publish. A final section offers suggestions for modernizing the Ottoman military. A key example notes that improved geographic knowledge and military organization allowed Christian Europe to conquer the Americas, as well as formerly Muslim lands (for example, India). Ibrahim notes that the Russian adoption of European methods quickly strengthened Russian positions and concludes: "If [Turks] learn new military sciences and are able to apply them, no enemy can withstand this state."[89] These new sciences and methods include the printing press, and Ibrahim's arguments on military modernization reflect his earlier arguments for print: they will preserve and extend Ottoman glory.[90]

The Müteferrika press's final printing mirrors its first. The publications of the Müteferrika press were bookended by two grand dictionaries: *Kitab-ı Lügat-ı Vankulu (Sihah El-Cevheri)* in 1729 and *Kitab-ı Lisan el-Acem el Müsemma bi-Ferheng-i Şuuri* in 1742. In *Vesiletü-t Tibaa,* Ibrahim specifically mentions the printing of dictionaries, and the first of his ten outlined benefits ties the importance of mastering Arabic to the availability of "accurate and comprehensive dictionaries." Müteferrika concretized this in his initial printing, and his introduction to that work reiterates the scholarly importance of dictionaries.

His final printing, also a dictionary, was the Persian-Turkish *Ferheng-i Şuuri*. This work reflects the earlier Arabic-Turkish dictionary in both scope and stature. Like the *Vankulu,* the work consists of two volumes. The first introduces Persian grammar followed by a registry of 1,844 Persian metaphors, sayings, and proverbs; the second presents the dictionary proper, with more than twenty-two thousand entries illustrated in proper usage.[91] European printers were already circulating Persian and Turkish dictionaries, but these works were printed in Latin type. *Ferheng-i Şuuri* was the first Persian-Turkish dictionary printed in Arabic type, the shared characters of the languages themselves.

Within the corpus of the Müteferrika press, the eighth book presents a small oddity. The book, titled *Grammaire Turque: Ou méthode courte et facile pour apprendre la langue Turque,* was printed in 1730. It is the only major Müteferrika production that consists primarily of Latin type, and it notably prefixes a list of thirty-eight errata. The French-language text targeted clerks of the French consulate in Constantinople, and it is not listed in Ibrahim's catalog of print runs. Jean Baptiste Holdermann, a French Jesuit who died shortly before publication, wrote the book, and it was urged on to completion by the French ambassador Marquis de Villeneuve. Villeneuve ordered two hundred copies for the education of consulate staff. The short Turkish grammar, interestingly, does not contain a four-form table with isolated, initial, medial, and final variants of each Ottoman letter. Instead, it includes an engraved table showing seven distinct *styles* of Arabic script. (See Figure 4.1.) Each letter is provided with a phonetic Latin-letter equivalent on the left and a Latinate name on the right. In between, the letter is written in seven of the most common Ottoman styles: *sulus (thuluth), reïhani (rayhan), jakuti* (a variant of *muhaqqaq*)*, nesqhi (naskh), tealik (ta'liq), divani (diwani),* and *kyrma* (a variant of *siyaqah*). A brief note states, "The Turks have many other styles of writing, which were omitted in the interest of space," and the accompanying text explains that the various styles represent distinct types of documents: *diwani* is used for business of the royal bureau, *ta'liq* is employed by judges, *kyrma* is used for record keeping, and so on.

Among the printings of the Müteferrika press, the *Grammaire Turque* is unique for its Latin typeface. According to Ibrahim's preface, Jonah cast the characters for the Latin and Arabic typefaces locally.[92] The book's "short and easy method" follows the organization of a three-column phrasebook. The central column presents Ottoman Turkish typeset in Arabic *(naskh)* script. The right-hand column offers a French translation. And the left-hand column transliterates the Ottoman Turkish using Latin letters. According to Louis Mathieu Langlès (1763–1824), Müteferrika hoped to reuse the Latin type for an ambitious multilingual dictionary. The proposed dictionary was organized around French words, with translations into Italian, Greek, Latin, Turkish, Arabic, and Persian. Printing would therefore have required three sets of type: Latin, Arabic, and Greek. Although Langlès claims that a folio-size sample page was printed and circulated, Müteferrika was unable to complete the project.[93] Had he done so, the book would have provided an incredible resource for Ottoman and European scholars. Multiple languages of import would have been collected and cross-referenced in one massive tome.

The publications of the Müteferrika press reflect Ibrahim's personal interests in language, history, geography, and tactics, and the corpus proposes a program of administrative and military reform in line with modern methods. Ibrahim argued that Ottoman scholars must familiarize themselves with European military, scientific, and technological knowledge in order to regain Islamic glory. The printing press itself offered a key example in this regard. Printing was never proposed as a replacement for scribal variety or a substitute for efficient traditions of Qur'anic and classical scholarship. Instead, the press provided a state-oriented tool for modernization and information management. Hidayet Nuhoğlu usefully defines the Müteferrika press as "the first printing house to be set up under the patronage and with support of a Muslim state in its lands with the aim of printing books belonging to and needed for the culture of the state."[94] Müteferrika was not the first to print the Turkish language, he was not the first to print using Arabic type, nor was he the first to print in Ottoman lands. But Ibrahim Müteferrika was the first Ottoman Muslim printer, the first to print locally with Arabic type for an Islamic readership, and the first to direct print in service to the Ottoman state. Publications targeted the administrative and military elite, and the Ottoman court partially subsidized the cost of printing. Printings included discussion of recent discoveries and current events, as well as useful reference works, all of which were rare in manuscript copy. The Müteferrika press, therefore, expanded the Ottoman textual landscape. In *Usül ul-hikem fi nizam il-umem,* Ibrahim was the first to print the Ottoman term *nizam-ı cedid* (a modern order).[95] The term would later become popular with Ottoman reformers and modernizers. The new order of *nizam-ı cedid* included—among other suggestions—a new textual order: the tactical adoption of print technology.

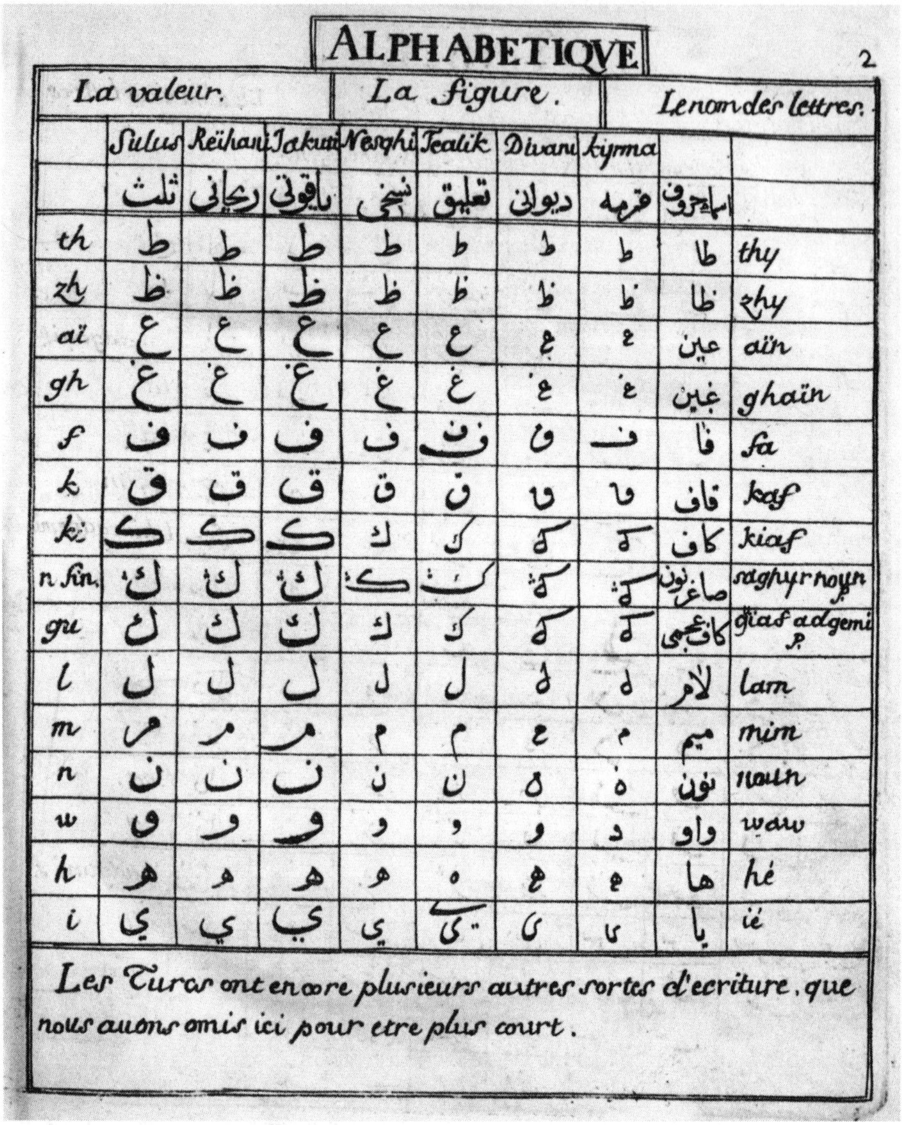

Figure 4.1. *Grammaire Turque* alphabet table

These engraved alphabetical tables were included in Jean Baptiste Holdermann's *Grammaire Turque* (1730), which was printed by the Müteferrika press. The tables display the Turkish alphabet in seven different styles of Arabic script. Their inclusion in the book, which was designed to teach Turkish to local French diplomats, conveys the importance of recognizing the stylistic differences of Ottoman handwriting. (Image courtesy of the Newberry Library.)

La valeur.	La figure.							Le nom des lettres
	Sulus	Reihani	Jakatt	Nerghi	Tealik	Divani	kyrma	
a								elif
b								ba
p								bai adgemi
t								ta
s								sa
dg								dgim
tch								tchim adgemi
h								ha
qh								qhy
d								dal
z								zal
r								ra
z								za
j								jé adgemi P.
s								sin
ch								chin
ss								sad
dh								dhad

Conclusion: Ottoman Print Culture

During the first centuries of movable type, the Ottomans had mixed relations with print. On the one hand, the *millets*—most noticeably the Jewish and Armenian communities—supported vibrant printing and publishing operations.

Constantinople-based printers exchanged works, equipment, and expertise with printers in Europe. On the other hand, no local attempts were made to adopt or apply the technology to Arabic script. Ottoman administrators warily perceived the spread of movable type printing across Europe, especially in relation to its political and religious ramifications. Given the instability of Europe, they had every right to be cautious. Print inflamed European factionalism and evaded local restrictions. Printers were as likely to distribute lucrative works of political sedition, as they were apt to share classical scholarship. And a number of printed works propagandized against the perceived Ottoman threat. If Ottoman sultans did indeed ban printed works, they may have targeted specific tracts that challenged their authority. Unlike weaker European states, the Ottoman realm was well organized, stable, and capable of enforcing local regulations. Moreover, a large community of scribes adequately addressed local textual needs. Scribes wrote in the aesthetically celebrated style of Ottoman *naskh* as well as a variety of alternative styles according to context and genre. Ottoman administrators may not have seen an initial need to adopt the new technology of movable type.

Arguments in favor of Ottoman printing began in the late seventeenth century. And once they arrived, they targeted new types of printed texts rather than wholesale mass production. As printing spread, it altered practices of research and scholarly exchange. Modern scholarship benefited from the printed circulation of recent discoveries and new findings, and Ottoman intellectuals began referencing these sources. But unlike classical Islamic works, newly printed texts were extremely rare in Ottoman markets. Ottoman elites recommended print as a tool for circulating novel forms and new ideas. A shift in geopolitical power heightened the sense of urgency. During the early years of print, Ottoman advance into Christian Europe appeared inevitable. But three centuries of European printing, navigation, and colonization balanced relations. Newly printed maps announced overseas routes, and European trade traversed the seas rather than overland routes across Ottoman domains. The accompanying advantages—both economic and strategic—weakened Ottoman positions on the global stage. Ibrahim Müteferrika responded by printing updated Ottoman maps. And his subsequent printings placed recent works of Ottoman scholarship in conversation with European developments.

Ibrahim Müteferrika was an eighteenth-century Ottoman diplomat. He applied the technology of movable type to the pressing needs of state. As a youth, he witnessed the printed exchange of competing ideas, and he later served as an ambassador and translator for visiting dignitaries. Ibrahim was familiar with European methods of scholarship and sought to adapt them for Ottoman contexts. The Ottoman court and local religious authorities not only condoned the Müteferrika press; they championed it. A religious decision *(fatwa)* and a royal decree *(ferman)* established the press, and later decrees partially subsidized the costs. Publications emphasized navigation, history, military modernization, and language education, all of which streamlined functions of state. When compared with Gutenberg and unregulated European printing, Ottoman print appears delayed. When compared with the embrace of printing as a vehicle of the state, the first Ottoman press sits squarely alongside European developments.[96] In comparison, the royal French Imprimerie nationale opened in 1640, and its distinctive typefaces debuted in 1702, less than twenty-five years before the Müteferrika press published its first book. The state adoption of print marks not the advent of a new technology per se but the tactical deployment of technology toward new regimes of textual management.

Ottoman *millets* employed print technology long before Ibrahim's birth, and Muslims continued printing after his death. But the Müteferrika press signals a shift in the technical and textual practices of Arabic script. Müteferrika introduced a mode of print culture—rather than the means of print technology—to Ottoman elites.[97] When Ottoman Muslims began printing, they learned to set type, prepare inks, and operate the requisite machinery from local Jewish printers. Movable type ceased to be a foreign technology. For the first time, members of an Ottoman Muslim community cultivated and developed the technical skills of printing. Their products modeled a modern printed mode of scholarly communication, rather than a replacement of earlier tradition. The new medium was not embraced for religious purposes, but neither were its benefits dismissed. The bureaucratic process of obtaining a religious *fatwa* and a royal *ferman* bridged the paradigmatic divide. Questions of print were answered via traditional channels of Islamic authority, and discussion addressed the types of texts suitable for printing. The distinction is subtle, but significant. Neither the royal *ferman* of Sultan Ahmet III nor the religious *fatwa* strictly prohibits religious texts. They *permit and endorse* the printing of educational and scientific texts. Print introduced new types of texts, with mechanical typefaces, and modern appearances, and these new forms circulated alongside the religious and classical products of scribal production.

The distinction of printed secular text and hand-produced religious text was one of practice and design. Although scribal *khatt* remained the ideal image of beautiful Arabic script, typographic *naskh* became the symbol of administrative and state modernization. Arabic letters, which already displayed a wide range of scribal styles, became yet more varied. The appearance and design of Arabic script continued to respond to its textual role. Many writings—and religious works in particular—remained handwritten. They retained classical form and preserved the visual idiom of Ottoman scribal tradition. Concurrently, new letters were cast in metal and pressed on the page. The typefaces of these new printings were modeled on Ottoman *naskh,* which was already the preferred scribal style for texts of scientific knowledge and general education. But the regularity, standardization, and repeatability of type conveyed the image of an orderly modern state. The new typographic appearance of *naskh* was "modern," and the circulated texts promoted modern scholarship. Ottoman printing began with feet pointed squarely toward the future. The printing of *naskh* heralded a new order *(nizam-ı cedid).*

Chapter Five

Questions of Script Reform

*I*n 1726, Ibrahim Müteferrika began printing secular and scholarly texts that catered to state interests. The Müteferrika's print shop was vetted, approved, and supported by the Ottoman political and religious bureaucracies. Two centuries later, in 1928, the modern Turkish republic adopted a new Latin alphabet. Both initiatives were state-sponsored and top-down. The state championed and instituted change in order to maximize and incorporate the potential of European print technology. The ability to produce and control identical copies enticed public authorities and political reformers.[1] Printed materials became instruments of administrative policy, vehicles of mass education, and engines of national solidarity. Two centuries after the Ottoman adoption of print, the ongoing impetus of bureaucratic and textual reform culminated in a new alphabet. When modern Turkey jettisoned Arabic script in favor of a Latinate alphabet, it signaled the historic, technical, and symbolic importance of movable type. The new Turkish letters proudly announced their individual modernity. It was a far cry from the multi-script structure of the Ottoman *millet* system, in which Arabic script unified the Ottoman Muslim community. Arabic script was recast as the marker of a Middle Eastern and dynastic past, whereas the new Latinate alphabet looked toward Europe and a secularized future.

Turkish language reform offers one of the most visible and dramatic transformations of modern nation building, but it was far from unique. Throughout the twentieth century, questions of script reform marched hand in hand with questions of modernization, nationalism, and political reform. Scripts, and their symbolic resonances, became politicized, and policies of "simplification" were debated across a variety of languages. In 1917, Aleksey Shakhmatov reformed Russian orthography for the Soviet Ministry of Popular Education, and the Soviet Union later consolidated the languages of its various republics under Cyrillic script.[2] Germany, under the Nazi regime, first praised the uniquely Germanic character of Fraktur, or black-letter Gothic, and later, in a 180-degree reversal, denounced the same typefaces as an obstacle to advancement.[3] And in 1956, China launched the first official edition of Hanyu Pinyin, the now common system of transcribing spoken Mandarin with Latin characters. Reforms were also debated for Hebrew, Korean, and Greek. The legacy of European colonialism, meanwhile, adapted Latin script to a wide variety of local and newly national languages. The wave of script, spelling, and language reforms was closely tied to the formation of new national identities.[4] Political justifications argued that reforms made languages easier to read and thereby increased literacy, an essential skill of modern citizenship.

Arabic script reform was hotly debated, culminating in a competition sponsored by the Academy of Arabic Language in Cairo. As elsewhere, the impetus was "simplification" of the script for modern technologies and increased literacy. Ultimately, however, Latinization and radical reform never posed a serious threat to Arabic script grammar. And the Academy of Arabic Language in Cairo did not announce a winner despite the numerous reform proposals that it received. Nevertheless, the debates point to a significant change in practices of script and written communication. Movable type printing, which became the vehicle of modern literacy, is best suited to scripts with a limited set of distinct characters. At the end of the eighteenth century, however, the new technology of lithographic printing challenged the hegemony of movable type. Lithography, which European printers reserved for illustrations, could faithfully reproduce the handwritten line. It was consequently applied to the mechanical reproduction of scribal copies of Qur'anic *masahif*, as well as Arabic calligraphic displays. Lithography's close connection to handwriting preserved nonlinguistic aspects of visual communication unavailable to movable type. But this inadvertently reinforced the traditional associations of scribal aesthetics. Movable type and "simplified" scripts, in contrast, became the symbol of modern communication.

Modern Turkish and Latin Letters

The "revolution" of the Müteferrika press occurred 275 years after Gutenberg, but Müteferrika was also ahead of his times. The Müteferrika press serves as an intellectual and technological preface to later shifts of Turkish modernization.[5] Ibrahim Müteferrika emphasized the utility of print for political and military reform. His writings and the publishing program of his press heralded broad changes in Ottoman textuality. He astutely emphasized the rising importance of new textual materials: accurate maps, discussion of recent discoveries, reference works, and official histories. Müteferrika's first printings were maps, rather than books, and the press championed politically useful texts. In Europe, the majority of early printed works were religious or popular texts. During the first century and a half of Ottoman printing, less than 20 percent of printed material addressed religious topics.[6] The vast majority of Ottoman printings were bureaucratic, scientific, or educational—the primary texts of modernization. Presses became vehicles of state, and bureaucratic modernization produced a flood of new types of text: from administrative forms to visual identity cards and postage stamps. These new forms of written and textual material fell outside the realm of scribal practice, and print answered the call.

From the 1840s to the 1870s, the Tanzimat reforms shifted Ottoman political structures closer to European models. Many of the reforms echoed suggestions forwarded by Ibrahim Müteferrika more than a century earlier. When Sultan Abdülmecid I signed the Tanzimat Fermanı in 1839, he enacted *nizam-ı cedid,* a new order. The edict extended national rights and protections to all Ottoman subjects, regardless of religion or sect.[7] It effectively ended the Ottoman *millet* system, which divided scripts and print technologies along identifiable religious lines. Under the *millet* system, Jewish, Orthodox Christian, and Armenian communities administered their presses semiautonomously. The Tanzimat reforms simplified the growing complexity of the system, which had swelled to include various Christian denominations as independents *millets.* The changes reflect an inherent tension of modernization: on the one hand, the state became more inclusive of its citizenry. On the other hand, this inclusivity was accomplished via the centralization of state power and the erasure of officially recognized diversity. Although presses that printed in the various *millet* languages continued to flourish, religious distinctions no longer defined political and judicial communities.[8] The new order applied government regulations universally to all Ottoman subjects. The ideal of a united nationalism replaced separate but sanctioned religious groups.

Other Tanzimat reforms included reorganization of the military, implementation of a civil legal code, the formation of modern universities, and establishment of a postal system. The country adopted a national anthem and conducted its first national census. A plethora of newly printed documentation concretized these changes. By 1875, more than 150 presses were working to support the nation.[9] Like the Müteferrika press, they were mostly secular and state-oriented. State-oriented printing distanced the traditional poles of Ottoman religious and state authority. The religious sphere retained a hold over classically religious texts, Arabic language, and the requisite modes of preprint circulation. Scribal *naskh* remained the dominant mode of Qur'anic copying. But the modern state was textually ascendant. Newly necessary texts included identity cards, census forms, postage stamps, training manuals, schoolbooks, and the musical score of the new national anthem.[10] These materials were written in Ottoman Turkish rather than classical languages, and they lacked precedent in the preprint organization of scribal design. In 1869, parliament ratified the Mecelle civil code. The Ottoman Mecelle was the first *sharia*-based legislation enacted exclusively by a sovereign nonreligious authority.[11] The numbered articles, written in Ottoman Turkish—and printed with *naskh* type—strove for linguistic clarity. Less than a decade later, article 18 of the 1876 Ottoman constitution declared Turkish, rather than Ottoman, the official language of state.[12] The previous *millet* structure organized written scripts according to religious affiliation; the new nation collected all *millets* under the banner of a shared vernacular.[13] Turkish, a *spoken* language, replaced the diversity of *written* scripts—Arabic, Hebrew, Greek, Armenian, and Latin—as the linguistic marker of community. And the mechanical standardization of printed typefaces replaced stylistic and scribal variety.

Perhaps no written form better exemplifies the shifting textual landscape of the nineteenth century than the printed newspaper. Newspapers circulated newly relevant knowledge, accounts of current events, and necessary information. Unlike earlier community texts, they were designed to be cheaply produced, widely distributed, and easily disposable. Readers across the nation saw the same printed words, read similar stories, and discussed shared topics.[14] Although disparate stories cover a wide variety of issues, the mosaic form of the newspaper conveys a unified experience of the day-to-day.[15] The import of a newspaper is stamped by its date. The dated masthead gathers relevant news, opinions, letters, weather reports, and advertisements as representative of a particular moment of historical time. Readers connect the dots of these disparate components, moving among and between the various elements. Newspapers connect readers across the present day and current happenings. And they too circulated outside the traditional channels of classical and religious texts. But whereas state-oriented operations, such as the Müteferrika press, targeted elite readers and administrators, periodicals directly addressed a growing reading public. In and around Istanbul, newspapers "spoke" to their audiences in the cadence of daily Turkish. The classical written forms of Arabic, Persian, and Ottoman were replaced with idioms of common usage.

Takvim-i Vekayi, the first Ottoman newspaper, appeared in 1831. It covered the nation with editions printed in Ottoman Turkish, Arabic, Persian, Greek, Armenian, and French. At this time, Ottoman lands remained multilingual and multi-scripted. The first privately owned and operated newspaper followed in 1840. William Churchill, an English merchant, launched *Ceride-i Havadis* (The Register of Events). The paper eschewed the formal prose of Ottoman literature in favor of simplified "journalistic language" *(gazeteci lisanı).*[16] *Ceride-i Havadis* sought to inform Ottoman readers of current events, and dedicated coverage of the Crimean war drove sales. Ibrahim Şinasi (1824–1871), a popular poet who eschewed flowery phrasing in favor of direct, everyday expression, penned the paper's first editorial.[17] Addressing the reading public at large, he staked the paper's reputation on writing that could be easily read and understood.[18] Printed script and spoken vernacular were moving closer together. Newspapers displayed Arabic script, but they represented Turkish speech. Şinasi later branched out to found his own paper, *Tasvir-i Efkâr* (The Picture of Ideas). *Tasvir-i Efkâr's* editorial pages provided a catalyst for new political ideas, and the simplicity of Şinasi's prose carried over into typographic design. The paper utilized a reduced set of type with only 112 forms, a sharp decrease from the 500 sorts of most Ottoman *naskh* typefaces.[19]

The journalistic focus on direct and accessible language had ripple effects on Ottoman writing practices.[20] The traditional courtly register of written Ottoman was incredibly complex. Rhetorical style was highly poetic, with a blend of Turkish, Arabic, and Persian structures that required readers to hold basic familiarity in all three languages. And it did not employ modern punctuation. Rather, rhyming words marked semantic stops. This, in turn, created a feedback loop: the need to rhyme increased the number of Arabic and Persian loanwords and further exaggerated semantic complexity. Rhetorical flourishes and poetic structure trumped clarity of meaning, the exact opposite of the everyday directness of journalistic prose *(gazeteci lisanı)*.[21] For Turkish speakers, the complexity of Arabic script and Ottoman phrasing became the visual symbol of linguistic confusion. The cursive *naskh* script, moreover, continued to cause problems for movable type printing. Most printed texts, newspapers included, were not vocalized with *tashkil*. Printed *naskh* frequently displayed only the consonants of Arabic script. This erased and occluded semantic differences of spoken Turkish. A key example noted that the words *oldu* (he became) and *öldü* (he died) became indistinguishable out of context.[22] Editors, readers, ideologues, and bureaucrats increasingly called for a distinctly Turkish script.

In 1862, Mehmed Münif Paşa argued before the Ottoman Scientific Society (Cemiyeti Ilmiye-i Osmaniye) that Arabic script presented a hindrance to Turkish literacy.[23] Arabic script remained a powerful religious symbol, but it no longer served as a useful vehicle of modern Turkish communication. Münif Paşa based his argument on difficulties and inconsistencies of phonetic representation. Like Müteferrika, he looked toward Europe as a bastion of modern science. Scientific literacy increasingly relied on European—rather than Arabic and Persian— loanwords, which were difficult to identify in unvocalized *naskh*. This created a barrier to scientific literacy. Paşa envisioned "a writing system that would be read as it was written, and be written as it was spoken."[24] Two years later, the Azerbaijani dramatist Mirza Feth Ali Ahundzade outlined a more specific proposal. Ahundzade suggested new vowel signs to facilitate the phonetic representation of Turkish.[25] Vowels would be placed between the consonants of Arabic script, functioning much as they do in the Latin alphabet. This would alter traditional Arabic script grammar. The visual representations of vocalization would descend from the higher levels of *tashkil* (layers 3–6) to merge with the line of primary text (layers 1 and 2).

While the Scientific Society voiced appreciation, it failed to enact any specific reforms.[26] The society stated that improvement of letters *(islah-i huruf)* was necessary, but they tactfully distanced script reform from contentious religious debates. Questions of Turkish literacy were framed as educational and scientific, not religious.[27] Arabic, as the language of the Qur'an, and Arabic script, as the visual representation of Arabic language, remained the pillars of religious authority. In an increasingly secularized society, the Turkish and Arabic languages demarcated distinct spheres of scientific and religious influence. The demarcation suggests that a specifically Turkish script might actually preserve, rather than undermine, the sanctity of Arabic. Assigning different scripts based on language and authority is not entirely unlike earlier scribal practices. It might not be a stretch to frame the distinction as a linguistic and scientific extension of stylistic variety: the traditional styles of *al-khatt al-mansub* signified Qur'anic and religious tradition, whereas *diwani* was a uniquely Turkish style of Ottoman political authority. What began as a stylistic and visual distinction of script had now become a linguistic distinction separating Turkish and Arabic. In 1926, Kılıçzade Hakki published an editorial that claimed "Gabriel didn't bring the Arabic letters." The controversial piece stated that the sacred nature of Qur'anic revelation did not extend to Arabic script.[28] Hakki's opinion contrasts sharply with the traditional position in which Islamic nations adopted Arabic script as a symbol of religious and cultural unity.[29]

During World War I, secular and utilitarian pressures placed new strains on written Turkish. The uneasy alliance of Arabic script and vernacular Turkish came to be seen as a military liability. The need for quick, reliable, and efficient communication trumped tradition. Minister of War Enver Paşa designed a specialty system called *hatt-ı cedid* (modern *khatt*), or *ordu elfibasi* (army alphabet) for military telegraphs. The system utilized only one form per character and included signs for both vowels and consonants. Character sequences displayed disjointed individual letters, rather than a unified cursive line. Enver Paşa rationalized *hatt-ı cedid* as a means of simplifying and speeding up essential communications.[30] Critics, however, argued that it did just the opposite. The new system frustrated telegraph operators, who needed to learn codes for unfamiliar new vowels and new sequences. And the system was never utilized outside the ministry. Yet *hatt-ı cedid* nevertheless demonstrated a working example of transmitting phonetic Turkish with non-Arabic symbols. Although it built upon the Arabic *abjad,* it discarded Arabic *script* in favor of disconnected letterforms.

The final break occurred in 1928. Under the leadership of Mustafa Kemal Atatürk, the new Turkish Republic pursued a strong secularist agenda. Modern Turkey distanced itself from the Islamic and Ottoman past. Traditional Ottoman society—handwritten with Arabic *naskh*—was swept under the carpet of history. Islam was removed as official religion of state, and local Islamic practice was Turkified.[31] Language reform was a cornerstone of the new nationalist identity. Reformers argued that a modern language implied a modern script. Scholars gathered to debate a new Turkish alphabet, and Atatürk demanded results. He requested that the new script be formalized within three months. Under intense political pressure, the commission unanimously agreed to adopt a Latinate alphabet as the official script of the new republic. The "Elifba Raporu" (Alphabet Report) was submitted under deadline, and, less than a week later, Atatürk unveiled the new Turkish alphabet. Speaking before a crowd of thousands in Istanbul's Sarayburnu Park on August 9, 1928, Atatürk declared Turkey free of the "incomprehensible signs" of Arabic script. Arabic script, he claimed, pointed to the past. The new Turkish letters announced a modern printed future: "Our nation [Turkey] will show, with its script and with its mind, that its place is with the civilized world."[32]

Far from simply providing the visual symbol of a new republic, the Turkish alphabet signaled a major shift in the relationship of writing, language, and script. Script reformers championed the notion that written communication should phonetically represent a spoken national vernacular. This is not a particularly radical claim in modern communication. Prior to the spread of printed vernaculars, however, such arguments were far from obvious. A "modernist" mode of representational script, in which written characters represent vernacular patterns of speech, replaced earlier practices of stylistic variation.[33] Printed newspapers and journalistic directness further diminished the gulf between vernacular speech and written style. But which speech and whose vernacular should written letters represent? Even the sounds of the national language, like the Latinate letters that represent them, were oriented toward Europe. The glottal stop of *hamza,* which remained common in southeastern regions of Turkey, was marked by an apostrophe rather than a letter, while the soft g received full phonemic status as a unique letter (ğ).[34] But the sound of ğ was far from universal; it was much more common in Istanbul and the European provinces than in other provinces. In his desire to purge Turkish of "Islamic" influence (for example, Arabic and Persian loanwords), Atatürk personally rejected letters that distinguished phonemic differences of spoken Arabic.[35]

Script reform unified Turkish as the language of a national-ethnic community, and the new Latin letters connoted European modernity.[36] Atatürk's comments on "incomprehensible signs" and "the civilized world" produce a cultural and rhetorical dichotomy: Arabic script, which recorded Islamic and Ottoman tradition, signals the past; Latin typography, with its implications of modern technology and European ascendance, signals the future. The shift from one to the other was a shift of mystique.[37] Rhetorical thrust is strengthened by Latin script's nonlinguistic "extras" (for example, ease of printability, integration with modern technology, affiliation with European science, etc.). Atatürk's announcement in Sarayburnu Park culminated in the unveiling of a lavish decorative plaque on which the new Turkish alphabet was carved in gold.[38] The golden letters display the Latinate face of modern Turkish. Yet the dramatic unveiling references a particularly scribal, even *calligraphic,* celebration of written characters. Artistic pieces of Ottoman calligraphy, such as *hilye* and *lewha,* applaud the visual qualities of fine writing and beautiful script. A particular subgenre of *lewha* known as *meshk* displays beautifully crafted Arabic letters, which did not necessarily combine into legible phrases. Atatürk's golden plaque presents a *meshk* of Latinate letters. The disconnected letters of the modern Turkish alphabet are well formed and clearly depicted. But the displayed forms do not combine to spell a spoken phrase.

Proposals for Arabic Script Reform

In Turkey, top-down policies were answered by grounded rationalizations of phonetic representation and the radical adoption of a new script. As an extra benefit, the modern Turkish letters easily aligned with dominant forms of print and text technology. Twentieth-century print technology built on the grammar of Latin script. Movable type remained the norm for long-form printed texts, and the Latinate model of a limited alphabet with discrete forms adapted easily to mechanical printing. The utility of isolated and discrete forms carried over into the new media of telegraphic and electronic communication. Non-Latin scripts, often referred to as "complex" or "exotic," did not. The perceived "complexity" was not a feature of the scripts per se; it arose from poor alignment with Latin-based technology. This led to script reform, or simplification, in order to assist mechanical reproduction. Results were rarely subtle and occasionally violent: structures were broken, postures were altered, details were erased, appendages were severed, and characters were eliminated. Arabic script was particularly "complex."[39] It posed a number of problems for Latin-centric technologies. Arabic script connects cursively. It flows from right to left rather than left to right. Letters rarely appear as isolated forms. Characters change shape according to context. Optional layers of diacritics appear in some texts but not others. These diacritical marks are layered above and below the line of primary text rather than inserted between characters, and so on.

A decade after Turkey's dismissal of Arabic script, the Academy of Arabic Language in Cairo commissioned a formal study of script reform.[40] The idea was not new. Münif Paşa's and Mirza Feth Ali Ahundzade's proposals before the Ottoman Scientific Society outlined changes to Arabic script, despite the fact that the language in question was Ottoman Turkish. Independent newspapers and printers also experimented with reduced sets of Arabic forms. These include Şinasi's *Tasvir-i Efkâr,* as well as numerous periodicals in the Levant and Egypt. In 1904, the *New York Times* ran a story on Salim Haddad. The article claimed that Haddad, who adapted Arabic script to the typewriter keyboard, had "conquered the multiform Arabic alphabet and reduced it to the requirements of a business office."[41] Modern businesses apparently required a script that aligned with hardware provided by International Business Machines (IBM). These disparate attempts—from competing printers, national assemblies, and technology providers—pulled the script in multiple directions. And they often produced more confusion than simplification. The Cairo academy sought a unified path moving forward. Primary concerns included the difficulty of setting vocalization marks for foreign names and a desire to make Arabic easier to read.[42] Mansur Fahmy, who formally proposed the study, boldly announced the academy's charge: "working by all possible means towards the simplification of the writing of Arabic letters, by inventing [a new system], and to make correct Arabic reading easier, but without abandoning the fundamental principles of the language."[43]

In 1944, the academy hotly debated two initial proposals. One, by Abd al-Aziz Fahmi, then chairman of the Committee on Writing at the Royal Academy of Arabic Language, followed the Turkish model. Fahmi proposed an extended set of Latin letters to represent Arabic, arguing that the prevalence of the Latin alphabet for the majority of world languages proved its efficiency and utility.[44] Fahmi's simplistic argument overlooked the complicated net of political, technological, and colonial forces by which Latin script spread across the world. But it carried rhetorical weight, and it was demonstrable with current technology. Fahmi, and the academy as a whole, assumed—perhaps rightly—that altering a script was easier than redeveloping the technological infrastructure of modern printing. A second proposal by Ali al-Gharim retained the cursive grammar of Arabic script. Al-Gharim suggested additional letters to represent vowel sounds.

These would replace the complicated multilayer system of typesetting *tashkil.* Already, two tendencies became apparent: (1) altering Arabic script in imitation of Latin script grammar or (2) preserving cursive Arabic structure through the addition of new forms. Neither path was obvious, nor did either of the initial proposals receive formal support. Instead, the academy launched an open competition for reforming Arabic script. The competition offered a monetary prize of 1,000 Egyptian pounds for the best solution. The submission deadline, which was originally set for October 26, 1946, was later extended to March 31, 1947. By that time, the academy had received over two hundred proposals.[45]

Five years later, the jury announced its decision: no winner. None of the proposals received enough support to merit academy approval. And no cash prize was awarded. Instead, the various submissions were classified into three groups: (1) proposals advocating a complete break with Arabic script in favor of Latinate letterforms, (2) proposals that retained Arabic structure while expanding the character set to include vowels and phonetic values, and (3) proposals that reduced the character set to a single form per letter.[46] The first strategy followed the lead of modern Turkey and Abd al-Aziz Fahmi. These proposals discarded the *naskh* tradition of written Arabic and adopted a foreign writing system. The second group, which resembled Ali al-Gharim's proposal, built new forms in line with the old rules. It preserved cursive structure and Arabic script aesthetics, but it flattened the layers of Arabic script by adding new characters. The third group pursued a hybrid strategy. It attempted to preserve Arabic aesthetics while reducing the character set so as to better align with movable type, typewriter, and electronic technologies. Some of the proposals in this group remained cursive in structure and resembled traditional forms; others adopted a Latinate structure of isolated printed characters. Some retained the traditional system of *tashkil* vocalization, others modified forms to address the difficulties of typesetting *tashkil,* and still others ignored questions of vocalization altogether. No single proposal adequately addressed all the committee's concerns. Hence, there was no winner. Adding more fuel to the fire, many of the submissions included typeset Qur'anic passages among their examples.[47] The radically nontraditional appearance of sacred text may have irked conservative readers and judges.

Debates on script reform continued at the 1956 Arab Academies conference in Damascus, as well as the 1958 and 1961 meetings of UNESCO's Confederation of Arabic National Committees. Ongoing discussion spurred a second wave of proposals. On December 19, 1959, the Academy of Arabic Language in Cairo cautiously recommended a subcommittee proposal. The proposed method, which addressed only typeset and typewritten Arabic, worked with as few as seventy-two letterforms.[48] But it was never widely adopted. Unlike Modern Turkish, modern Arabic dialects were spoken across a wide geographic region, phonetic range varied greatly, and Arabic served as the national language of multiple countries with competing agendas. Pashto, Persian, and Urdu were also designated as national languages, and they too continued to use Arabic script for their own alphabets. Although a few of the academy's proposals addressed non-Arabic language characters (such as the additional letters employed for Persian and South Asian languages), universal Arabic script reform would necessarily affect a transnational public of readers and speakers of multiple languages. Unlike the Turkish Alphabet Commission, the academy could not enforce a top-down mandate.[49] Radically altering a writing system shared by such diverse constituencies promised deep political battles and high logistic hurdles. Implementations of Arabic script reform—when they were enacted—developed as entrepreneurial ventures or, at best, single-nation strategies. The following sections highlight selected proposals. Although they are far from comprehensive, they demonstrate the range of debate and its technical ramifications.

The 1948 Memo of Mohamed Nadim

In 2010, Dr. Natalia Suit discovered an exciting primary document in the Dar al-Kutub archives. It was a photocopy of a handwritten memo in *ruq'ah* script. The memo was bound together with another text, and it was not listed in the library catalog. The author, Mohamed Nadim, served as director of Printing Operations at Dar al-Kutub during the 1940s and sat on the review committee for proposals submitted to the Academy of Arabic Language in Cairo's award competition. Nadim penned his memo shortly after the academy's initial deadline of 1947. He summarizes key historical moments in Arabic printing before outlining a series of recommendations. The tone is highly practical and focuses on the means that operational presses have employed for tackling challenges of Arabic printing. A key concern involves the different practices of government presses and privately run print shops. Nadim proposes a workable middle ground for government presses seeking to remain competitive, while preserving Arabic literary aesthetics and the shape of the script.

Nadim begins with a direct admission that the morphological structure of Arabic script poses great difficulty for print technology. He wishes to facilitate the technological process of Arabic printing while maintaining the precision of current forms. Familiarity, Nadim argues, is conducive to accurate reading. Traditional Arabic characters should not be replaced by radically novel forms. Next, a brief historical timeline discusses three stages of Arabic printing. Each stage is marked by a reduction in the number of printing sorts. First, Muhammed Ali Pasha founded the El-Amiriya Press (the Bulaq Press) in 1820. El-Amiriya was the first Egyptian governmental press. It utilized a set of more than 900 sorts, which were modeled on handwritten *naskh*. In 1902, a government-appointed committee reduced the number of letter sorts to 464. The process was contentious, and the appointed calligrapher nearly abandoned his post over disagreements surrounding cursive structures. Finally, in 1948, Nadim proposes a system of only 116 sorts. Adopting a modern attitude, he distinguishes Arabic printing, as a means of disseminating education and knowledge, from Arabic calligraphy, as a traditional and fine art.

Nadim differentiates between Arabic letters that "overlap" and "interlock." These different types of cursive connections were the source of disagreement among committee members in 1902. The eventual compromise preserved a diverse set of ligatures with a final set of almost 500 forms. However, the typesetting of these complex forms disrupts the horizontal line. This, in turn, complicates the placement of *tashkil,* which has become increasingly necessary for modern education and foreign names. Nadim's suggestion maintains a consistent horizontal line by removing, whenever possible, vertical letter connections and complex ligatures. When necessary, distinct lines of *tashkil* run above and below the primary line of *rasm,* much like railroad tracks. Nadim's character set includes 113 letters (twenty-eight isolated forms, twenty-nine initial variants, twenty-seven final variants, twenty-nine medial variants) and three overlapping ligatures (the word "Allah" and two variations of *lām-alif*) for a total of 116 letter shapes. Eighteen marks of optional *tashkil,* ten numerals, and thirteen punctuation marks complete the set, for a grand total of 157 sorts.[50]

Nadim's final section criticizes the operations of Egyptian state presses. Due to the prevalence of interlocking characters and complex ligatures, there is no consistent method of typesetting *tashkil.* Furthermore, lines of *tashkil* are incredibly narrow and require a great deal of patience and dexterity. Incorrect placement of *tashkil* increases error, and this, in turn, hinders reading comprehension.

Nadim contrasts the convoluted practices of state-run operations with independent presses, which have already discarded interlocking letters. He notes that readers of the newspaper *Al-Ahram* first resisted the change, but they eventually grew accustomed to the reduced character set. Similar reductions spread across a wide variety of periodicals. Unfortunately, however, private presses were inconsistent in the reduction of forms. Different presses employ different character sets, different numbers of sorts, and different methods of marking *tashkil*. Nadim urges the heads of private presses to convene and agree on common practice. He believed that his proposed system would facilitate the process while preserving the traditional aesthetics of Arabic script. In his final words, Nadim asks the Ministry of Finance to order the state-operated El-Amiriya Press to adopt the recommended changes. If not, he warns, Arabic printing will continue to be subject to technological hurdles and grave inaccuracies.

The Unified Arabic Alphabet of Nasri Khattar

Nasri Khattar's Unified Arabic Alphabet remains one of the most recognizable and successful projects of Arabic script reform. (See Figure 5.1.) Khattar simplified the Arabic script to one form per letter.[51] The letters do not connect cursively; they are both discrete and unconnected, like the letters of the Latin alphabet. Khattar's Unified Arabic Alphabet unites the various initial, medial, final and isolated forms of Arabic letters into a single standardized character. The basic alphabet includes thirty characters: the twenty-eight letters of the Arabic *abjad,* the essential *lām-alif* ligature, and the *tā' marbutah.* Later iterations added signs for *hamza* and *alif maqsurah. Tashkil* can be layered over and under individual forms similar to traditional script. Khattar recalls that his initial eureka moment occurred in 1932.[52] While teaching an Arabic typewriting class, he accidentally struck the same form of the letter *hā'* in both instances of its use in *"ahlan wa sahlan."* The first instance normally takes the initial form of *hā',* and the second instance takes one of a variety of medial forms. But the typewritten message remained legible even when the initial form was used in both instances. This sparked the idea of an Arabic typewriter alphabet in which each letter received a single shape.

Khattar tirelessly promoted Unified Arabic throughout his distinguished career. After graduating from the American University of Beirut in 1930, Khattar studied architecture at Yale and Columbia Universities in the United States. In

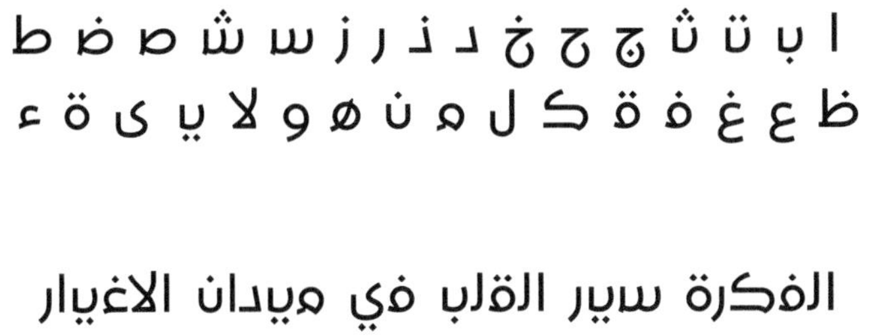

ظ ض ص ش س ز ر ذ د خ ح ج ث ت ب ا

ء ة ى ي لا و ھ ن م ل ک ق ف غ ع ط

الفكرة سىر القلب في مىدان الاغىار

Figure 5.1. The Unified Arabic Alphabet

Nasri Khattar's Unified Arabic Alphabet reduced Arabic script to one isolated form per letter. The reform idea was inspired by a typewriter keyboard. The line of text on the bottom transcribes the same phrase used for the calligraphy examples in Chapter 2 and the other figures in this chapter. (Figure created with Pascal Zoghbi's UA Neo B font, which is based on one version of Khattar's Alphabet. Font images courtesy of Pascal Zoghbi.)

1939, seven years after his eureka moment, he was appointed chief architect of the Lebanese pavilion at the New York World's Fair. The pavilion featured a Remington typewriter outfitted with an early version of Unified Arabic.[53] Khattar later apprenticed with Frank Lloyd Wright at Taliesin in Spring Green, Wisconsin.[54] Wright's modernist ideals of minimalism, functionality, and aesthetic reduction greatly influenced Khattar's designs. Khattar pitched his alphabet to IBM (International Business Machines), and Thomas Watson, who was then head of the company, became an enthusiastic admirer. Watson sponsored a prestigious launch party for the Unified Arabic Alphabet at New York's Waldorf Astoria Hotel.[55] And Khattar was subsequently appointed IBM's "ambassador" to the court of King Farouk in Egypt. While there, he partnered with Dr. Frank Laubach to combat illiteracy. Laubach's book *Teaching the World to Read* (1946) champions Unified Arabic as a major advancement in the fight against Arabic illiteracy. Laubach boasted that students could learn to read Unified Arabic in one-tenth the time it takes to learn traditional *naskh*. Per Watson's request, Laubach and Khattar presented King Farouk with an Arabic translation of the United Nations charter printed in Unified Arabic. This was the first text written on IBM's new Unified Arabic typewriter. Khattar twice submitted Unified Arabic for consideration by the Academy of Arabic Language in Cairo: once in 1947 and again in 1957.[56] His proposal received strong consideration, but, like all the other submissions, it failed to win the academy prize. Khattar remained resolute. He applied for, and received, a patent from the U.S. Patent and Trademark Office, and the American Type Foundry (ATF) began marketing a metal typeface of Unified Arabic in 1950.[57]

Khattar directly acknowledged his radical break with handwritten and scribal aesthetics. In a 1955 article titled "Unified Arabic, Weapon against Illiteracy," he writes that "a sober analysis of Arabic vs. Roman systems will undoubtedly reveal that advances by the latter are not due to its superiority as an alphabet, but rather its printability."[58] Khattar argued that printed characters should not mimic the appearance of hand-drawn forms. Printing was a specialized technique in need of specific technical elements. He drew parallels with the adoption of Roman type during the Italian Renaissance. Roman type broke with the scribal appearance of Latin cursive and returned the Latin alphabet to ideal shapes of individual letters. Printed Latin and handwritten Latin cursive continue to function side by side despite drastic visual differences. Khattar similarly positioned Unified Arabic as a complement, rather than a replacement for handwritten script. He argued that printing and cursive handwriting advantageously coexist in modern English, and that Arabic can benefit likewise. Khattar's idea can even be seen as an extension of scribal practices of stylistic variety, in which differences in appearance signify diverse genres and audiences. The suggestion that printed letters have their own distinct uses resonates with Ibrahim Müteferrika's claims two centuries earlier. Both Khattar and Müteferrika argued that print produces different types of text than those written by hand.

Khattar's driving force was the fight against Arabic illiteracy. The Unified Arabic Alphabet tackled the problem with a two-prong design strategy: (1) retain, as much as possible, the recognizable and identifying features of isolated Arabic letters and (2) enhance the printability of Arabic characters by adapting them to modern technologies. Khattar's letter shapes were highly influenced by his modernist sensibilities. The earliest designs share aesthetic qualities with popular sans-serif Latin typefaces of the mid-twentieth century, such as Univers and Helvetica. The letters appear highly rationalized, strongly geometric, and more abstract than those proposed by Khattar's contemporaries. Embracing the crispness of modernist form, Khattar broke entirely with scribal imitation. The handwritten line of *naskh* traces a gesture. Type, in contrast, is engineered: drawn, designed, and carved for implementation in a technical system. Khattar referred to his work as "typographic engineering."[59] Drawing on the language of architecture and industrial design, He framed Unified Arabic as a solution to a usability problem. Khattar engineered Arabic script to solve compatibility issues with international standards and infrastructural technologies.

On the production side, Unified Arabic facilitated printing. The full repertoire consisted of only thirty letters. This is even fewer than the number required to print uppercase and lowercase letters in English. The low number increased the speed and efficiency of both typesetting and typewriting. The smaller character count also reduced the cost of producing typewriters and the overall cost of adapting Arabic to modern communication systems. On the consumption side, Khattar argued that Unified Arabic facilitated reading comprehension. Readers need to recognize only thirty characters rather than the multiple forms of traditional *naskh*. Moreover, the geometric openness of Unified Arabic supported legibility at smaller sizes, and the alphabet shared identical line spacing with bilingual texts printed in Latin letters. The simplicity and flexibility of the system were especially appealing to corporate sponsors and technology manufacturers, who adapted the alphabet across a range of materials and products: from typewriters to metal typefaces, to signage and digital systems. Unified Arabic translates to Latinate computing environments as easily as it did to printing systems. In 2013, Lebanese designer Pascal Zoghbi worked with Camille Khattar—Nasri Khattar's daughter and the trustee of his estate—to adapt Unified Arabic as a fully functional Unicode font. Rana Abou Rjeily's Mirsaal typeface, which is highlighted in her book *Cultural Connectives* (2011), is another descendant of Khattar's approach. Abou Rjeily shares Khattar's philosophy that simplified geometric forms assist literacy and cross-cultural understanding.

Arabe Standard Voyellé-Codage Arabe (ASV-Codar)

The Arabe Standard Voyellé-Codage Arabe (ASV-Codar) system of Ahmed Lakhdar-Ghazal successfully migrated Arabic script into a range of modern technologies. The project obtained substantial technical and political success. The Moroccan government officially endorsed it and independently implemented ASV-Codar as a national standard. In 1958, Professor Lakhdar submitted ASV-Codar to the competition sponsored by the Academy of Arabic Language in Cairo. His proposal described the system as "a typeface designed to allow the setting and dissemination of Arabic texts, taking into account the use of all modern techniques: printing and typing, informatics, data transmission and telecommunications."[60] At the time, Professor Lakhdar directed L'Institut d'Études et de Recherches pour l'Arabisation (IERA) at Mohamed V University in Rabat. The institute worked to adapt Arabic language and script to modern technologies, linguistics, and information systems. Morocco promoted IERA, and ASV-Codar in particular, through educational and literacy campaigns. King Hassan II personally championed the program, and *Manar al-Maghrib* (The Moroccan Lighthouse) utilized ASV-Codar to typeset its articles.[61] The newspaper targeted newly literate readers and appreciated ASV-Codar's easy inclusion of *tashkil*. The system allowed articles with full vocalization to be typeset quickly and efficiently. Based on this record of success, UNESCO enthusiastically debated ASV-Codar in both 1958 and 1961. The United Nations Development Program (UNDP) financially supported the development of an ASV-Codar *naskh* typeface in 1975 and funded training workshops for ASV-Codar type designers in the early 1980s.[62] The system has been successfully implemented across a wide variety of technologies, including cast-metal movable type, Linotype, Letraset, typewriter balls, microfilm, phototypesetting, and computerized text.[63]

ASV-Codar can be implemented on two levels. (See Figure 5.2.) The "pure" system consists of 84 character sorts, and the "total" system expands the set to 107. The systems are fully interchangeable, and they are compatible with the number of keys on a standard alphanumeric Latin keyboard. Whenever possible, ASV-Codar abstracts Arabic letters to a single form. The letters connect cursively on a consistent common baseline. The system also contains three appendix forms, which provide terminals for letters in a final or isolated position. Most significantly, ASV-Codar incorporates *tashkil* vocalization as distinct sorts. *Tashkil* is marked above or below a connecting bar placed between letters.[64] The *tashkil* sorts appear after the consonants they modify, and they are typeset on the same line as the primary letters. This allows both vocalized and unvocalized texts to be transmitted, or typeset, as a single sequence of characters. The pure system consists of the following 84 characters:

- 33 letters: the 28 consonants of the Arabic *abjad*, plus *hamza*, a final *yā'* (which remains distinct from medial *yā'*), *alif maqsurah, tā' marbutah*, and final / isolated *hā'* (which resembles a dotless *tā' marbutah*).

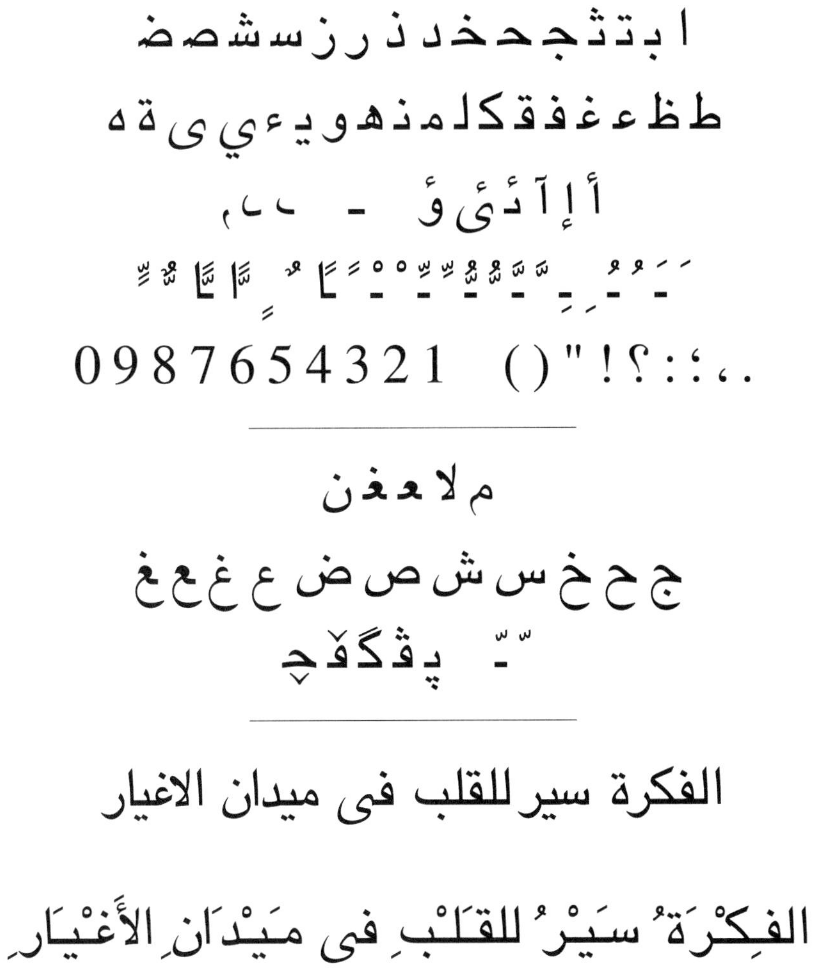

ا ب ت ث ج ح خ د ذ ر ز س ش ص ض

ط ظ ع غ ف ق ك ل م ن ه و ي ء ى ة ه

أ إ آ ئ ؤ ـ ٬ ٫

٠٩٨٧٦٥٤٣٢١   ( ) " ! ؟ : ؛ ،.

م لا ع غ ن

ج ح خ س ش ص ض ع غ غ

پ ڤ گ ڨ چ

الفكرة سير للقلب فى ميدان الاغيار

الفِكْرَةُ سَيْرُ للقَلْبِ فى مَيْدَانِ الأَغْيَارِ

Figure 5.2.   The LAKHDAR typeface / ASV-Codar

Yannis Haralambous's LAKHDAR typeface re-creates the glyph set of Ahmed Lakhdar-Ghazal's Arabe Standard Voyellé-Codage Arabe (ASV-Codar) system. The "pure" system above the first dividing line contains eighty-four glyphs covering the Arabic language. The "total" system adds the twenty-three glyphs below the line, expanding coverage to Persian, Ottoman, and local Moroccan languages. The lines of text on the very bottom use the system to transcribe the same phrase used for the calligraphy examples in Chapter 2 and the other figures in this chapter. (Image courtesy Yannis Haralambous.)

- 6 *hamza:* 5 variations of *hamza* in combination with the stems of *alif, wāw,* and *yā',* plus a separate character for *alif maddah.*
- 1 unmarked connecting bar.
- 3 appendixes for word and letter terminals: the *bā'* type, the *sīn* type, and the *jīm* type.
- 22 vocalization characters: 7 forms of isolated *tashkil* for all *harakat* and *shaddah* combinations, the same *tashkil* paired with a connecting bar, and 8 forms of *tanwin.*
- 10 numerals: the western Arabic digits employed in Morocco and shared with Latin script (1, 2, 3, 4, 5, 6, 7, 8, 9, and 0).
- 9 punctuation marks: period, comma, semicolon, colon, question mark, exclamation point, quotation marks, and right and left parentheses.

Like other single-form proposals, the pure ASV-Codar system sacrifices familiar forms of isolated and final letters to preserve a one-to-one correspondence between letter and shape. Aesthetic and formal variations were added to the total system for designers wishing to include a wider, more traditional character set. The total system also includes characters representing foreign, or non-Arabic, phonemes. It adds 23 characters to the pure system:

- 6 primary aesthetic variants: final / isolated *lām,* final / isolated *mīm,* final / isolated *nūn,* the *lām-alif* ligature, and the inverted triangle shape of medial *'ayn* and *ghayn.*
- 11 secondary aesthetic variants: final / isolated forms of *jīm, ḥā', khā', sīn, shīn, ṣād, ḍād, 'ayn* (2 varieties), and *ghayn* (2 varieties).
- 5 non-Arab letters: three phonemic representations commonly used across languages that employ Arabic script (the *bā' rasm* with three sublinear *nuqta* for the p sound, the *fā' rasm* with three supralinear *nuqta* for the v sound, the *kaf rasm* with a light supralinear line for the g sound) and two letters employed in local Moroccan dialects (the *fā' rasm* with a supralinear caron and the *jīm rasm* with a sublinear caron).
- 2 *shaddah* characters: isolated *shaddah* and isolated *shaddah* paired with a connecting bar. In the pure system, *shaddah* is always accompanied by a vocalization mark.

ASV-Codar produced a powerful combinational system. Despite their some-what rigid appearance, characters preserve, as much as possible, the primary structural appearance and visual peculiarities of cursive *naskh*. The innovation of casting discrete letter terminals retains a limited amount of contextual vari-ation while adding only 3 sorts to the total count. The 107 sorts of the total system support multiple Arabic script languages, and the number is less than the number of sorts in the complete Latin character set. The character count answers IERA's charge of adapting the Arabic script to both print and electronic communica-tion system. Early character encoding schemes consisted of seven bits, which produce 128 distinct code points. Encoding all 107 of the total ASV-Codar system preserves 20 code points for use as markup and control characters. The system can efficiently transmit either vocalized or unvocalized Arabic script as a single string of characters in a seven-bit digital system.

The Lure of Latin Script

Other proposals, following Turkey's lead, suggested the replacement of Arabic characters with Latin ones. Abd al-Aziz Fahmi's 1944 proposal was one of the first to take this route. Fahmi substituted a single Latin-like form for each Ar-abic letter. In order to retain a semblance of handwritten Arabic, Fahmi's let-ters adopted a scriptlike appearance and connected cursively. They resembled the decorative Latin script typefaces such as Newlywed Script and Lucida Hand-writing. Latin letters were assigned based on phonetic similarities: ā represented the Arabic *alif,* b represented *bāʾ,* s represented *sīn,* and so on. Other classes of letters, such as the *jīm, ṣād,* and *ʿayn* classes, acquired new forms loosely reminiscent of their isolated Arabic forms. In line with Latinate structure, Fah-mi's letters read from left to right, rather than the traditional Arabic direction of right to left. Fahmi also introduced the Latinate concept of uppercase and lowercase for differentiating proper and common nouns and indicating sentence breaks.[65]

A 1955 proposal by Yahya Boutemène followed a different track. (See Figure 5.3.) The phonetic similarities of b and *bāʾ* or m and *mīm* did not concern him. Instead, Boutemène analyzed the distinctive structural features of Arabic let-ters. He assigned each Arabic letter a Latin alphabet letter, a modified Latin letter, or sometimes a Greek letter that mimicked the Arabic letter's dominant visual traits. Thus, the lowercase Latin letter l was used to represent the Arabic

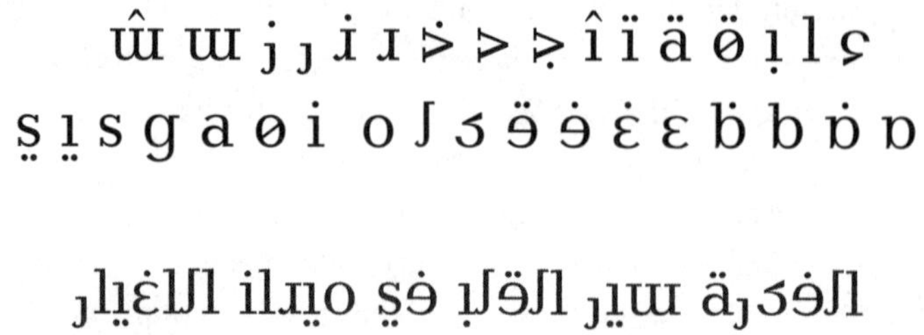

û ɯ j ɟ ı ı ɹ ⪢ ⪢ ⪦ î ï ä ö ı ı ç

ṣ ḷ s ɡ ə θ i o ʃ ɔ ə̈ ə̇ ɛ̈ ɛ b̈ b ḅ ɒ

ɹₗₐɛ̈ΣΣ ilɹo ṣ⪦ ṇ̈θʃΣ ɹₗɯ ä̈ɹɔ⪦ΣΣ

Figure 5.3. The Boutemene typeface

Yannis Haralambous's Boutemene typeface re-creates the letters of Yahya Boutemène's reform proposal for Arabic script. Boutemène assigned each Arabic letter a visual analogue based on the Latin alphabet. The line of text on the bottom transcribes the same phrase used for the calligraphy examples in Chapter 2 and the other figures in this chapter. (Image courtesy Yannis Haralambous.)

letter *alif.* Fahmi's system, in contrast, used a cursive letter l to represent *lām.* The lowercase Latin letter l shares a phonetic overlap with the Arabic letter *lām,* but it visually resembles the isolated *alif.* For the Arabic letter *nūn,* which is identified by a single *nuqta* above its primary *rasm,* Boutemène borrowed the lowercase Latin letter i, with its single dot above a simple stem. The *bā'* class letters were similarly built around the stem of an undotted i (ı): *tā'* became ï (with the two dots of a diaeresis, or umlaut, above the stem); *thā'* became î (with a circumflex above the stem), and *bā'* became ı (with a single dot below the stem). The medial form of the Arabic letter *yā'* was represented with two dots below the stem of the ı. Other visual equivalencies include the lowercase letter s for *alif maqsurah,* ö for the isolated *tā' marbutah* (and ä for *tā' marbutah* in the final position), an upside-down m for the *sīn* class, an upside-down r for the *dāl* class, and a v rotated 90 degrees for the *jīm* class. The Greek letter epsilon (ε) represented *'ayn,* and a dotted epsilon represented *ghayn.* A few characters were uniquely designed for the set. *Lām* was represented by a modified lowercase letter l, which displayed a small hook on the bottom left. The shape, which resembles the integral symbol used in mathematical notation, distinguished *lām* from *alif,* which used an unmodified lowercase Latin letter l. *Kāf* was represented by the bottom two-thirds of a clipped numeral 3. And the same symbol rotated 180 degrees became *hamza.*[66]

Although Boutemène's proposal was never formally implemented, it raises a series of intriguing questions. All written forms have a dual character. They have both visual shapes and linguistic, symbolic, or phonetic meanings.[67] Fahmi's 1944 proposal emphasizes the latter and borrows the phonetic values of Latin script. Boutemène borrows the other half of the equation. He highlights writing as a *visual* medium. Boutemène did not phonetically apply the Latin alphabet to Arabic sounds; he used Latin-based shapes to create a uniquely Arabic character set. He wrote the Arabic language with Latin script grammar. Representationally, Boutemène's proposal operates very similarly to the Unified Arabic Alphabet: one distinct form per letter. But Boutemène's forms are more Latinized than Nasri Khattar's. They are Latin shapes in all but representation. The complete set consists of thirty-four characters: the twenty-eight letters of the Arabic *abjad* plus *hamza, alif maqsurah,* two variants of *tā' marbutah,* and a second variant for both *yā'* and *hā'.* The thirty-four characters map easily to keyboard inputs, and they seamlessly integrate alongside the Latin, Greek, and Cyrillic alphabets.

Boutemène's innovative decision to reform script through aesthetic, rather than phonetic, similarities foreshadowed later techniques of digital design. In the 1990s and early 2000s, Arabic designers sought to benefit from visual variety and the availability of Latin fonts. Adopting strategies reminiscent of Yahya Boutemène, they rotated, dissected, and rearranged Latin letters to create Arabic characters.[68] In programs such as Adobe Photoshop, the Latin letter m can easily be rotated 180 degrees to resemble *sīn,* the Latin letter j can substitute for *zā',* or letters can be chopped up for component parts.[69] (See Figure 5.4.) The dissected and modified forms imitate Arabic characters while preserving the visual consistency of a Latin font family. The Arabic shapes replicate the width of strokes, the contrasts of thick and thin, the sweep of curves, the points of terminals and serifs, and various other delicate details that distinguish Latin typefaces.

During the mid-1990s, Ahmad Humeid pursued this strategy while working for *Byte: Middle East.* When the American edition of *Byte* adopted a sleek sans-serif masthead, Humeid wished to parallel the visual impact. He chopped, manipulated, and rotated elements of the Latin font Helvetica Narrow to piece together a complementary sans-serif Arabic font, which he labeled "Ahmad."[70] Arabic chat alphabet, or Arabizi, offers another example. Arabizi uses Latin letters to represent the Arabic language. The informal alphabet developed for Arabic text messaging on cell phones and personal devices that support only Latin script.[71] Arabizi is a hybrid system, halfway between Fahmi's phoneticism and Boutemène's visual resemblances. Many Arabizi equivalencies

Figure 5.4. Arabic letters hacked from Helvetica

The top line displays the Arabic word *risala* (written message) as depicted by the Geeza Pro Arabic font. The second line mimics this word with chopped-up letters of the Latin font Helvetica Bold. From right to left, the bottom word is built from the tail of a lowercase letter g (for *rā'*), an upside-down lowercase letter m (for *sīn*), a capital letter L (for *alif*), the mirror image of a capital letter L (for *lām*), and the loop of a lowercase letter a topped with two periods (for the *tā' marbutah*). (Image produced in Adobe Creative Suite.)

are phonetic, such as b for *bā'* and l for *lām,* but others are visually inspired, such as 3 for *'ayn* and 7 for *ḥā'*. Trapped in technologies designed for the Latin alphabet, Arab youth were forced to integrate Arabic language into the available character set.

For technologists, Latin script promised easy integration with modern communication and printing systems. For other reformers, the attraction of Latin script arose from cultural and symbolic resonances.[72] The Latin alphabet was perceived as a modernizing force, with Latin script opening the gateway to democracy, industrialization, and future development. Writing in 1955, Salama Mousa argued that the adoption of Latin letters would "mark a change in psychological attitude." With a new alphabet, Mousa continued, Arabs "would welcome modern industrial civilization, with its moral, cultural, and spiritual values. . . . Problems that are now difficult to resolve would present less difficulty. . . . [Arabic] *Weltanschaung* would be changed from one which looks backward to one which looks to the future."[73] The distance of history highlights the colonial tone of Mousa's statements, but his arguments are not too far afield from ideas circulated in Turkey, where they had realpolitik and powerful linguistic consequences.[74] The enormous advancements in communication technologies during the twentieth century tempted newly independent countries to adopt Latin script for competitive advantage. Latin script offered the promise of immediate access to global networks of infrastructural and media technology. On the other side of the aisle, Arabic speakers increasingly perceived Arabic script as the symbol of independence from a colonized past. For Arabic nationalists, cursive *naskh* was the mark of national freedom and ethnic pride. Arabic script protects and preserves the holy text of the Qur'an, it visually references the golden age of Islamic civilization, and it signals the arrival of newly independent Arab states on the global stage. The adoption of Latin-like letters can never erase the scientific, literary, and philosophical contributions of Arabic script. *Naskh* continues to unify Arabic and Islamic identity, and it points the way toward non-Western visions of modernity and futurity.[75]

The Question of Lithography

Script reform movements catered to the technical constraints of movable type printing and, later, a limited number of typewriter keys. Printer's grids requested a limited number of homogeneous characters that fit together to form neat lines of text. This implied that greater attention to detail and relatively higher levels of skill were required for Arabic script when compared with the discrete forms and comparatively consistent letters of Latin script.[76] Modeling the subtle and delicate lines of *naskh* required great precision from type designers and punch cutters. The resulting character set often included a large number of complex ligatures in addition to forms of individual letters, and the various sorts need to align perfectly in order to mimic cursive connections. The large number of sorts and their specific alignments, in turn, demanded meticulous accuracy and exactitude from typesetters. The temptation to reduce the number of forms is apparent. Not only would this reduce the number of sorts needing to be cast; it would also reduce the complexity of and possible combinations needed for piecing the sorts together. Scripts were conformed to meet the needs of the technological system; they were reformed to fit into type cases and printer's grids.

Script reform movements underscore a conceptual and technological division separating text and image. Movable type is text, or, rather, movable type is potential text. Movable type offers a collection of combinatorial forms that can be strung together to construct and hold passages of text. Once printing is complete, the pieces are disassembled and the next text is built from the same blocks. Handwriting is much closer to an image. The scribal hand that writes does not cease to draw.[77] Handwriting traces the visual marks left by an expressive gesture of the body. This overlap of writing and drawing disappears with movable type. Typography is a technical process of construction. It is writing with performed types (type-graphy) rather than writing by hand. In print copy, the expressive and performative act of "writing" occurs prior to typesetting. Textual content is then dressed in an appropriate typeface, which was also designed prior to typesetting and, usually, with little or no knowledge of the textual content it will eventually hold. The aesthetic qualities of a typeface are drawn by a type designer (a role quite different from that of "writer") and molded into hard metal by punch cutters. Finally, the hand that sets the type is neither the hand that composed the passage nor the hand that drew the type. Movable type isolates aesthetic design, expressive content, and technical assembly as three moments of practice.

The separation of text and image did not port easily onto "complex" non-Latin scripts such as Arabic. Script reform addressed the mismatch by altering the visual quality of the script. The forms became easier to draw and cut as type. Letters and forms were simplified, bent, and broken until they fit within useful blocks of movable type. An alternative solution would alter the technological infrastructure, rather than the script. "Complex" scripts are only complex as movable type; they are much simpler to reproduce with other technologies. The persistence of scribal pens in Ottoman circles, even as print was reshaping European society, was not solely, or even predominantly, conservative. The technology of reed pen on paper developed hand in hand with aesthetics of cursive *naskh* and practices of stylistic variety. Movable type printing could not replicate the drawn communication of Arabic script. In the late eighteenth century, however, a new method of printing could. The new method, lithography, supported better integration of text and image: images could now be incorporated directly into text, and text could appear as complex as a hand-drawn image. Lithography can mechanically reproduce complex scripts without requiring script reform. Typography, in contrast, transforms handwriting into type characters: "in [the former], letters and words are joined 'naturally' in unbroken script, in the other, they are joined mechanically. Conveyed in an idiosyncratic, individual hand, the lithograph text may be more comfortable to read, at least in certain times and places, whereas typography, employing a standard, potentially universal type form, may be relatively uncomfortable to read, again in certain times and places."[78]

Lithographic printing relied on the simple fact that oil and water do not mix. And the material requirements were incredibly simple: grease, lampblack, water, paper, and polished stone, usually limestone. It required neither precast metal type nor complex machinery. First, the image or text is drawn or written on stone with a greasy crayon. Next, the stone is washed with water and lampblack is applied. Then the stone is washed again. The water washes away the lampblack, except where lampblack stuck to grease (since the grease repels water). Finally, paper is applied to the stone, which transfers a mirror image of the writing-drawing onto the paper.[79] Consequently, the entire production cycle of lithographic printing could occur locally without the need to import heavy and expensive foreign equipment. When playwright Alois Senefelder (1771–1834) invented the method, he introduced it to the Bavarian court by replicating a handwritten note before their very eyes.[80] A few decades later, Muhammad Azhari performed a similar demonstration for the Dutch consul in Sumatra. Azhari extemporized a poem of welcome and printed it on the spot.[81] In Muslim communities that lacked a previous commitment to movable type printing, lithography spread like wildfire. The British introduced lithography to India in 1824, and in the first year alone, more than seventeen thousand books were produced. Within a few years, well over a hundred locally run lithographic presses had sprung up across the country.[82] In Persia, the first lithographic press opened in Tabriz in 1835, which already had an earlier typographic press. But movable type quickly fell out of favor compared to lithography.[83] By 1860, lithographic presses were competing in all major Persian cities.[84] Similar trends occurred in Southeast Asia, where Muslim printing was dominated by lithography from the nineteenth until the middle of the twentieth century. Within fifty years of its introduction, lithography had become a powerful force in Arabic script printing from Persia to Malaysia. Lithography reproduced the two-dimensional design "complexity" of scribal lines.[85]

Attempts to re-create scribal appearances in print were nothing new. European incunabula mimicked Latin manuscripts before diverging into more simplified printed aesthetics. Gutenberg's cases contained more than twice as many sorts and ligatures than later became standard, and the Gutenberg Bible, in particular, imitated pre-print predecessors, even to the inclusion of hand-drawn and hand-colored rubrication.[86] When Ibrahim Müteferrika adopted European printing techniques two hundred years later, he also adopted the European style of printed text. Müteferrika's earliest printings appear formal and sparse, with minimal aesthetic decoration. His later printings, however, in an appeal to readers more comfortable with manuscript appearances, added opening pages and decorative borders that mimicked manuscript style.[87] With lithography, printers no longer needed to mimic manuscript appearances. Lithographic printing "altogether lacked the mechanical rigidities of type. Its complete flexibility in reproducing graphic forms . . . was critically important for its success in the Islamic world, for it meant lithography was capable of reproducing calligraphy. . . . A book printed by lithography was essentially a manuscript reproduced."[88] Readers accustomed to manuscript styles, and those who simply preferred them, could purchase lithographic reproductions.

If lithography removed the need for script reform, why then did reform movements still occur? Why did Turkey adopt Latin letters, and why did the Academy of Arabic Language in Cairo launch its competition? For one, both countries adopted movable type printing prior to the spread of lithography. State-oriented presses in Turkey and Egypt invested heavily in movable type equipment and machinery. And they doubled down on the press as an agent of change. In European tradition, the revolutionary potential of print sprang from movable type. Movable type—beginning with Gutenberg and the printing of the Bible—was seen as the symbol and mode of modern textual communication. Movable type formed the technological foundation of a grand historical narrative that invoked secularization, industrialization, and modernization. Lithographic printing is minimized as a footnote to these deeper currents, which, as the Eurocentric narrative goes, began much earlier. In Europe, lithography replaced engraving, and it was used primarily for image reproduction: illustrations, maps, figures, and diagrams.[89] In the Euro-American context, lithography was rarely seen as a revolutionary development.[90] Ian Proudfoot distinguishes between Arabic script countries that followed the European manner of movable type and those that embraced lithography. Both Turkey and Egypt mimicked the European model of movable type for textual communication, supported by illustrative lithography. The commitment to movable type—infrastructural, economic, and ideological—ultimately buoyed appeals for script reform. The symbolic resonances of the European technology, rather than purely technical reasons, exerted a powerful influence.

In the nineteenth century, a wave of mass printing swept across the Arab and Islamic world. Muslim states increased their support of journeymen who developed the necessary skills of typesetting and printing while working abroad.[91] These early technocrats then returned to open local presses in service to modernization and state development. From Müteferrika onward, the dominant drivers of Arabic printing in the central Middle East were government ventures. Muhammad Ali followed a similar secularist model in the establishment of the El-Amiriya Press at Bulaq in 1820. The prime movers spurring print in both Turkey and Egypt were state bureaucrats and literary elites.[92] And they tacitly adopted the European model of separation between typographic text and lithographic image. Press machinery and movable type alternatively arrived via Christian missionary societies. Missionary presses imported European equipment to circulate devotional texts and support local operations. Examples include the American Church Missionary Society, which founded an Arabic language press in Malta in 1822 and relocated to Beirut in 1834. An Arabic language Bible printed by the Beirut Press won a gold medal at the Paris Exposition of 1878.[93] In Palestine, Austrian Catholics and British Protestants established competing missionary presses in 1848, and Roman Dominicans imported press machinery to Iraq in 1859. Missionary presses diverged ideologically from, and were occasionally directly opposed to, locally run state-sponsored administrative presses. But the technological models of the competing camps held much in common. The European ideal of a "republic of letters" provided a shared undercurrent. Both state-oriented and missionary presses utilized print as a vehicle for education and community formation, and both sides preferred typographic printing, with its requisite heavy machinery and considerable investment.

Yet, one key text remained detached from movable type and the new channels of movable type printing: the Qur'an. Throughout the nineteenth and twentieth centuries, the majority of printed Qur'anic *masahif* were lithographically reproduced, even in Turkey and Egypt, where presses favored the European model of movable type.[94] The Qur'an specifically references "the pen" as an instrument for conveying the divine message. Qur'anic *masahif,* copied by pen, preserved and celebrated the divine text. Movable type, in contrast, removes pens from the equation of written communication. Typeset passages are organized and composed rather than traced by pen. Lithography short-circuited these concerns: it reinserted the primary importance of the pen and copied the lines of well-formed *naskh.* Lithographic printing was also less reliant on expensive foreign equipment than typographic printing, which assured the ritual purity of Qur'anic *masahif.* If movable type sacrificed the pen for mass distribution, lithography offered a new synthesis: "Lithography brings together, in hybrid fashion, two authorities—that of the person and hand, buttressed by the human collation system, with that of the alienated truth value of mechanical reproduction."[95] Lithography mechanically reproduced the gestural pen and visual design of manuscript *masahif*.

In 1874, Cevdet Paşa published the first *masahif* printed in Ottoman lands. While the Ottoman Scientific Society debated the initial script proposals of Münif Paşa and Mirza Feth Ali Ahundzade, Cevdet Paşa began working on a vernacular Turkish translation of the Qur'anic text. Ultimately, however, he printed an Arabic language *mushaf* rather than a Turkish-language interpretation. Paşa was an entrepreneur and a secularist with no formal religious authority. His ability to print Qur'anic *masahif* therefore demonstrates a tectonic shift in Ottoman textual and religious authority that occurred between the eighteenth and the nineteenth century. When Ibrahim Müteferrika and Said Çelebi wished to open a secular and administratively oriented press in the 1720s, they validated the enterprise with both a royal *ferman* and a religious *fatwa*. The pair asked for and received a religious judgment, despite a carefully worded question that specifically excluded books of religious content. A century and a half later, when Cevdet Paşa wished to print the most sacrosanct book of Islamic tradition, he obtained only governmental permission.[96] He neither asked for nor received a religious *fatwa*.

Nevertheless, Paşa visually preserved an incredibly important mark of Islamic tradition: the handwritten line of *al-khatt al-mansub*. His print edition lithographically reproduced the scribal pen of Şekerzade Mehmet Efendi, who meticulously copied the text in the style and template of Şeyh Hamdullah. Later editions lithographically printed the styles and scripts of comparably famous Ottoman calligraphers, such as Hafiz Osman (d. 1698 c.e.) and Hasan Çelebi.[97] Lithography copied the exemplars and pinnacles of Ottoman scribal tradition. It printed the ideal image of handwritten Ottoman *naskh* rather than re-forming *naskh* into rigid boxes of movable type. Even in Turkey—where typographic printing was the norm for textual materials, and calls for radical script reform were gaining steam—the interaction of scribal tradition and lithographic printing proved mutually beneficial: "On the one hand, major works of the famous calligraphers were made accessible to a broader audience by printing. On the other hand, lithography helped calligraphers to continue making a living."[98] Professional scribes sold lithographic reproductions of manuscript copies and calligraphic works. As a result, the nineteenth century saw a major uptick in calligraphic and visual experimentation with Arabic script. Complex puzzlelike compositions, zoomorphic and figurative motifs (*resim yazı,* or picture writing), intricate *hilye* designs, and mirrored writings *(müsenna)* all increased post-print. All these designs could be copied and printed via lithography, without recourse to reform or simplification.

The lithographic printing of Qur'anic *masahif* continued a long theme of Islamic and Arabic textual practice. Qur'anic *masahif* have always removed themselves from the prosaic world of mundane texts. The earliest *masahif* were bound as codices to differentiate them from secular texts written on scrolls. Later, Qur'anic copyists resisted the marking of *tashkil* and the cursive *naskh* styles of professional scribes. Long after *naskh* became the dominant bookhand, Qur'anic *masahif* continued to be written in unvocalized archaic *Kufic*. When Qur'anic copyists finally adopted the *naskh* styles, the meticulously produced *muhaqqaq* style was reserved as particularly hieratic. Ottoman practice subsequently elevated and distinguished the Qur'anic text as a book apart by canonizing formal *mushaf* templates, with the dominant templates drawn from the examples of Şeyh Hamdullah.[99] When Cevdet Paşa lithographically printed the Qur'anic text in 1874, he reproduced a copy of Hamdullah's template. Qur'anic *naskh* refused to reform per the wishes of movable type. A similar bracketing move occurred in 1938, when Abdullah Yusuf Ali published what would become one of the most popular English interpretations of the Qur'an.[100] The text of Ali's English translation is typeset with Latin letters. The accompanying Arabic script employed photolithography to reproduce the hand-drawn *naskh* of calligrapher Pir Abdul Hamid. Yusuf Ali explained his design decision as follows: "calligraphy occupies an important place in Muslim *art,* and it is my desire that my version should not in any way be deficient in this respect."[101] The typographic English, by implication, is *artistically* deficient, while the Arabic original displays the handwritten image of divine text.

Conclusion: Type-Writing

Turkish language reform, Arabic script reform, and lithographic printing all carry assumptions about written communication and technology. The new Turkish alphabet replaced Arabic script with Latinate letters that were perceived as symbols of the future and more conducive to modern communications. Arabic reform movements preserved the visual character of Arabic script while adapting it to movable type and print technology. And lithography introduced a form of mechanical reproduction that copied the handwritten line. The simplicity and local control afforded by lithography pushed back at the dominant model of printing with movable type. But lithography's success was tempered by another new technology: the typewriter. The typewriter operates exactly as its name suggests. It allows users to write with type. Whereas earlier print technologies supported print production, the typewriter targeted authors and writers.[102] Typewriter-equipped authors could write, for the first time, directly with type. This concretized the popular separation of hand-drawn script and typed characters.

The typewriter keyboard privileged a consistent character set over aesthetic variation. As much as typewriters opened up new genres of compositional style, they closed a door on handwritten styles of scribal variation. Every typewriter typed the same shapes, even if they composed very different texts. For efficient usage, the number of common characters cannot exceed the number of keys, or double the number with a shift function. The Latin typewriter supported around ninety forms, including uppercase and lowercase variants of each letter, numerals, and select punctuation marks. Most cases of Arabic movable type, in contrast, contained well over five hundred sorts. These included positional variants for each letter, multi-letter ligatures, and *tashkil*. The pairing of Arabic type to keyboard layouts therefore necessitated a drastic reduction of forms. Nasri Khattar's Unified Arabic alphabet was directly inspired by the typewriter, while other Arabic script reformers—including Abd al-Aziz Fahmi, Yahya Boutemène, and Ahmed Lakhdar—took the limited character set of the typewriter as both the starting point and the rationale for their reform suggestions. Most reform suggestions clocked in at just over 100 Arabic characters, including Mohamed Nadim's proposal for 116 sorts and Ahmed Lakhdar's "total" ASV-Codar system of 108. More radical suggestions went even lower: the Unified Arabic alphabet contained 30-some characters and Yahya Boutemène's Latinate proposal needed only 34. Both of these systems could be efficiently typewritten without recourse to a shift key.

Printing houses and publishers continued to handle mass production and distribution—at least until the personal computer heralded the era of desktop publishing—and they too were increasingly constrained by keyboards. Indeed, the first Latin-letter keyboard controlled a Linotype machine, and it did not by any means resemble the now familiar QWERTY layout of typewriters and personal computers. By the twentieth century, Linotype had become the industry standard for periodical printing and other jobs requiring quick turnaround. Rather than setting individual pieces of movable type, the Linotype machine released matrices to cast an entire line of type. Lines of type were then stacked and printed, greatly increasing the speed of typesetting and production. As the name implies, Linotype machines prescribed a highly linear arrangement of written characters. Before designing any characters, type designers waited for keyboard layouts to be finalized, since the placement of the keys and the matrices they released influenced the size, shape, and width of the corresponding characters.[103] When applied to non-Latin scripts, this effectively imposed script reform without political debates and formal competitions: linear variation was brought in line with the requirements of the machine. The number of ligatures that reflected *naskh*'s vertical bounce was further reduced, and the four-form model of Arabic script was more stringently enforced. This demarcated a technological crossroads at the dawn of the digital era: Would *naskh* continue to be reformed and redesigned in order to efficiently meet the demands of technology, or would new digital technologies be designed to better represent *naskh*?

Chapter Six

Arabic Script on Computers

*I*n the twentieth century, a range of new technologies altered the transmission and design of script. By the end of the century, an enormous
volume of written communication circulated as natively digital text, either on
screen or as digitally printed material artifacts. The digital canvas is much more
open than grids of movable type. It supports a more fluid cursive line, more
subtle visual complexity, and more contextual variation. Digital remediation
suggested new methods for representing and sharing non-Latin scripts. This
fertile period of technical reorganization coincided with proposals, projects,
and contests of Arabic script reform. Utilitarian adaptions to print technology
were reforming and "simplifying" Arabic script just as newer technologies were
beginning to move the script beyond print. Computerized and digital systems
eased, to some extent, the persistent challenges of typesetting Arabic script. Digital characters were coded to multiple variants, rather than cast as individual
metal sorts. And computerized selection, rather than a human typesetter, selected the proper form of an Arabic letter: isolated, initial, medial, final, or otherwise. The possibilities of digital form revitalized Arabic script design, and the
ongoing changes herald a return of visual and scribal variation. New fonts, new
characters, and new textual forms dance in the light of digital screens.

 These changes—much like earlier transitions to proportional script and
movable type—recirculate perennial questions of written form, recognition, and

repetition. In the tenth century, *al-khatt al-mansub* formalized *naskh* as a proportional and repeatable style of handwriting. In the fifteenth century, movable type replaced handwritten scribal styles with repeatable metal sorts. And the twentieth century replaced metal sorts with repeatable code. The transformation to digital code alters the character, and characters, of Arabic script. Digital characters operate simultaneously as abstract coded representations and specific visual representations. A coded letter j remains the letter j regardless of its outward dressing as Times New Roman or Helvetica Narrow. And the coded letter *jīm* remains *jīm* even as it changes shape according to word position and chosen font. Coded characters are both discrete and repeatable, like movable type, and contextually fluid, like scribal forms. A wide range of visual variation can represent a single digital character, and appearances can change with the click of a mouse. Another significant shift entails increased communication across multiple human and technical actors. Both humans and devices read and write digital text. The automated interaction of technical networks is more extensive than ever before. Digital devices read text as code and write that code as visual form. Consequently, the design of digital writing operates on multiple planes. Computer engineers, font designers, and writers all shape the appearance of text. Encoding schemes define the unique characters of a script and the ways in which those characters interact, while fonts dress those coded characters in a variety of outfits.

Encoding Arabic

The coding of characters benefited Arabic typesetting, as computers were programmed to tackle the question of contextual variation. Due to the large number of contextual forms, Arabic typesetting was difficult, expensive, and time-consuming. Sorting through the various options and selecting the proper form demanded time, close attention, and knowledgeable staff. Computers shifted selection duties to devices. Digital keyboards code keystrokes into electric or digital signals. Inputs are coded for digital transmission, and transmissions are decoded on the other end of the connection. Transmitted codes are received and acted upon by devices, which retranslate code into onscreen or printed characters. Lines of script were decomposed into preset variations of coded characters and programmed in dialogue with each other. Character sets could become larger, more refined, and more complex. But the new technology built on legacies of movable type. It did not simply replace earlier technologies and render them moot.[1] Coded character sets remained closely tied to the analytic model of movable type.

In the 1970s, computerized typesetting machines radically quickened the process of selecting and composing Arabic sorts. Walter Tracy, then chief of type design for Linotype-Paul, championed the advances in an article titled "Arabic without Tears" (1976). Tracy describes the benefits afforded by machines such as the Linotron 505C and the Linofilm VIP. These machines merged the computerized selection of sorts with filmsetting and photocomposition. Based on keyboard inputs, the computer selected and outputted a preprogrammed Arabic form. The programmed forms included positional variants of the standard four-form model, as well as complex multi-letter ligatures:

> The programs take care of a number of different functions. The most important is the process of character selection; that is to say, it is the computer which decides whether the appropriate form of a letter to be used in response to the key-stroke is to be the initial, medial, final, or unconnected version of a letter. A second function of the program is to select the logotype represented by two separate character keystrokes: for example, the operator may key the letters "l" [*lām*] and "m" [*mīm*] and the computer will recognize this as a particular logotype—of which there are nearly a hundred in the total character array. . . . [T]he operator does no more than key an elementary version of the final requirement, the tape codes being translated by the computer into instructions . . . in the Arabic program, to produce the right form of letter or logotype, the correct placement of vowel signs, the insertion of extension strokes and so on. The computer does the difficult work; the operator gets it easy—and easy work is, with ordinary luck, accurate work.[2]

Users input characters via the keyboard, and the computer outputs the appropriate form. In cases of movable metal type, contextual variations resided in distinct physical locations. Typesetters needed to know a letter's position within a word before referencing the case and selecting the proper form among more than five hundred sorts. In computerized input, the human user simply needs to strike a key. The keyboard position of a particular Arabic letter remains the same regardless of whether that letter appears at the beginning, middle, or end of a word. Sequences are typed letter by letter, and the machine produces the appropriate form based on the sequence of keystrokes. Computational algorithms quickly sort contextual forms and select the best option according to adjacent characters and the surrounding text.

The second half of Tracy's equation was photocomposition. Although the computer selected contextual variants from a wide range of forms, the resulting characters were not yet fully digital. Instead, the resulting printed text was developed from film and character designs migrated to filmic negatives. Photocomposition was described as the "greatest step forward since the invention of moveable type."[3] It extended the open planar affordances of lithography to typographic printing and replaced the sculptural forms of three-dimensional metal type with two-dimensional shapes.[4] Lines became finer, edges more specific, and definition greater. Character shapes were no longer constrained by the material qualities of metal typecasting, such as brittleness or the bleed of ink in the transfer to paper. For the first time, it became possible to "design a typeface without any reference to the behavior of steel, under the shaping tool, or under the blow that sinks the punch into the matrix-metal."[5] The resulting possibilities allowed characters to adopt a wide variety of shapes, sizes, and connections that were previously impossible. Unlike metal type, film negatives could be layered and developed as a complex image.[6] For cursive scripts, the layering of negatives allowed letters to connect from any direction: horizontal, vertical, or diagonal. This set a new high-water mark in typographic detail, with noticeable benefits for Arabic script, mathematical equations, and beyond.[7]

Computerized photocomposition marks a key transitional point between movable metal type and digital text. But not all keystrokes resulted in photographically printed hard copy. Other characters remained onscreen as rough assemblages of blocklike pixels. Initial iterations of fully digital text reversed the aesthetic and planar openness of photocomposition. Fine lines disappeared yet again, as the low resolution of early digital forms restricted characters much more than movable type ever did. Even metal type was analogically carved by hand. Type designers enjoyed a wide degree of analog freedom in the casting of forms, provided the resulting character sets could fit together as a line of type that adequately held ink to paper. Early screens significantly limited aesthetic freedom. Grids of pixels replaced the relative openness of metal casts and photographic film. Limitations in screen resolution made all scripts, Latin letters included, rough around the edges. Character shapes were built of large, unsubtle blocks. A limited number of pixels—which were initially rectangular but eventually became square—could be turned on or off.[8] Consequently, letter terminals were truncated, curves were squared, and open counters were exaggerated. The resulting blocklike constructions mimicked letters, but they certainly did not replicate handwritten scribal forms. Later, instructions for drawing character outlines replaced the rough pixel bricks of bitmapped fonts.[9] The needle swung back the other way as vector outlines once again supported smoother and subtler forms. But screen resolution remained an important factor in the final display.[10] More significantly, the materiality of the text had changed. The material artifacts of movable metal type and film negatives disappeared. Written characters, both bitmaps and vector outlines, became digitally native. They were coded and saved as binary strings of zeros and ones.

Much like movable type, early coding schemes were drawn from the script grammar of printed Latin: a limited collection of disconnected and individually identifiable letters rendered in sequence. The binary coding of computerized text began with Latin script and Western languages before spreading to non-Latin scripts and non-European languages. And the coding schema that would have the greatest effect on computational text was the American English–centric ASCII, the American Standard Code for Information Interchange. ASCII was first published in 1963, and an updated 1967 version solidified the structure that has remained in use ever since. In 1968, the Johnson administration mandated that all U.S. computers support ASCII encodings. Given U.S. technological and economic dominance, ASCII also operated as a de facto international standard. ASCII has shaped, and continues to shape, the history of global computing. It codes all letters, numbers, and characters into binary sequences of eight zeros and ones. The capital letter A, for example, was encoded as 0100 0001, the capital letter B was encoded as 0100 0010, and the lowercase letter a was encoded as 0110 0001.[11] This resulted in the now-standard 8-bit byte of computer memory. As an American standard, it assigned these points to characters used in American English. It includes fifty-two Latin letters (twenty-six uppercase and twenty-six lowercase), ten numerals, and thirty-one punctuation marks for a total of ninety-five characters. The other code points were assigned to control characters, such as "escape" and "delete." All together, ASCII encoded a total of 2^7 characters, or 128 distinct code points.[12]

The globalization of computing unveiled ASCII's America-only bias. The accented Latin letters common to European languages were not included, nor were any characters from non-Latin scripts. Increases in computer memory and processing doubled the character count to twenty-eight, or 256 distinct code points. In Europe, the additional code points encoded non-English letters and accents, including those with a diaeresis or umlaut (for example, ï or ü), cedilla (ç), and tilde (ñ).[13] Non-Latin scripts, such as Arabic, Cyrillic, Greek, and Hebrew, assigned the newly available code points differently. Arabic schemes, for example, retained ASCII's basic Latin set of 128 characters while assigning higher code points to Arabic forms. The resulting coding scheme could represent both English, the dominant language of international computing, and basic Arabic. Other languages and scripts similarly retained ASCII while assigning higher code points to letters or forms of their own. Consequently, ASCII text easily transferred across machines, even if the machines employed different encoding schemes. Non-ASCII characters, in contrast, became jumbled. The same code point might repeat an accented Latin letter in Europe, an Arabic letter in the Middle East, a Cyrillic letter in Russia, a Hebrew character in Israel, and an ornament or dingbat in the United States.

Transmitting non-ASCII text required higher-level computer protocols that could shift between various encoding schemes.[14] In 1988, the International Standards Organization (ISO) addressed the issues with the publication of two standards: ISO 2022 and ISO 8859. ISO 2022 standardized the exchange of information across multiple code sets, with specifically reserved control characters for switching directly between assigned sets.[15] The sets themselves were defined by ISO 8859. The ISO 8859 standards defined 8-bit coding schemes for Latin, Cyrillic, Arabic, Greek, Hebrew, and Thai scripts, and ISO 2022 provides the mechanism for switching between the various encoding schemes of the ISO 8859 family.[16] Although the system worked well for European languages, it was a stopgap measure for global communication. The ISO 8859 family specifically excluded Asian scripts, such as Chinese, that required multiple-byte (more than 8-bit) encoding schemes. And the defined Arabic scheme (ISO 8859–6) encoded only the twenty-eight letters of the basic Arabic-language *abjad* and the most basic of the *tashkil* marks. It did not encode the additional letters required for major languages such as Farsi and Urdu, the necessary *lām-alif* ligature, Arabic punctuation marks, or the precise *tashkil* necessary for Qur'anic passages.

Electronics companies addressed the vacuum by creating proprietary code sets. Texas Instruments, NCR computers, and IBM all developed competing Arabic script encoding schemes.[17] Many of the corporate schemes included additional Persian letters and, occasionally, Arabic script letters for other non-Arabic languages. But encodings were incompatible across companies, and, sometimes, even schemes from a single company assigned Arabic code points differently depending on the local market. IBM character sets, for example, were language- and country-based. Arabic, Persian, and Urdu received distinct IBM code charts, all of which differed from IBM's bi-scribal Arabic / French scheme that targeted North Africa. During the 1990s, software operating systems replaced hardware companies as the dominant players. And this further muddied the waters. Microsoft Windows, the most popular operating system in the Middle East, utilized the Windows-1256 scheme for Arabic script. Although Windows-1256 supported a wide range of Arabic script languages, the encoding order followed no rational arrangement. The twenty-eight letters of the Arabic *abjad* were interspersed with characters from the extended Latin set, such as the ç and accented é common in Arabic countries that also employed French. Meanwhile, the additional letters required for Farsi, Urdu, and other Arabic script languages were scattered throughout the coding scheme in no particular order. The MacArabic scheme, in contrast, followed a more rational arrangement.[18] The basic Arabic *abjad* preserved the order set forth in ISO 8859–6, which was then followed by additional letters for Farsi, Urdu, Ottoman, and other languages. But the Windows and Mac schemes—unfortunately, yet unsurprisingly—were incompatible. The code points representing *hā'*, *wāw*, and *yā'* in Windows-1256 represented *mīm, nūn,* and *tanwin-dammah* in Mac-Arabic, while the MacArabic code points for the same three letters (*hā', wāw* and *yā'*) represented ç, é, and è in Windows-1256. Hence, Arabic texts—unlike ASCII—could cross platforms only if they were translated from one encoding scheme to another.

Arabic Script in the Unicode Standard

By the end of the twentieth century, the resulting confusion produced Unicode. The Unicode Consortium formed in 1991 to promote an international standard and universal encoding scheme. It began with the stated goal of unifying "the many hundreds of conflicting ways to encode characters, replacing them with a single, universal standard."[19] Unicode offered a simple solution to the plethora of overlapping and competing encoding schemes: rather than increasing the number of encoding schemes, Unicode increased the number of bits per character.[20] The Unicode Standard 1.0 stated the following goal: "Unicode provides a unique number for every character, no matter what the platform, no matter what the program, no matter what the language."[21] Unicode first doubled the size of characters from 8 bits to 16 bits. This increased the number of available code points from 2^8 (256) to 2^{16} (65,536), and the bit count would eventually double again to 32 bits per character. The 32-bit encoding scheme supports 1,114,112 distinct code points.[22] Version 7.0 of the Unicode Standard (2014) assigned 112,956 of these to characters of all the world's scripts and writing systems. With more than one million code points still available, the Unicode Standard contains ample room for future expansion. Unicode also reserves 6,400 code points for private use.[23] Users can locally assign the reserved code points to characters not included in the Unicode repertoire.

Unicode was specifically designed to be universal, efficient, and unambiguous. Universality entails a character repertoire large enough to contain all written characters in general use. Unicode also sought to maintain backward compatibility with ASCII, as well as a number of other encoding standards. Universal coverage included contemporary usage as well as historical encoding schemes. The second trait, efficiency, implies that the code is easy for computers to parse. A single, fixed code for each and every character supports efficient sorting, transmission, search, and display.[24] Finally, the standard is unambiguous. A Unicode code point always and everywhere represents the same character. Another defining feature is Unicode's *character-glyph* model, which differentiates between *characters* and *glyphs*. Characters are abstract representations of semantic value, whereas glyphs are the shapes of characters. Characters are code, and glyphs are visual representations of coded characters when they are rendered or displayed.[25] Unicode encodes characters, not glyphs.[26] For example, the capital letter B and the lowercase letter b have distinct semantic value: B indicates proper nouns or the beginning of a sentence. The letters B and b are therefore distinct Unicode *characters*. But the visual contrast between a lowercase Times New Roman letter b and a lowercase Helvetica letter b do not differ semantically. They simply display different *glyphs* of a shared character. For Arabic letters, the visual differences of isolated, initial, medial, and final forms are all glyphs of a single character. One character maps to multiple glyphs depending on context and word position. For ligatures, such as *lām-alif*, the opposite occurs: multiple characters (*lām* and *alif*) combine to form a single glyph.[27]

Unicode organizes characters into blocks, or planes, based on script rather than language. It therefore encodes characters of Latin, Arabic, and Bengali *scripts* rather than letters of the English, German, Arabic, Farsi, Bengali, and Assamese *languages*. A script is defined as a collection of characters used to represent a group of related languages, and the majority of common scripts are encoded in Unicode's Basic Multilingual Plane (BMP).[28] Unicode also contains blocks for symbolic systems (for example, mathematics, astronomy, engineering), historical scripts no longer in use (for example, cuneiform, Egyptian hieroglyphics, Greek Linear B), and a very large block of CJK (Chinese, Japanese, Korean) ideographs. The upper blocks contain code points reserved for private, or use-specific, designations.[29] Every Unicode character is labeled as U+*nnnn,* where *nnnn* represents a four-digit hexadecimal number (16 binary bits). The capital Latin letter A, for example, is U+0041, and the Arabic letter *alif* is U+0627. Ranges of Unicode characters follow the notation U+xxxx–U+yyyy, where xxxx and yyyy are the first and last character values in the range.[30] The primary Arabic characters occupy U+0600–U+06FF, which represents the hexadecimal binary range of 0000 0110 0000 0000 to 0000 0110 1111 1111, or one plane of 256 distinct code points.

Unicode's Arabic block resides within the Middle East-I grouping of the General Scripts Area of the Basic Multilingual Plane. The Middle East-I group contains all modern Middle Eastern scripts, including liturgical scripts, that flow from left to right. It includes Hebrew, Arabic, Syriac, Samaritan, and Mandic, all of which have a common origin in the Phoenician alphabet.[31] The Arabic block encompasses all the characters required to represent any language that currently employs, or historically employed, Arabic script. The range of languages includes Arabic, Persian, Urdu, Pashto, Sindhi, Uyghur, Hausa, Wolof, Afrikaans, Ottoman Turkish, Malay, and Uzbek, among others. The basic Arabic plane (U+0600–U+06FF) encodes characters for the most common languages: Arabic, Farsi, Urdu, Pashto, Malay, Sindi, Uyghur, and Ottoman Turkish. To preserve backward compatibility, letters of the primary Arabic *abjad* and basic *tashkil* are encoded in the same relative positions as the 1989 standard ISO 8859–6. Additional Arabic characters are encoded in the Arabic Supplement (U+0750–U+077F), Arabic Extended-A (U+08A0–U+08FF), Arabic Presentation Forms-A (U+FB50–U+FDFF), and Arabic Presentation Forms-B (U+FE70–U+FEFF) blocks. The Arabic Supplement block contains Arabic script letters used by the languages of northern and western Africa, such as Fulfulde, Hausa, Songhay, and Wolof, as well as letters used by the non-Urdu languages of Pakistan.[32] The Arabic Extended-A range encodes letters, vowel signs, and tonal marks needed for less common Arabic script languages from Africa, the Philippines, and Myanmar. This block also includes a number of specialty signs employed only for Qur'anic annotation. The Presentation Forms are included primarily for the sake of compatibility with earlier encoding schemes. They encode positional variants of Arabic letters (initial, medial, and final positions) as unique characters as well as ligatures for common words and phrases. For example, the word "Allah," the honorific *salla ilahu wa alahe wa-sallam*, and the *bismilla ar-rahman ar-rahim* are all encoded as single characters in the Arabic Presentation Forms. Whenever possible, however, Unicode recommends constructing these compounds from multiple single-letter characters rather than using the legacy ligature character.

Unicode effectively tackles a number of challenges that haunted previous Arabic encoding schemes. Arabic script displays a large number of glyphs, its cursive structure dictates that character shapes shift according to context, and it flows from right to left. Although none of these issues is unique to Arabic script, the intersection of all three creates particular challenges. Arabic script shares the first issue, a large number of glyphs, with Chinese and a number of Asian scripts. Indeed, the number of Chinese ideographic characters dwarfs the number of Arabic forms. The Unicode CJK (Chinese, Japanese, Korean) blocks of Han ideographs contain tens of thousands of unique, and semantically distinct, characters. The complete set of Arabic script blocks, in contrast, encode approximately 1,250 characters. And the number shrinks to less than 400 once the legacy characters of the Presentation Forms are removed. Despite the size of the Chinese Han character set, and as complex as individual Han glyphs may appear, they are nevertheless distinct forms.[33] Unlike Arabic, Han characters do not connect cursively. They therefore function much like an extremely large set of disconnected letters. Computationally, a string of unique CJK Han characters is little different from a string of unconnected Latin letters: ABCDEF. The incredibly large number of characters caused problems in early computing, but it was easily addressed by Unicode's 32-bit character length as well as drastic increases in processing power and data storage.

Arabic script, however, displays multiple glyphs per character. Arabic's necessarily cursive grammar dictates that character shapes shift contextually according to word position and the surrounding characters. Arabic script also includes a variety of *tashkil* and other marks that modify and layer above or below other characters. As a result, a large number of glyphs and combinations can arise from a small number of characters. The number of characters required for any given Arabic script language is actually quite low. A minimum of twenty-eight letter characters can semantically represent the Arabic language, whereas the minimum required for English is twice as many: the twenty-six uppercase and twenty-six lowercase letters receive distinct code points. But the relationship reverses for glyphs: Arabic displays more than twice as many glyph variations as English. English letter characters typically display only one glyph regardless of context. The 128 code points of Latin ASCII are therefore roughly equivalent to the number of sorts required to set English with movable type. Arabic letter characters display, at minimum, two or four glyph variations. Ligatures, vertical connections, and optional *tashkil* further increase visual variety. Consequently, most sets of Arabic movable type included approximately five hundred sorts, more than double the number required for setting Latin type. Different Arabic sorts for isolated, initial, medial, and final forms were set according to context. Unicode preserves this diversity of visual glyphs while reducing the number of requisite code points. The set of letters is encoded as distinct characters only once. These are mapped to multiple glyph variants, and computational protocols apply the proper glyph according to context.

Arabic Unicode characters default to their requisite cursive connections and contextual variations. Two special characters can modify these connections when necessary. These are Unicode's zero-width non-joiner (U+200C) and zero-width joiner (U+200D) characters. Both characters reside in Unicode's general punctuation block.[34] Like *tashkil,* the zero-width non-joiner and the zero-width joiner modify surrounding characters. But unlike *tashkil,* neither displays a visual representation or glyph. The "zero-width" description refers to the amount of visible space claimed by these characters on screen or in print. Although their encoding width is the same bit-length as any other Unicode character, their representational width is zero.[35] Instead, the characters influence the connectivity of Arabic script and other cursive characters.[36] The zero-width non-joiner (U+200C) separates a character from the preceding character. It inserts a zero-width "space" between characters that would normally connect. The zero-width joiner (U+200D) does the opposite: it forces a character to appear as if it is cursively connected to the previous character, even if no such character exists. This allows initial, medial, and final forms of Arabic letters to be displayed, even when context suggests another more appropriate form. (See Figure 6.1.) For example, U+062C represents the Arabic letter *jīm*. The sequence <U+200D, U+062C>, *jīm* preceded by a zero-width joiner, will display the final form of the character: *jīm* acts as if it is joined with the previous character, even if that character is a space or a traditionally non-connecting character. The sequence <U+062C, U+200D>, *jīm* followed by a zero-width joiner, displays the initial form; *jīm* acts as if it will join the following character. And the sequence <U+200D, U+062C, U+200D>, *jīm* both preceded and followed by a zero-width joiner, displays the medial form: *jīm* acts as if it connects with both the preceding and the following character. The four-form tables of Arabic script, which are common in educational textbooks and academic studies such as this, would be impossible without the zero-width joiner. The column of medial forms in Figure 1.1 of Chapter 1 displays Arabic Unicode characters bracketed by a zero-width joiner character on either side.

Arabic script's final coding challenge is directionality. Like all scripts in Unicode's Middle East-I grouping, Arabic script flows from right to left. With movable type, this was less of an issue. Typesetters simply set Arabic type in the direction opposite that of Latin lettering. With computing, a sequence of code represents characters, and the computer determines whether to render the sequence from right to left (Arabic), left to right (Latin), top to bottom (Chinese), or another direction. If a text contains more than one direction, such as a bilingual Arabic-English text, the processor needs to display the relevant strings of characters in an order that makes sense to the reader. Formatting becomes even more complicated if a text includes numbers, more than two languages, or multiple nested language changes. Even before rendering, computers process sequences of code in a particular order, and most computer code is written in the Latinate direction of right to left. This poses problems for Middle Eastern scripts that run in the opposite direction. One solution, visual ordering, stores all characters in a consistent order regardless of script direction. If a computer system renders characters from left to right, scripts such as Arabic and Hebrew can be coded and saved in reverse order. They would be rendered in reverse order (from left to right) onscreen but appear legible to readers whose eyes move in the opposite direction. Visual order simplifies text rendering since the

نشخ
The Arabic word *naskh* **in defualt presentation.**
The word is composed of the letters *nūn* (in initial variant),
shīn (in medial variant), and *khā'* (in final variant).

ذ ش خ
The three letters modified by zero-width joiner (ZWJ).
Nūn displays initial variant, *shīn* displays medial variant, and
khā' displays final variant despite the spaces between letters.

ن ش خ
The three letters modified by zero-width non-joiner (ZWNJ).
Isolated variants are displayed for all letters despite absence of
space characters between letters.

ن ش خ
The three letters separated by spaces.
All three letters display the isolated variant by default.

Figure 6.1.   Zero-width joiner and zero-width non-joiner
Unicode's zero-width joiner (ZWJ) and zero-width non-joiner (ZWNJ) characters alter
the glyph variant of the character to which they are attached. For Arabic script, this
allows any of a letter's positional variants (initial, medial, final, or isolated) to be displayed
regardless of whether or not the characters are separated by spaces. (Image produced
in Adobe Creative Suite.)

computer system does not need to switch directions. For this reason, it was often
employed as a convenient workaround for early Middle Eastern and multi-script
computing. Between 1997 and 2003, the Israeli government officially backed
visual order as the preferred method of representing Hebrew on the World Wide
Web.[37] This jump-started the Hebrew internet and quickly increased the number
of Hebrew web pages, despite the overriding Latin-script bias and left-to-
right directionality of early HTML.

But a consistent left-to-right visual order complicates text processing. Hebrew and Arabic words need to be inputted, stored, and searched backward,
which is anything but the ideal of natural language processing. The contextual
shaping and cursivity of Arabic script also made visual order less attractive than
it was for Hebrew. Hebrew characters are distinct, and glyphs can easily string
together in reverse order. For Arabic script, programming selects the proper contextual variant according to word position. In left-to-right visual order, the
first stored character of an Arabic letter block receives the final form of the letter,
while the final stored character of a letter block receives the initial form. Pro-

gramming selection protocols in reverse order further complicated an already complicated system. Unicode, therefore, adopts a different strategy. It preserves the logical order in which characters are understood by readers, and it stores Middle Eastern scripts in logical—rather than visual—order. This greatly simplifies algorithms of contextual glyph selection. The initial character in a string receives the initial form, and the final character receives the final form. Logical order preserves semantics for human users, who read and input text, as well as digital devices, which process, search, and format text. Unicode assigns all characters an inherent directionality, and the Unicode Bidirectional Algorithm (Unicode Standard Annex #9, or UAX#9) defines how to handle characters in multidirectional strings.[38] Scripts typically possess strong directionality: Arabic and Hebrew characters have a strong right-to-left directionality, Latin and Cyrillic have a strong left-to-right directionality, and so on. Unless a system is given explicit instructions to do otherwise, Arabic and Hebrew characters will render from right to left, while Latin and Cyrillic characters will render from left to right.

But not all of Unicode's solutions are without controversy. Unicode privileges fully formed letters of Arabic script. It therefore combines i'jaam, such as nuqta, that differentiate consonants with the primary rasm. Unicode encodes the collection of rasm and i'jaam as a single character.[39] The standard assumes that Arabic letters always display requisite nuqta. Some of the earliest historical Arabic texts, however, do not contain nuqta, as these marks were developed later to assist readers unfamiliar with the written language.[40] These texts, in which unspecified rasm deliberately encode a level of ambiguity, cannot be accurately represented by Unicode. Setting them with a standard Arabic font inserts nuqta where none appear. For Unicode, i'jaam are not optional and cannot be parceled separately from rasm. This undermines Unicode's claim of "covering the needs of both modern and historical texts."[41] The absence of undotted rasm does not cover the typesetting needs of a variety of Arabic texts, including Qur'anic masahif, from the eighth through the twelfth century. Other layers of Arabic script, such as tashkil, remain optional in modern communications, and Unicode encodes them as such.[42] The codes for tashkil and other modifying characters are transmitted directly after the characters they modify. Thus, a fathah (U+064E) placed above the letter jīm (U+062C) is saved in the logical order of jīm-fathah, or <U+062C, U+064E>. Still elsewhere, a singular shape receives multiple encodings. The hamza shape, for example, is encoded as a stand-alone character (U+0621), as a diacritic placed above the preceding character (U+0654), and as a diacritic placed below the preceding character (U+0655).[43] In a number of non-Arabic languages, the *hamza* shape combines with other forms, either as *i'jaam* for or as a base form that takes *i'jaam,* to form letters. Such letters are encoded as precomposed characters, preserving the practice of combining *rasm* and *i'jaam* for letters.

Some distinct shapes of Arabic script, such as *nuqta,* are not encoded separately in Unicode's preferred usage blocks. Other shapes, such as *tashkil,* are encoded separately, and their application is optional. And yet other shapes, such as *hamza,* are encoded in multiple instances. Add in the multiple forms expected for each Arabic letter (isolated, initial, medial, and final), and the number of total glyphs begins to rise. Unicode's blocks of Arabic Presentation Forms raise the number even higher. The Presentation Forms encode additional letter variants and / or combine multiple Arabic characters into complex ligatures. The result is a large amount of redundancy. Most Arabic letters have at least five Unicode character designations and at least one of these characters has multiple positional glyphs associated with it. The letter *bā',* for example, is encoded as a stand-alone character (the preferred encoding), in each of its four positional variants (for legacy encodings), and in more than 20 multi-letter ligatures. The letter *jīm* contributes to more than 80 ligatures, and the number for *mīm* exceeds 150. Unicode can, and indeed prefers, to combine stand-alone characters into ligatures. But an Arabic font still needs to output and save those glyphs individually in order for them to appear. Although only a limited number of total glyphs are required to typeset Arabic, this limitation reinscribes a preference for Arabic simplification into digital environments. A sophisticated typographic representation of Arabic script still requires a large number of individually designed, coded, and saved glyphs.

Designing and Rendering Arabic Fonts

The Unicode character set defines the glyphs—linguistic and otherwise—that type designers create. Constructing these forms from scratch frees Arabic script from preexisting constraints of Latinate aesthetics and Latin-based technologies. At the same time, Arabic and Latin types increasingly circulate alongside and in dialogue with each other. And despite its limitations, Latin-infused type design provides time-tested and workable solutions to common pitfalls and complex problems alike. Reconsidering the broader landscape of type design and the Latinate legacy of typographic history is not a task to be taken lightly.[44] Latinate models can usefully guide, but they should not determine, Arabic type. Strategies range from adding Arabic characters to a preexisting Latin font family to borrowing formal design constraints, to deconstructing and repurposing Latin forms. In each case, the resulting Arabic forms maintain a degree of visual resemblance to the Latin originals. As digital texts began to circulate globally, the need for bilingual fonts grew accordingly. Visual cohesion across multiple scripts is incredibly useful for presenting dual-language or multilingual texts.[45] When they appear together, multiple scripts should display harmony, and they should cooperate in terms of line spacing, justification, and layout. The characters of diverse languages and scripts—such as Arabic and English—should "speak" in a similar register.

In the early 2000s, Syrian designer Yassar Abbar found design inspiration in the sans serif Latin typeface Univers, which was designed by Adrian Frutiger in 1954.[46] Abbar imported the Latin notions of x-height and a consistent baseline into Arabic font design. Arabic scribal tradition bases proportions and builds outward from the *nuqta*. Latin designs, in contrast, construct letters within a grid of externalized measures (such as x-height). By importing Latin measures, Abbar created a framework for designing Arabic forms with Latin norms. The resulting letters preserve sizing across the two scripts, and they may appear together (or even alternate within a passage) without radically altering the appearance of Latin text blocks. But foreign measures deviate from local norms and risk damage to a script's internal stability. Critics warn that "by replacing a script's traditional proportions with arbitrary ones inherited from the Latin master, we weaken the natural formation of word shapes."[47] The universal adoption of Latin norms elevates Latin script grammar to an unwarranted position of continuing global prominence. Once again, non-Latin scripts are expected to conform to European structures of text and technology. International parties failed to agree on Arabic script reform during the era of movable type, and there is even less reason to expect wide agreement during the digital era. At the same time, the polarization of such debates masks practical realities. Although its predominance diminishes with each passing year, Latin typography does indeed maintain a powerful position in digital environments. Standing on those typographic shoulders, Yassar Abbar saw new paths beyond currently perceived obstacles.

The Typographic Matchmaking project sponsored by the Khatt Foundation for Arabic Typography was perhaps the most ambitious effort to design Arabic companions to Latin fonts. The project culminated in the 2007 release of six Arabic fonts along with a book documenting the design process.[48] It began in 2004 during a series of discussions at ATypI (Association Typographique Internationale) meetings in Prague, and Huda Smitshuijzen AbiFarès founded the Khatt Foundation the same year. The foundation inspires cross-cultural dialogue through design programs focused on the Arab world and the Middle East. For Typographic Matchmaking, "the main thrust of the project is to address the modernization of Arabic textfaces and to develop quality Arabic fonts that will on one hand set the benchmark for future developments in this field, and on the other create good matching fonts for existing Latin font families. The project aims to provide design solutions for legible Arabic fonts that answer the dual-script needs of contemporary design in the Arab world."[49] The stated goal specifically identifies a direction of movement from Latin models to Arabic companions, and a cross-cultural focus infused the project from the outset. "Quality Arabic fonts" and "matching fonts for existing Latin font families" were seen as mutually reinforcing and beneficial, rather than antagonistic. Designs that matched successful Latin fonts would benefit and improve the usability and quality of digital Arabic. During the matchmaking design phase (2005–2007), less than a few dozen high-quality Arabic fonts were in wide circulation. Latin typefaces, in contrast, numbered well into the thousands. Even Greek script, which globally has a much smaller reading audience than Arabic, counted a few hundred varieties at the time.

To rectify the situation, the Khatt Foundation played matchmaker. It paired five Dutch type designers with Middle Eastern and Arabic designers familiar with Arabic script. Participants came from diverse backgrounds, and they had varying levels of technical and linguistic expertise. The Dutch partners were accomplished font and type designers. They possessed a high degree of technical knowledge and skill, and they entered the project with a portfolio of successful typefaces. "Each Dutch designer was asked to select one appropriate font from his existing typefaces, and then in collaboration with his Arab partner to design a matching Arabic version."[50] Their Arabic partners were successful designers in their own right, albeit less professionally recognized as a group. They were mostly early-career professionals, and the project offered them the opportunity to share their work with a wider international audience. More significantly, Arabic participants contributed primary familiarity with Arabic language and Arabic script, and they were more accustomed to the pitfalls and challenges of designing bilingual and trilingual texts. Most of the Dutch designers began the project unfamiliar with the technical specifics of Arabic script. Typographic Matchmaking introduced them to the process and difficulties of translating Latin aesthetics into the idiom of another script.

Matchmaking teams were formalized in 2005, and the final fonts were released at a design symposium and launch party two years later. The result was "Arabic type with a Dutch flavor."[51] The five teams and their designs were (1) Peter Bilak and Tarek Atrissi, who designed an Arabic companion to Fedra; (2) Martin Majoor and Pascal Zoghbi, who designed Arabic Sada as a companion to the Latin font Seria; (3) Fred Smeijers and Lara Assouad, who designed an Arabic companion to Fresco; (4) Gerard Unger and Nadine Chahine, who designed an Arabic companion to Big Vesta;[52] and (5) Lucas de Groot and Mouneer al-Shaarani, who designed TheMix Arabic, a hybrid member of the Thesis font family. The original design brief limited the project to useful book faces for running text, excluding display faces and fanciful or idiosyncratic alphabets. More specifically, the brief stipulated the following requirements:[53]

- The Arabic font and its Latin counterpart were to have the same visual size at the same point size.
- The Arabic fonts were to be designed in two weights: a regular or book weight for running text and a bold weight for headings.
- The Arabic fonts would have the same "look and feel" as the Latin fonts, with similar design details like stem weight, color, letter contrast, and stroke endings.
- The results should be truly bilingual (for example, the fonts should be suitable for Arabic and Latinate languages both individually and in conjunction).
- The character set should accommodate both the Arabic language and Farsi.[54]
- The fonts would be professionally produced and compliant with commonly used Arabic desktop publishing software.

The idea of matching Arabic and Latin typefaces was far from novel. Multi-script typography is almost as old as movable type itself.[55] Nevertheless, designing fonts for multiple scripts and languages poses a unique set of challenges. The fonts should preserve the distinctive structure and grammar of each script, while balancing each other amicably and aesthetically: Do characters of the two scripts walk at the same pace? Do they do similar types of work? Are they suitable for the same types of texts? Do they imply a shared tone of voice? Do they color a page similarly?[56] Pairing scripts of different directionality, such as Latin and Arabic, further complicates matters. Lines of text begin on opposite sides, either running counter to each other or converging toward the center. And they converge toward a common center by different gaits. Latin letters appear distinct and emphasize verticality; Arabic letters connect cursively and emphasize horizontal flow. Both the directionality and the internal contrasts of Latin and Arabic letters pull in opposing directions. Peter Bilak, one of the project participants, contrasted the "musical" rhythm of Arabic script with the cold "logic" of Latinate spacing.[57]

The various design teams tackled these challenges with overlapping as well idiosyncratic strategies. Latin fonts typically display a consistent baseline and three levels of vertical contrast: x-height, ascenders, and descenders. Beginning with Latin models, Typographic Matchmaking did not challenge these Latinate measures. But Arabic script displays a much wider degree of vertical bounce than Latin script. Scribal models may employ five or more levels of vertical alignment.[58] As a consequence, Arabic typefaces often appear much smaller than Latin counterparts of the same point size.[59] Many Typographic Matchmaking fonts addressed this issue by adopting generous x-heights with comparatively short ascenders and descenders.[60] This allowed Arabic script to retain some degree of vertical motion without overly compressing counters and curves. The teams designing Fresco and Big Vesta specifically adopted this strategy as a conceptual starting point. (See Figure 6.2.) The team working with Fedra, which already displayed a large Latin x-height, defined two middle heights for the Arabic companion.[61] This introduced additional levels of Arabic bounce within the dominant Latin structure. And the team designing Sada increased visual size by opening the counters of Arabic letters. To preserve Arabic script's horizontal rhythm, most fonts curved the baseline connections of Arabic letters.[62]

The Matchmaking design teams all worked with a shared Basic Arabic and Persian character set. The set covered most of Unicode's Arabic block (0600–

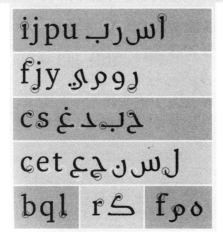

Figure 6.2. The Fresco Arabic font

The Typographic Matchmaking fonts Fresco and Fresco Arabic display visual consistency across Latin and Arabic letters. The top compares the baselines and vertical spacing of the two fonts. The bottom identifies shared formal characteristics, including serifs and letter terminals. The Fresco Arabic font was designed by Lara Assouad and Fred Smeijers, as part of the Khatt Foundation's research project "Typographic Matchmaking." (© 2007. Khatt Foundation and the designers; image courtesy of Lara Assouad and Huda Smitshuijzen AbiFarès.)

06FF), select characters from Unicode's Arabic Presentation Forms-B block, numerals, punctuation marks, and basic mathematical operators.[63] Letters received either four glyphs (initial, medial, final, and isolated) or two (final and isolated) according to standard usage, and *tashkil* were drawn from both the standard Arabic block and presentation forms. The Presentation Forms duplicated and combined various glyphs as independent characters in order to preserve compatibility with non-Unicode encoding schemes. Despite the combined Arabic and Persian *abjads* possessing only thirty-two letters, the teams created nearly three hundred distinct glyphs for their working fonts. Design guidelines identified common strokes that could be copied across letters for consistency and similarity.[64] These included vertical stems, horizontal strokes, terminals, and configurations of *nuqta*. To preserve the look and feel of the Latin originals, the teams often applied strokes, curves, serifs, and terminals to both scripts. Elsewhere, the horizontal emphasis of Arabic script replaced the vertical emphasis of Latin. Fedra, for example, inverted the angle of contrast: the thickest horizontal in Latin became the thickest vertical in Arabic. And Sada moved contrast weight from diagonals to verticals, since Seria, its Latinate model, applied contrast weight to horizontals rather than diagonals.

The *Typographic Matchmaking* book usefully documents the teamwork that went into the final fonts, including background research, initial concept, and development phases. The designers' comments and reflections pull back the curtain on a professional practice that often remains hidden. As Nadine Chahine observes in her final remarks: "Type design is a private endeavor with a very public appearance."[65] The public community that reads, looks at, appreciates, and chooses fonts is rarely privy to the work that builds the final product. The project therefore increased the visibility of Arabic type design, culminating in five new professional-quality Arabic fonts. Final remarks from Dutch participants emphasized theoretical takeaways and the ways in which working with a foreign script altered their practice and perspective: "As a non-native speaker, you'd better be careful and keep your mind open. . . . Type design knowledge and shape sensitivity alone is not enough by far."[66] The Arab designers were similarly challenged, but they also highlighted practical concerns, such as skills learned in collaboration or the discovery of novel techniques: "Initiatives like this project—researching and coming up with fresh new ideas to tackle the question of typographic adaptations—are very rare in [the Middle East]. . . . This project was an opportunity to apply the methodology and approach in designing roman/Dutch typefaces to that of Arabic type."[67] Additionally, the Arab practitioners were more likely to celebrate the release of five new Arabic fonts.

The project successfully shared cross-cultural typographic knowledge, professional insight, and technical expertise. The results merge the successful track record of Dutch designers with the primary-language familiarity of Arabic designers. They also produced working fonts for a growing community of Arabic designers. Designing Arabic companions for successful Latin fonts initiated a visual and cross-cultural dialogue. In Unicode's extensive code banks, Latin and Arabic companions coexist within a larger set of shared characters. A set of matching fonts greatly facilitates the design and typesetting possibilities of multi-script communication. Yet the direction of dialogue mirrored the longer history of movable type printing. Print technology flourished in Europe and was later transferred to non-European languages and non-Latin scripts. By moving from Latin originals to Arabic companions, Typographic Matchmaking replicated this technological transfer.[68] But the designers did not do so unconsciously; it was a practical and utilitarian decision. The project accepted Latin typography as the historical basis and dominant mode of digital communication, and it sought to balance the design needs of end users with budget and technical limitations.[69] The resulting fonts were useful, professional, and high-quality. They could integrate seamlessly into digital environments and common practices. The project organizers specifically targeted multiple-script support across a range of digital devices and platforms.[70]

Typographic Matchmaking boldly suggests type design as an answer to "the dichotomy of globalization versus local tradition."[71] It looks to a digitally native future in which new letterforms address the new concerns of digital communication: "Arab type designers are breaking new ground with largely experimental typefaces; they question conventional calligraphic styles, reinterpret them by taking advantage of the available technological possibilities and limitations, and often move beyond the rules of pen-drawn letterforms."[72] The prevalence of digital platforms requires a new vision for Arabic script, and project organizers criticized both the Arabic calligraphic tradition and script reform movements as out of touch with the realities of contemporary visual culture.[73] In her opening comments, Huda Smitshuijzen AbiFarès argues for a new and contemporary approach to the design of Arabic type: "Arabic calligraphy continues to be one of the most beautiful and expressive calligraphic traditions. However, there is still a need for Arabic to evolve into an equally beautiful and expressive type."[74] Contemporary fonts must "strike a balance between aesthetic judgments with social concerns and practical constraints" (such as technical support, bandwidth, network standards, and preexisting font-rendering protocols).[75] To answer this call, Typographic Matchmaking sought a fusion of old and new, East and West, traditional and modern, Arabic and Latin. It targeted young Arab designers who "embrace Western ideologies" of type design and digital communication, while "appropriating and subverting them to their own ends and needs. . . . When designing Arabic fonts, one must assume the responsibility of taking creative risks that may challenge established conventions; of recognizing present realties of contemporary design and visual branding; of being ready to constantly question what we take for granted; and of setting the stage for constructive discussions around the future of Arabic type."[76]

One particularly constructive—and occasionally contentious—discussion addresses the ways in which computers handle the relationship between Arabic characters and displayed glyphs. Seeking to promote readily usable professional fonts, Typographic Matchmaking designs visual glyphs for Unicode characters; it does not address the way in which those characters are processed. Other projects tackle these more abstract discussions head-on. DecoType, a name derived from "Designers of Computer-Aided Typography," began in the 1980s. Thomas Milo, one of company's founders, observed a wide gap between everyday practices of Arabic script and dominant modes of typographic representation.[77] Fonts and typographic technologies were unable to accurately model the intricacies of Arabic script, and the DecoType team—consisting of Thomas Milo (linguist), Mirjam Somers (graphic designer), and Peter Somers (aeronautical computer engineer)—sought a clean break with pre-digital typographic technology. DecoType asked what an organic digital font technology closely modeled on scribal Arabic would look like. The result was the Arabic Calligraphic Engine (ACE), which, given the fact that the resulting technology is not limited to Arabic, was later renamed the Advanced Composition Engine without altering the acronym. The name change stresses the fact that ACE is not technically linked to the qualitative term "calligraphy." ACE technology is content-neutral. It neither imposes nor demands calligraphic aesthetics, despite its ability to model complex calligraphic and scribal relations. Nor is the engine limited to Arabic or *naskh* style of Arabic script.[78] The Decotype team initially rejected *naskh* as too complicated and inconsistent to turn into typography, and instead ACE was primarily developed to handle the *ruq'ah* style, which, in Milo's view, provided a usable model of Arabic script, without sacrificing any of the script's essential characteristics.[79] ACE has also proven to be particularly useful at typesetting Persian and Urdu text in the hanging style of *nasta'liq*.[80] And the implications of the technology are much broader than any single script.

ACE is not a simply another Arabic font, font family, or style of writing. ACE is not a font at all, it is a font technology. It powers an alternative engine for rendering, representing, and designing digital text. Milo has worked with the Unicode Consortium since its beginnings in the late 1980s, and ACE was one of the first technologies to deploy Unicode as the basis of multilingual and multiscript global communication. But ACE also pushes back against common practices of Unicode implementation. Fonts typically interact with Unicode as a series of character glyphs. Designers construct glyphs, and font-rendering technologies string those glyphs together, and sometimes combine them, to visually represent a sequence of Unicode characters. Characters are processed and displayed in a roughly one-to-one mapping of character and glyph (the Unicode "character-glyph model"). Even Arabic characters, with separate glyphs for isolated, initial, medial, and final positions, follow this principle: the standalone character maps to one glyph, the character at the beginning of a letter block maps to another glyph, the character in the middle of a letter block maps to a third, and the character at the end of a letter block maps to a fourth. Ligatures combine multiple characters into a single glyph, but each of these combinations is designed and programmed individually. Mapping all the possibilities and variations of cursive Arabic combinations is a herculean task. ACE therefore digs deeper into the structure of Arabic script and upends the simple mapping of characters to glyphs. ACE does not adopt the character-glyph model.

Instead, ACE interacts with Unicode as computational code rather than simply a sequence of pictures. Like any font technology, ACE takes Unicode as its input, processes the code, and outputs strings of glyphs. The difference is one of abstraction and occurs during the interstitial step of processing the code. Traditional fonts remediate the linear boxes of metal type by processing Unicode characters as predesigned glyphs. Images of glyphs are strung together one after another, like the setting of movable metal type. ACE deviates from this simple equation and frees the typographic line from preset boxes. (See Figure 6.3.) ACE parcels the letters and forms of Arabic script into visual elements and strokes, rather than boxes. It then arranges the elements in space, and the outputted shapes are mapped back to Unicode characters. The one-to-one mapping of character to glyph is a legacy of movable type, and the system works adequately for Latin script and similar systems, which string together horizontal sequences of isolated and distinct visual characters. Arabic script is modeled very differently, and this discrepancy inspired calls for reform. Arabic script was redesigned to answer the needs of movable-type technology. The creators of ACE flipped this approach on its head. They sought to preserve the script and reform the technology. ACE jettisoned earlier models of font technology and designed a new model, which it based on analysis of Arabic script.

ACE draws on Thomas Milo's seven-layer model of Arabic script. Successive layers expand outward from the line of primary letterforms, or *rasm* (see

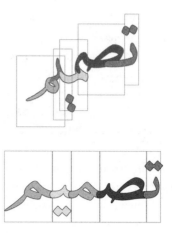

Figure 6.3. Glyph boxes and letter strokes

The bottom line displays the glyph boxes for the letters of the Arabic word *tasmeem* from the Adobe Arabic Naskh font. The boxes align horizontally with very little overlap. The top line displays the same word set with DecoType's Advanced Composition Engine (ACE). ACE models the individually strokes of the letters. It does not arrange predetermined boxes. For comparison's sake, this figure superimposes the glyph boxes from the bottom line on the ACE-rendered word. Note how the boxes do not align horizontally and display a great deal of overlap. (Image produced in Adobe Creative Suite. DecoType image courtesy of Thomas Milo.)

Figure 1.2 in Chapter 1). Logical characters are not simply sequenced horizontally. Rather, logical relations develop through the interactions of layers, which models the way in which Arabic script developed historically.[81] Despite having twenty-eight letters, the Arabic *abjad* contains only fourteen basic letter shapes, or *rasm* (level 1). Languages that adopted Arabic script preserved this structure. New letters arose through the variation of *i'jaam* (level 2) above or below the strokes of *rasm*. The seventeen basic *rasm* have remained consistent across languages.[82] For example, the Arabic letters *bā'*, *tā'*, and *thā* all belong to the *bā'* class of letters, as do the Persian letter *pe* and the Urdu letter *ṭe*. All these letters share an identical base shape *(rasm)*, which is differentiated by the addition of *i'jaam* (*nuqta* or other forms). But Unicode's character model does not identify Arabic letter classes; Unicode combines the logical layers of *rasm* and *i'jaam* into graphemic letter characters. There is one Unicode designation for the letter *bā'*, another for *tā'*, a third for *thā'*, and so on. Consequently, there is no way of knowing that these letters possess a logical relationship at the archigraphemic

188

level of shared *rasm*. This useful and pertinent information is not encoded. Critics have therefore suggested that Unicode may benefit from a reconceptualization in which letters are logically decomposed into *rasm* and additive *i'jaam*.[83]

DecoType's Advanced Composition Engine (ACE) reclaims letter classes as both semantically relevant and useful for design. Rather than mapping one or more Unicode characters to distinct visual glyphs, ACE combines visual elements and then maps them back to Unicode characters. The technology does not design the appearance of these visual elements; it leaves design to the designers. But it alters what forms designers design and the logical way in which those forms interact. ACE facilitates a stroke-based method for designing and rendering digital Arabic script. In lieu of individual glyphs per letter, it exploits recurring shapes in order to minimize font size. ACE begins with *rasm*, the basic skeletal structure of cursively connected letters. It then adds *i'jaam (nuqta)* that differentiate letters, followed by the vocalization marks of *tashkil,* and finally, when necessary, decorative elements surrounding the text. This allows letters of a particular letter class to follow shared rules of stroke shaping, stroke connection, word spacing, the placement of *i'jaam,* the placement of *tashkil,* and so on. All changes flow downward in logical succession. Changes to the strokes of the primary *rasm* will influence the placement of all other layers successively, changes in the placement of *i'jaam* will influence to placement of *tashkil* and the higher layers but will not alter the primary forms of *rasm,* and so forth. All changes in placement, design, and organization of elements alter only the relations further downstream.

Designers who work with ACE design fonts differently than designers who draw the glyphs of individual characters. Letters and glyphs are built outward in layers. Since letters of a particular class replicate the shapes of their shared *rasm,* those shapes should appear consistent regardless of the surrounding *i'jaam.* Typically, designers copy and paste these common forms from glyph to glyph. The Typographic Matchmaking guidelines, for example, identified a number of common strokes and shapes that could be copied across glyphs. If multiple letter variants or complex ligatures are required, these shapes are copied into yet more glyphs. ACE handles such "copying" computationally.[84] Once a *rasm* shape is designed, it is applied to all letters of its class. The form itself does not need to be copied from glyph to glyph. The same is true for other shapes and arrangements of shapes, such as collections of *nuqta* and the placement of *tashkil.* Once a specific shape or a formal relationship is designed, ACE applies the design wherever it occurs. And the system dynamically generates the necessary glyphs. A designer can choose to specify and individually calibrate particular glyphs. But it is not necessary to do so. The entire range of generated glyphs can be called into service without individual attention.

The combinatorial possibilities reduce the number of individually designed elements while multiplying the number of glyphs. Whereas the Typographic Matchmaking teams designed (or copied across) approximately 300 individual glyphs for simple coverage of the Arabic and Persian languages, ACE can generate Unicode's entire repertoire of Arabic script characters with a similar number of shapes.[85] With only three hundred to four hundred designed strokes, ACE can support all characters of all languages, past and present, that employ, or have employed, Arabic script, from the common languages of Arabic, Persian, and Urdu to Ottoman, Malay, Wolof, Songhay, and regional Pakistani dialects. Limiting discussion to isolated letter variants and the Arabic-language *abjad,* ACE can generate the three letters of the *bā'* class from two shapes: the *bā'* class *rasm* plus *nuqta.* Adding the *sīn* class *rasm* bumps the numbers to five letters from three shapes. Adding the *jīm* class *rasm* increases the numbers to eight letters from four shapes. And so forth. Expanding this example to include non-Arabic languages produces more than twenty letters from the same four shapes.[86] A typical font requires approximately 180 glyphs for basic Arabic-language coverage. A DecoType font built for ACE provides the same functionality with around one hundred shapes—a 45 percent decrease in the number of individually designed forms.

ACE models a digitally native means of rendering and drawing text. It rewrites script dynamics for a computational medium rather than remediating the legacies of movable type. The resulting freedom reactivates the layers of Arabic script—from the base of *rasm* to the highest levels of decorative ornamentation. As a result, manuscript models, scribal forms, and complex calligraphic compositions become typographically viable. (See Figure 6.4.) A number of academic publishers, including Brigham Young University Press, New York University (NYU) Press, and Brill, employ ACE software for typesetting classical texts.[87] DecoType *naskh,* designed and typeset with the support of the Advanced Composition Engine, provides the Arabic font for NYU Press's Library of Arabic Literature series. A note, "About the Typefaces," at the end of every book describes it as "the first and only typeface in a style that fully implements the

وَعَمَلِيَاتُ ٱلِٱقْتِرَاضِ مِنَ ٱللُّغَاتِ ٱلْأُخْرَى تَتِمُّ بِفَوْضَنَةٍ مُطْلَقَةً وَلَا تَنْسَجِمُ

وَآلَاتُ ٱللُّغَةِ نَفْسِهَا فِي تَوْلِيدِ ٱلتَّوَسُّعُ. وَمِنَ ٱلْمُتَدَاوِلِ بَيْنَ ٱلْمُخْتَصِّيِنَ فِي عِلْمِ

ٱللُّغَةِ ٱلِٱجْتِمَاعِيِّ أَنَّ ٱلْأُمَمَ ذَاتَ ٱلثَّقَافَاتِ ٱلْمُتَرَسِّخَةِ لَاتَسْتَطِيعُ ٱلنُّهُوضَ دُونَ

ٱلِٱعْتِمَادِ عَلَى لُغَاتِهَا، وَأَنَّ لِلغَةِ دَوْرًا بَارِزًا فِي عَمَلِيَّةِ ٱلنُّهُوضِ وَأَثَرًا بَلَغَ ٱلْوَقَعِ فِي

ٱلتَّنْمِيَةِ بِمَفْهُومِهَاٱلشَّامِلِ. فَكُلَّمَاٱتَّسَعَتْ قَاعِدَةُ ٱسْتِعْمَالِ لُغَةٍ مَا، وَتَدَاوُلُهَا

بَيْنَ صُفُوفِ مُتَكَلِّمِيهَاكَانُواأَقْدَرَ عَلَى ٱلْفَهْمِ وَٱلْإِفْهَامِ وَأَكْثَرَ وَعْيًابِٱلْأَشْيَاءِ

وَٱلْأَفْكَارِ، وَأَسْرَعَ إِلَى ٱلِٱخْتِرَاعِ وَٱلِٱبْتِكَارِ. وَيَتَأَيَّدُهَذَاٱلزَّعْمُ بِتَجَارِبِ بَعْضِ

وعمليات الاقتراض من اللغات الأخرى تتمّ بفوضنة مطلقةً ولا

تنسجم وآلات اللغة نفسها في توليدالتوسع. ومنالمتداول بينالمختصيين

في علم اللّغة الا جتماعيّ أنّ الأمم ذات الثقافات المترسّخة لا تستطيع

النهوض دون الا عتماد على لغاتها، وأن للغة دورًا بار زًا في عمليّة

النهوض وأثرًا بلّغ الوقع في التنمية بمفهومها الشامل. فكلّما اتّسعت

قاعدة استعمال لغةٍ ما، وتداولها بين صفوف متكلّميها كانوا أقدر

على الفهم والإفهام وأكثر وعيًا بالأشياء والأفكار، وأسرع إلى

Figure 6.4. Typesetting with ACE

The same passage in the same ACE font typeset with different spacings. The passage on the top displays "calligraphic spacing" modeled on manuscript samples. The passage on the bottom displays "classical typographic spacing" modeled on movable Arabic type. Note how the calligraphic spacing is set much tighter while also displaying more visual complexity. (Image courtesy of Thomas Milo.)

principles of [Arabic] script grammar."[88] Arabic scribal practices informed textual presentation through a range of techniques that were lost in the transition to movable type: from stylistic variety, to complex ligatures, to unique connections among particular letter sequences, to the placement, or even the absence, of *nuqta*.[89] DecoType ACE reclaims these past affordances, which traditional typography cannot accurately reproduce. It transforms scribal models into fully searchable Unicode text without compromising visual and aesthetic sophistication. The Dr. Peter Karow Award for Font Technology & Digital Typography recognized the promise and possibilities of this approach in 2009.[90] Thomas Milo and DecoType were awarded for thinking, quite literally, outside the boxes of movable type.

Implications of Digital Arabic

Digital Arabic script draws on the past but is not beholden to it. Computation offers the chance to remediate the benefits and aesthetics of both scribal and print legacies without being constrained by the limitations of either. As with any new medium, digital text will challenge expectations. Novel traits will arise, past traits will be lost, and others will be regained. The limits of writing will be pushed to new extremes. Developing technologies, venues, and means of circulation will reimagine the shape of script. Digital communication traverses multiple devices and multiple interpreters; texts are read and processed by machines and human readers alike. Unicode serves both sets of readers. It provides a communication standard for encoding abstract semantic characters of plain text. Devices implement the standard to read, transmit, process, and render the code as visible glyphs and writing. For human readers, the process culminates in the perception of a glyph. Yet the visual component of writing stands on a foundation of code, which remains hidden and out of sight.[91] Writing has always been both linguistic and visual. Increasingly, scripts are also becoming invisible. Unicode, and digital coding schemes more generally, represent written characters as sequences of binary code. Devices read and process the code, which is rarely—if ever—perceived by human readers.

In the grand scheme of Unicode, alphabets, characters, and notational systems with drastically different histories and voices gather on a shared stage. The mutual interaction of diverse writing systems is bound to alter relationships and appearances. Characters will open to new experiences and new forms of text. Digital texts are incredibly flexible. They can shift according to context, surrounding characters, and textual patterns. At the same time, digital characters are precisely defined: they are assigned specific code points, they are classified with specific directionality, they are specifically quantified, and they are programmed with specific glyphs. Novel characters, some of which are themselves invisible, also shape the stage. Digitally native entities, such as the zero-width non-joiner (ZWNJ), take their place alongside traditional letters. Although the ZWNJ has no visual representation, its ontological position as a "character" is coded the same as any perceivable written character. The ZWNJ is an invisible character. If it steps on stage, the visible characters will act and appear differently. The how of the matter—the exact costumes, appearances, and fonts—are beyond the precise scope of Unicode. Unicode encodes only "enough information to permit the text to be rendered legibly, and nothing more."[92] It leaves appearances to other standards, programs, and protocols. Unicode simply suggests that all written characters—current and historical, visible and invisible— should stand on equal footing.

Both Typographic Matchmaking and DecoType raise pertinent questions about writing's global stage, the characters it supports, and the characters' footing. Typographic Matchmaking champions the extension of professional quality Arabic fonts that can integrate seamlessly and operate alongside their Latin counterparts. The project inserts Arabic script and Arabic designers into global networks of multilingual computing. The cross-cultural dialogue of Arabic, Latin, and other scripts elevates the quality, availability, and compatibility of fonts for all writing systems. DecoType addresses a deeply different, although not mutually exclusive, concern. DecoType's Advanced Composition Engine (ACE) operates at the level of computational abstraction. It tackles the aesthetic and technical challenges of typesetting Arabic script grammar. Drawing on careful analysis of scribal models, it rebuilds the technical infrastructure that builds upon and interacts with Unicode. Despite their differences, Typographic Matchmaking and DecoType share the foundational belief that the future of computing will remain multilingual and multi-script.[93] In doing so, they map a field of concern all too absent from dominant models that overemphasize the Latin alphabet. Embracing their challenges broadens the global discussion of scripts and written communication. The flexibility of the digital moment affords an opportunity to initiate and emphasize efforts that originate beyond the dominant Latinate paradigm.[94] Which lost strategies of Arabic scribal design will be recovered, and how? What aspects of print will be extended, and why? In the tenth century, vizier Ibn Muqlah established a proportional foundation for the enduring *naskh* styles of Arabic script. From the fifteenth century onward, those proportions were challenged, questioned, and occasionally reformed by print. Now, digital technology takes center stage. How this new equilibrium ultimately chooses to honor and code Arabic script remains to be written.

Coda

Beyond Arabic

The mirror of Arabic script reflects a necessary counterpoint to histories of communication that unintentionally—or deliberately—position Latin orthography as both the pinnacle and the foundation of written form. The historical marriage of Latin script and movable type in the fifteenth century, and a second marriage of the English alphabet and computerized ASCII in the twentieth, convey an aura of inevitability. Latin script, with a limited number of discrete letters—both consonants and vowels—arranged in neat horizontal lines, provides the de facto model of efficient, legible, and searchable mass communication. But the historic success of printed Latin does not imply the inevitability of continued dominance. Throughout history, styles of script and entire systems of writing have risen and fallen in response to new technologies, new languages, and new ideas that require transcription. Latin letters are already ceding ground to new shapes, foreign characters, and emojis at a rate that was unforeseen even less than a decade ago. As these changes unfold around us, we have a unique opportunity to reconsider earlier transformations of script, ponder what was lost, and ask what might be regained. Technologies of script and written characters circle one another in a dance of constraints and openings. For much of printed history, Arabic danced outside the dominant narrative. Inviting it to enter the fold alters the rhythm and rhyme of written communication.

For more than five hundred years, the cross-pollination of calligraphic and typographic practice pushed Arabic script in novel directions. Movable type parceled cursive Arabic into static, consistent, and repeatable positional variants. Calligraphic practice responded by becoming even more complex. From the fifteenth century onward—concurrent with the spread of print—examples of Arabic calligraphy display an increasing array of intricate compositions, figurative pictures drawn in script, and optical puzzles, almost as if the handwritten cursive line was challenging the medium of print to keep up. Print, in turn, answered qualitative complexity with quantitative distribution. Print-based education increased literacy rates, and new readers became acclimatized to simplified forms. During the twentieth century, script reform was predicated on the assumption that structural simplification benefits legibility and literacy. Yet cursive Arabic endured and migrated into the digital realm. In the Unicode Standard, digital Arabic script takes its rightful place alongside Latin script and all other writing systems, past and present. Standing on equal footing, Arabic script—and non-Latin models more generally—announce new vistas of written communication and textual form.

The future imaginaries of digital typography, Latin and otherwise, find historical precedent in Arabic script. The "script" styles of Latin fonts, which mimic Latin cursive handwriting, have blossomed in complexity. The exemplary Zapfino font contains well over 1,400 glyphs, including ten variants for the lowercase letter e alone. When it debuted in 1998, Zapfino was heralded as a major breakthrough in digital typography: "Herman Zapf has managed to take Zapfino *beyond a digital font* into the realm of electronic calligraphy, normally only achievable by very skilled hands."[1] But computerized systems were already handling automatic glyph selection from a large repertoire of Arabic ligatures more than two decades before Zapfino arrived on the scene. And DecoType's Advanced Composition Engine (ACE) could re-create Zapfino's 1,400 glyphs with fewer than two hundred strokes.[2] Animated type opens another exciting avenue of textual and visual possibility: "Motion enlivens typography by adding complexity and dimension to flat letterforms. . . . [It] allows type to grow, shift, transform, shrink, and stretch."[3] And yet again, digital Arabic script preceded the trend. The contextual variation of cursive characters causes them to grow, shift, and transform: "Typing in Arabic, one witnesses a little animated movie in which the letters change shape according to what comes next."[4] Calligraphic variations and animated characters, both of which are celebrated as radical and futuristic *options* for digital Latin typography, were structural and practical *necessities* for digital Arabic much earlier.

In the twenty-first century, an increasing chorus of voices challenge Latin script as the preeminent model of digital text. The global Internet, supported by Unicode, affirms the importance of multi-script communication. Accurate representation of one's native script has become a linguistic and cultural right. Historically, the limited choices of non-Latin typography led readers to accept substandard representations as acceptable typographic norms.[5] Labeling scripts as "complex," "foreign," or "exotic" implied a Latinate center to the textual universe. Yet Latin script represents the native languages of less than 40 percent of the world's population. The vast majority of human languages employ scripts that have been simplified and reformed in the name of technological efficiency. Online threats of monolingual and mono-script domination remain, but they are overtly acknowledged and tempered with healthy skepticism. Critics challenge dominant encoding schemes: "While positive benefits may accrue to minority languages from Unicode . . . benefits to minority languages do not necessarily translate into benefits to those who [use] them. Unicode may give the linguistically oppressed peoples of the world an online voice, but . . . that voice is mostly provided by American multinational corporations."[6] They question assumptions of typographic design: "The eurocentric notion that Latin typography should serve as a role model for typographic cultures with a shorter history should be re-evaluated in order to initiate and emphasize efforts that stem from the very culture a design is aimed at."[7] And they suggest alternative sales models: "If non-Latin types are no longer to be regarded as secondary to [sales] of Latin, nor vernacular fonts as peripheral to machine sales, then a new approach to the typographic development of indigenous scripts is vital."[8]

Digital Arabic, moreover, accrues benefits that extend beyond linguistic representation. As early as the 1970s, technologists championed the lessons that computerized Arabic offered mathematical typesetting.[9] Mathematical notation, like Arabic, combines into richly layered visual structures. The appearance and significance of mathematical characters vary in relation to context and surrounding characters. As with Arabic script, horizontal and vertical relationships are equally significant. A baseline numeral 2, a 2 below the vinculum (the crossbar of a fraction), such as in ½, a 2 above the vinculum, and a superscript 2, or 2^2, all represent drastically different mathematical meanings. Skills learned in programming the placement of Arabic *tashkil* above and below the primary line of characters and the selection of Arabic letterforms according to word position (initial, medial, and final forms) transferred to mathematical typesetting. Similar programs selected among multiple bracket heights in response to contained equations, or they stacked mathematical operators, superior figures, second-degree superiors, and so forth. Not all of these advances migrated into the digital era. Popular word-processing and design programs still struggle with the proper representation of complex mathematical formulas. Academic and scientific publications in which these formulas are essential often rely on TeX, a fully digital and computational typesetting system released by Donald Knuth in 1978.[10] TeX allows writers, mathematical and otherwise, to insert code that renders equations and complex formulas in proper spatial arrangement. These affordances have made TeX an unofficial scientific and mathematical standard, and computer scientists have even applied TeX to the typesetting of complex Arabic texts.[11] More generally, the success of TeX in the scientific realm opens the possibility of moving beyond fonts for non-Latin scripts. Alternative programs, such as DecoType's ACE, may become the norm for Arabic typesetting in the same way that TeX has become the norm in scientific circles. The fluidity of digital code frees scripts from the confines of substandard rendering protocols. We might even imagine a future in which Unicode's various scripts and blocks receive targeted software that will optimize accurate representation on a script-by-script basis.

The complexities of Arabic script and mathematical equations build a shared case against the legacy of Latin script. A defining characteristic of this legacy is the easy separation of plain text from rich text.[12] Plain text consists simply of coded characters: letters, words, spaces, numbers, punctuation, and so on. Rich text, in contrast, consists of plain text formatted with information about a text's visual appearance, its document structure, its language(s), and so on. Stylistic options such as **bold,** *italic,* and <u>underline</u> are differences of rich text, as are formatting choices of font, font color, and font size. Changes in the font or color of the current paragraph would not alter the underlying characters of plain text. The Unicode Standard does not address rich text. It provides a technical standard for encoding plain text, which it defines as "a pure sequence of character codes" or "the underlying content stream to which formatting can be applied." More specifically: "Plain text must contain enough information to permit the text to be rendered legibly, and nothing more."[13] The distinction implies that legibility can separate from the specifics of written appearance. But the limits of the phrase "and nothing more" are difficult to define. In many cases, separation of semantic information and visual presentation is not clearly delineated. Where does plain text end and rich text begin? Scribal practices, for example, encoded meaningful and "semantic" information in the style of script. The Arabic styles of *thuluth, muhaqqaq, ta'liq,* and *diwani* visually signified differences of genre, content, and role. At what point do these stylistic differences become semantically necessary for the rendering of legibility? Urdu almost always employs the *nasta'liq* style of Arabic script, which differs widely in appearance from *naskh*. Outsiders often do not even recognize them as the same script.[14] Yet Arabic and Urdu letters share character codes, despite their drastically different shapes and the fact that literacy in one style does not necessarily transfer to the other.

Once again, mathematical necessity demonstrated the limits of the digital standard. Unicode's Mathematics block contains a large section titled "Mathematical Letterlike Symbols" in which "rich text" variants are coded as unique characters. The mathematical bold capital **A** (U+1D400), mathematical italic capital *A* (U+1D434), and mathematical bold italic capital *A* (U+1D468) all receive unique code points. And all three forms of mathematical A differ yet again from the capital letter A of Latin script (U+0041), which may or may not be formatted with bold and / or italic qualities in rich text. These letters appear identical, but they are coded very differently. Whereas Latin capital letter A is a linguistic character, the other three "letterlike" symbols are mathematical characters. Per Unicode's explanation, "alphanumeric symbols are typically used for mathematical variables; those letterlike symbols that are part of this set carry semantic information in their type style."[15] The "rich" differences of "type style" are semantically relevant for mathematical characters. But the Unicode Standard cautions that these characters should be used only for mathematical purposes. Mathematical characters are not indexed, processed, or searched as linguistic characters: a mathematical A is not equivalent to a linguistic A. Confusing these characters unsettles textual relations and established protocols. But cannot the same be argued for the stylistic variations of linguistic characters? For astute Ottoman readers, a phrase penned in the hieratic *muhaqqaq* style was not "mathematically" equivalent to a similar phrase penned in the imperial *diwani* style. Confusing *muhaqqaq* and *diwani* would have unsettled "semantic" equations of religious and secular authority, with drastic effects for both the established protocols of Ottoman bureaucracy and the functioning of its human agents.

Such thought experiments, which challenge the philosophical and computational division of plain and rich text, are hypothetical. But they nevertheless underscore the difficulty of isolating abstract meaning from visual form. The line separating the characters of plain text and the formatting of rich text remains negotiable. And that line is bound to move as technical and visual practices of compositional writing merge with textual design. Users can now exert more control over digital fonts, frames, code, and graphics than ever before. Writers and readers alike are increasingly attuned to visual design and stylistic variety, and growing numbers of users have a favorite font—or an opinion on Comic Sans. Fonts and styles can change with the click of a button, and contemporary word processors support an increasingly wide array of layout and aesthetic choice. This "breakout of the visual" heralds new practices and possibilities of written expression.[16] As familiarity with the available options increases, compositional writing will cease to be the inputting of "plain text." Future writers will employ images, colors, and novel characters for communicative effect. Hybrid practices of design writing will produce visually *rich* scripts and textual communications.[17]

Throughout history, Arabic script has adopted different styles on different media for different audiences. Such diversity challenges us to appreciate the communicative role of scribal and visual variety. It inspires a retrofuturology in which the exploration of past techniques inspires future possibilities. The current excitement surrounding digital design looks to the future and the openness of the digital canvas. But innovative design has always kept one eye on the past, where it locates novel forms of textual organization, knowledge representation, and information visualization. Arabic script is one of the oldest scripts in continuous usage, and proportioned Arabic handwriting of the tenth century remains easily legible to modern readers, despite the fact that we are now much more accustomed to digital tablets than reed pens. Arabic script is classical. It is modern. It is secular. It is religious. It is local. It is international. It is prosaic. It is sublime. The history of Arabic script displays an incredibly wide range of calligraphic, technical, and typographic experimentation. Time and again, writers, designers, artists, and technologists have demonstrated the script's visual flexibility and its adaptability to new materials. May these past examples inspire future experiments of digital form. On today's digital screens, Arabic script is electronically illuminated and glows from within.[18] May these letters of light illuminate new pathways to the future.

Notes

Bibliography

Acknowledgments

Index

NOTES

Introduction

1. The approach outlined in *Comparative Textual Media: Transforming the Humanities in the Postprint Era* (Hayles and Pressman 2013) informs the current study. The "comparative" aspect of this 2013 edited collection, however, contains very little cross-cultural examination of non-Latin scripts.

2. Hudson 2002, 41.

3. Sheila Blair's masterful and comprehensive *Islamic Calligraphy* (2006) touches only lightly on printed Arabic, despite the more than five hundred years that Arabic calligraphy developed alongside and in dialogue with printed text. Blair's introduction outlines difficulties of early Arabic printing, chapter 11 mentions Ottoman print adoption, and a brief concluding section, "Printing, Typography, and Computer Graphics," examines contemporary practices. *The History of the Book in the Middle East* (2013), edited by Geoffrey Roper, usefully collects key articles addressing both manuscript and print culture, but it does not extend into the digital era.

4. Although scripts represent language, the visual and aesthetic qualities of writing models communicative systems that differ from spoken language. Technologies, arts, and religion provide alternative modeling systems, all of which challenge natural spoken language as the primary semiotic model. Bennetta Jules-Rosette develops this methodological approach in *The Messages of Tourist Art: An African Semiotic System in Comparative Perspective* (1984) and *Terminal Signs: Computers and Social Change in Africa* (1990). For focused discussion of the approach in relation to computer technology, see Jules-Rosette 1990, 100–103.

5. Abulhab (2006, 295) suggests the term "Arabetic" to unify the diverse styles of Arabic script: "It has enough flavor of Arabic for the Arabs to appreciate and take appropriate

credit for. But at the same time, it is not pure 'Arabic,' which can justifiably cause sensitivity and may even sound dismissive of those historically crucial and defining contributions of non-Arab users, calligraphers and civilizations to the Arabic language and script. Arabetic is a single, inclusive and unambiguous word to address all these scripts at once without compromising their distinct and unique characteristics."

6. For extensive and thoughtful examinations of Arabic script in Africa, see Mumin and Versteegh 2014.

7. Bloom 2001.

8. Milo's (2002a) insightful article outlines the seven-layer model of Arabic script grammar in relation to Unicode and digital typography. A more technical presentation can be found in Milo 2002b.

9. See, for example, Febvre and Martin 1958 and Eisenstein 1979. The key works of European print history helped launch an entire field of study.

10. Carla Hesse (1996) attentively warns against conflating the printing press (a *means* of cultural production) with print culture and the "modern literary system" (a *mode* of cultural production). The former spread across Europe in the fifteenth century, while the latter was not formalized until the eighteenth century.

11. Proudfoot 1997.

12. Ross 2012, 126–127.

13. Sampson 1985, 38. Cf. Rogers 1995, 46: "The study of writing systems is as subject to ethnocentric bias as most work in cultural areas. Titles like Our Glorious Alphabet are somewhat extreme, but at a more subtle level, there is no lack of articles extolling the virtues of a particular writing system."

14. Gitelman 1999, 229.

1. The Layers of Proportional *Naskh*

1. Rice 1955, 6; Blair 2006, 158; George 2010, 135.

2. Ibn al-Nadim 1970, 1.

3. Ibid., 28–29.

4. Ibid., 15.

5. Gruendler 1993, 132. The quoted passage combines phrasing from the body of Gruendler's text and note 190 on the same page.

6. Al-Bagdadi 2005, 92. The ontological and textual uniqueness of the Qur'an was reflected in the materiality of the text and the styles of script with which it was copied. These traits materially distinguished copies of Qur'an from more prosaic writing. For a useful introduction explaining how the Qur'an is not a "book" in the conventional sense of the word, see Sells 1999.

7. Madigan 2001, 36–37; Al-Bagdadi 2005, 95–96.

8. A. Y. Ali 1982. See also Blair 2006, 31–33.

9. Ibn al-Nadim 1970, 10–12.

10. George 2010, 89–90.

11. Ibid.; Donner 2010, 208–211.

12. Welch 1979, 31.

13. Ibn al-Nadim 1970, 10.

14. Ibid.

15. Ibid., 15.

16. The examples that follow are summarized from Gruendler 1993, 132–138.

17. Karabacek 1991, 70; Bloom 2001, 53.

18. George 2010, 56–60. George meticulously reconstructs the template and demonstrates its formal consistency.

19. Ibid., 58.

20. Déroche et al. 2006, 205–224.

21. Bloom 2001, 53.

22. Kennedy 2015.

23. Bloom 2001, 124–159.

24. Milo 2002a, 2002b.

25. The analytic shift from linguistic grammar to script grammar "weaken[s] the attachment to natural language as the only modeling device." Jules-Rosette 1993, 273.

26. George 2010, 58. Early Abbasid Qur'ans occasionally have page breaks in the middle of words.

27. Milo adapts his terms for script analysis from technical terms of spoken linguistics. Grapheme, archigrapheme, and allograph are scribal parallels to phoneme, archiphoneme, and allophone. Milo 2002b.

28. Daniels 2014, 30.

29. Gruendler 2012, 101.

30. The lack of *i'jaam* serves as a literary trope in Sinan Antoon's (2007) eponymously titled novel *I'jaam: An Iraqi Rhapsody*.

31. Daniels 2014, 30.

32. The common form of "Allah" is a notable exception. The name often displays layers 1–6, even if the surrounding text displays only layers 1 and 2.

33. Milo 2002a, 126n5: "Without altering the Qur'anic text, diacritics facilitated memorization of the text in a properly recited form."

34. Houston 2012, xii; 2004, 299.

35. Ibn al-Nadim 1970, 7. For a more recent summary of the birth and early spread of Arabic script, see George 2010, 21–31.

36. George 2010, 107, 143–144; Gacek 2009, 289–290. Red and green dots were the most common, although yellow and blue dots were occasionally used to signify alternate readings. The use of color to layer additional meaning embraced the visual affordances of writing, which need not be limited to monochromatic text. Ignace Gelb lists "the principle of color" and "the principle of position" as two distinct methods of marking written difference. Gelb 1952, 18–19.

37. Al-Khalil is also credited with drafting the first comprehensive Arabic dictionary. For a recent discussion of his process, see Dichy 2014.

38. Safadi 1979, 14; George 2010, 91.

39. Ibn al-Nadim 1970, 9–19.

40. For perspective on Ibn Muqlah's precise contributions, see Abbott 1939b; Tabbaa 2002; George 2010, 134–143. Tabbaa links Ibn Muqlah's scribal innovations to a religious and political movement enforcing a specific ideology. George criticizes this approach with

a focus on more gradual, bureaucratic change. According to George, Ibn Khallikan, who wrote three centuries after the death of Ibn Muqlah, is the first person to credit the vizier with the invention of proportioned script.

41. The new style, which George labels "broken cursive," preceded Ibn Muqlah by almost a century, and George therefore argues against the vizier's import. George 2010, 134–143.

42. Grabar 1992, 69–70. See also Abbott 1939b. Although slightly dated, Abbott's early study remains a useful introduction, which clarifies the contributions of Ibn Muqlah and argues against earlier suggestions that Ibn Muqlah developed new styles of script.

43. The trajectory of adopting new technologies for secular texts first applies not only to visual marks (e.g., *tashkil, al-khatt al-mansub*) but also to the medium that held the marks. Paper was first used for secular text in the ninth century but adopted for Qur'anic *masahif* only during the tenth century. George 2010, 125.

44. Ibn Khallikan 1970, 269.

45. E. Robertson 1920, 60–61; via Rice 1955, 6.

46. Mansour 2010, 49: "He made proper use of his ability to paint and illuminate and painters, like calligraphers, can easily spot fluency and sure strokes from stiff and indecisive ones."

47. Blair 2006, 162. The poem is included in Blair's comprehensive book on Islamic calligraphy. It was also translated by master calligrapher Mohamed Zakariya (2003).

48. Mansour 2010, 52; Rice 1955.

49. Bloom 2001, 109.

50. There is no consensus as to the exact name of the script that Ibn al-Bawwab used in his surviving *mushaf,* partially because the specific styles as they were later understood were not yet defined. Mansour 2010, 160.

51. George 2010, 127–134.

52. Grabar 1992, 73.

53. Blair 2006, 242–243.

54. Qadi 1959, 58: "[Yaqut] cut the end of the qalam. Thus, he altered both the rule and the writing, because writing is subordinate to the qalam. For this reason, his writing is preferred to that of Ibn Bawwab for its fineness and elegance, and not for the sake of the basic rules; for the essence of writing, it is the same as invented by Ibn Muqlah from the circle and the dot. And he took the foundation from the dot and adopted it. In these styles of writing Yaqut showed solidity, beauty, and clarity—none better than he has ever been found! He wrote in these six styles of writing with extreme elegance and beauty." See also Rosenthal 1971, 26.

55. Blair 2006, 245–246.

56. Rosenthal 1971, 4: "The different styles were handed down on the authority of the men around Muhammad in an uninterrupted chain of transmitters unto Ibn Muqlah and Yaqut."

57. The popularization of the Qur'anic text on paper parallels the popularization of biblical translations during the Protestant Reformation. In Islam, the availability of paper opened access to the written Qur'an through the application of more easily legible styles. In Christianity, availability of paper opened access to the Bible through the printing of vernacular translations.

2. Ottoman Script Design

1. Grabar 1992, 60. Grabar notes that the Greek word *kalligrpahos,* as opposed to *kalligraphia,* means simply "scribe."

2. Ibid., 66.

3. Marks 2010, 199.

4. Lupton and Phillips 2015, 13: "Point, line, and plane are the building blocks of design. From these elements, designers create images, icons, textures, patterns, diagrams, animations, and typographic systems."

5. Ingold 2007, 128.

6. Acar 1999, 26–27; Derman and Çetin 1998, 37. Jamal Elias relates a similar story in which Ibn Muqlah retreats for forty days in order to improve and refine Arabic letters. Elias 2012, 239.

7. Type designer Erik Spiekermann describes a similar method for updating and adapting historical examples: "I look at that for a long time . . . and I draw it and I sketch over it. Then I put it away, and the next day, I draw it from memory." Spiekermann 2011.

8. Stanley 2004, 56. Common Ottoman form defined *masahif* of fifteen lines per page on sheets measuring 18 by 12 centimeters. A ruling board, or *mistar,* used prior to writing, ensured consistency of line spacing from page to page. The *mistar* delineated borders, frames, and lines of text with thread. Pressing the paper onto the *mistar* would impress the template upon the paper.

9. Mahir 1999, 31.

10. Schimmel 1984, 36; Ülker 1987, 60.

11. Stanley 2004, 56.

12. Ülker 1987, 79; Blair 2006, 492.

13. Sheila Blair notes that Hafiz Osman lightly altered Hamdullah's style of *naskh* by "smoothing out the strokes, reducing the number of swooping tails and sublinear flourishes, and opening up the spaces between letters and words so that the layout is more compact and regular." Blair 2006, 483.

14. Acar 1999, 218.

15. Associations of the *hilye* components with parts of the body—the *başmakan* as head, the belly of the *göbek,* and the *etek* as foot or skirt—convey a bodily portrait-like quality. Elias 2012, 239; Marks 2010, 235.

16. Adapted from Grabar 1992, 74.

17. The text of Osman's *hilye* presents a description of the Prophet Muhammad as relayed by his nephew 'Ali. An English translation of the passage can be found in Blair 2006, 483–484.

18. The brief descriptions of specific styles draw heavily on Adam Gacek's *Arabic Manuscripts: A Vademecum* (2009) and the descriptions in Sheila Blair's *Islamic Calligraphy* (2006) and Uğur Derman and Nihad M. Çetin's *The Art of Calligraphy* (1998). The books that introduced me to the concept of stylistic variety as a marker of genre are Wijdan Ali's *What Is Islamic Art?* (1996), Muammer Ülker's *Başlangıctan Günümüze Türk Hat Sanatı (The Art of Turkish Calligraphy from the Beginning up to the Present)* (1987), and Yasin Safadi's *Islamic Calligraphy* (1979).

19. Mohamed Zakariya provided the translation. The passage appears in Ibn 'Ata'Allah 1978.

20. Gacek 2009, 274.

21. Qadi 1959, 56.

22. Gacek 2009, 164.

23. Mansour 2010. Mansour provides a close examination of *muhaqqaq,* its history, its traditional hieratic character, and the shape of each of its letters.

24. Schimmel 1984, 23; Mahir 1999, 12.

25. Gacek 2009, 160; Qadi 1959, 137.

26. Gacek 2009, 223.

27. Safadi 1979, 20.

28. Gacek 2009, 223.

29. Ibid., 264: The prevalence of unorthodox connections made *tawqi'* a common base style for writing *musalsal,* or chained, compositions. *Musalsal* compositions deliberately deviate from proper script grammar and connect all letter blocks in a single unbroken line.

30. Blair 2006, 516–517. Blair analyzes a collection of *hadith* written for Süleyman's son Mehmet. The Arabic traditions of the prophet are transcribed in *tawqi',* while the accompanying Persian commentary is written in *ta'liq.* The Abbasid and traditional Arabic connotations of *tawqi'* distinguish it from the Persian connotations of *ta'liq* script.

31. See, for example, Derman 1998. Derman lists the genealogies of famous scribes and the teachers from whom they received *ijazah.*

32. The *ketebe,* or the calligraphers' signature, was a mark of pride and individuality in an otherwise regulated system of scripts. The signature allowed scribes to design their own logotype: incorporating additional flourishes such as decorative serifs or intertwined loops that made their *ketebe* visually unique.

33. Gacek 2009, 165.

34. In appearance and form, the Persian variety of *ta'liq* more closely resembles the Ottoman script *diwani.* Gacek 2009, 263.

35. Blair's opening discussion of Arabic script explores how the script's flexibility allowed it to adapt and emphasize the linguistic features of diverse languages. Arabic emphasizes the verticality of repeated *alifs,* Persian highlights the flowing curves of final *yā'* and *nūn,* and Turkish builds upon the repeated cross-strokes of *kāf* and *gāf.* Blair 2006, 11–15.

36. Derman and Çetin 1998, 42.

37. Blair 2006, 433; Gacek 2009, 166.

38. E. J. Wright 2012, 234–239.

39. W. Ali 1996, 45.

40. Blair 2006, 508.

41. Gacek 2009, 252.

42. Fekete 1955. Fekete learned *siyaqah* from Turkish prisoners while held in a concentration camp during World War I. See also Bagheri 1998.

43. Gacek 2009, 252.

44. Darling 2012, 180.

45. T. F. Mitchell 1953.

46. Derman and Çetin 1998, 40–41.

47. *Ghubar* refers to the smallest and airiest variety of script. The term *hurde* was used for scripts written with a thinner pen than normal, but larger than *ghubar.* Acar 1999, 286.

48. Acar 1999, 228. Upon obtaining the throne, the sultan would select a new *tughra* from a variety of compositions presented before him. Once a design was settled upon, the *tughra* form remained consistent throughout the sultan's reign.

49. Blair 2006, 509; via Wittek 1948. See also Acar 1999, 227–228.

50. Warde 1955.

51. Morison 1936.

52. For a methodological introduction to infrastructural inversion, a practice in which invisible technologies are problematized and made visible, see Bowker and Star 1999. Typically, infrastructural technologies are only noticed when they break down. For example, readers are more likely to comment on a typeface if it is difficult to decipher.

53. A fun take on typographic rules and the ways they have been broken is Felton 2006.

54. The dominant Ottoman styles remain recognizably distinct, much like modern fonts. But they are not as easily exchanged as digital fonts; a scribal style cannot be altered without recopying an entire document. Typographers receive textual copy and dress it in the proper uniform. Scribes dressed the copy during inscription. There is no equivalent of "plain text" in a scribal environment. The style of script is applied and inscribed at the time of production. The formalized proportions, shapes, and ligatures of a particular style of manuscript copy were regulated and maintained as it was written. The font and style of script—the attributes of "rich text"—were chosen before production, and texts were directed to specialist scribes trained in the requisite style.

55. Bringhurst 1997, 1.1.1: 17.

56. Ibid., 1.3: 24.

57. Citations to Bringhurst contain both section and page numbers. The section numbers are relatively consistent across all versions of his text. Page numbers are from the 1997 second edition.

58. Bringhurst 1997, 1.2.4: 22.

59. Ibid., 6.1.1: 93.

60. Ibid, 6.1.2: 93. Letterpress also differs from photographic typesetting. Letterpress adds bulk to the form, whereas serifs and fine lines appear reduced in photographic typesetting.

61. Ibid., 6.1.4: 94–95.

62. Karabacek 1991, 70.

63. Bringhurst 1997, 6.2.1: 95.

64. Ibid., 6.3.1: 98–99.

65. Schimmel 1970; Blair 2006, 433; Gacek 2009, 166.

66. Bringhurst 1997, 6.5.1: 102.

67. Ibid., 6.4.1: 99–102.

68. White 2011, 177.

69. Bringhurst 1997, 1.2.3: 21–22.

70. Ibid., 1.2.5: 23–24.

71. *Diwani*'s aestheticized appearance might tempt us to classify it as a display style. And indeed, *diwani*-inspired forms are often used for decoration and display in modern advertising and design. But the formalized style of Ottoman diwani was not simply for creative display. It served as the official style for a particular format of document. It therefore complicates the binary distinction of display styles and text styles. As a text style, it transcribes

particular content; as a display style, it privileges aesthetics and complicates legibility. *Diwani* scrolls—despite their relative illegibility—authorized holders to act in particular ways.

72. While the linguistic content of an Ottoman *ferman*—written in the *diwani* style and topped with an ornate *tughra*—communicates to a limited audience of knowledgeable readers, the aesthetic display communicates its import to a much wider audience. This "double writing" draws upon conventional expectations (both linguistic and stylistic) in order to reach multiple audiences. Jules-Rosette 1984, 227.

73. Ruder 2013, 66.

74. Bringhurst 1997, 1.1.3, 19–20: "There is a style beyond style." The concluding sentences, from "the interaction . . ." to ". . . grace and vitality" borrow heavily from Bringhurst's poetic phrasing.

3. European Printing and Arabic

1. The use of the phrase "agent of change" is deliberate. Elizabeth Eisenstein's book *The Printing Press as an Agent of Change* (1979) remains one of the best and most thorough examinations of early European printing and its broad ramifications. Other scholars have suggested that the modern literary system of print was negotiated over time, rather than springing from a specific technology. See, for example, Johns 1998 and Hesse 1997.

2. Ibid., 60, 375.

3. Osborn 2008, 20–28.

4. Eisenstein 1979, 375.

5. Eisenstein 2011, 34–35: "Luther and other reformers embraced print because they needed to spread the word before the imminent end of the world. It was the moment to share everything widely." In Christian Protestant narratives, Ottoman expansion into Europe was seen as an omen of the "imminent end."

6. Schneider 2001, 199–206; Graham 1987, 146–148.

7. Connell 2015, 24, 99n3; Gilmont and Maag 1998, 1. For the original passage in Latin, see Luther 1912, 1:153 (no. 1038).

8. Füssel 2003, 170–171; Olson 1994, 153.

9. Manfred Schneider locates Christian precedent for Luther's translation strategy in the writings of Saint Paul: "St. Paul, the media specialist of the Apostles, radicalized the difference inaugurated by Jesus and his reporters: namely, that God's power and the medium of his revelation consisted in spirit. This spirit is, according to St. Paul, not chained to the letter." Schneider 2001, 202–203.

10. M. U. Edwards 1994, 111.

11. Ibid. "Scripture interprets itself" was a Protestant rallying call. By rearranging the text, prioritizing elements, and adding new components, Luther ensured that at least his *printed translation* of scripture interpreted itself.

12. Eisenstein 1997, 1055.

13. Ibid., 1062.

14. M. U. Edwards 1994, 129.

15. Hindman and Farquhar 1977, 16.

16. Bloom 2001.

17. Bobzin 2002, 165.

18. The application of lithography to Arabic script is discussed in Chapter 5.

19. Eisenstein 1979, 335.

20. The early replacement of scrolls with a biblical codex benefited scholarly and religious practices of reading across multiple texts. Eisenstein 1979, 334; Chartier 1995, 19.

21. Avakian 1978, 266.

22. Nasr 1994, 48. According to Nasr, if the Qur'an appears incoherent or difficult to understand, it is not the text that is out of alignment but the readers themselves.

23. Madigan 2001, 75.

24. Ghaly 2009, 8: "Printing of the Qur'an was not a pressing need for the Muslims [who were surrounded by the text in recitational form]. On the contrary, preserving the sacredness and aura of the Qur'an, in both oral and the written forms, were seen sometimes as obstacles to make use of this new technology in order to produce this sacred text."

25. Another common reason for not printing the Qur'an, according to European commentators, was Muslim aversion to applying pressure to the pages of the holy text. Walsh 1828, 16: "The reason they assigned was characteristic of [local Muslims]—they said it would be an impiety if the words of God should be squeezed and pressed together." For discussion of the various ways that printing compromised the traditions designed to preserve inimitable sacredness of the Qur'an, see also Ghaly 2009. Digital design may not be subject to the same faults. Stolow (2010) explores the ways in which digital design can reinvigorate scripturalism.

26. Bloom 2001, 55.

27. Johns 1998, 31; Mahdi 1995, 4.

28. Steinberg 1996, 98. Steinberg presents a list of additional biblical misprints, most of which are drawn from M. H. Black's "The Printed Bible" (1963), in *The Cambridge History of the Bible*.

29. Faroqhi 2000, 95.

30. Messick 1993, 126.

31. McLuhan 1962, 327.

32. Bobzin 1999, 2.

33. Ingold 2007, 124.

34. Reuwich's woodcuts heightened the book's allure, and *Peregrinatio in Terram Sanctam* became incredibly popular. The Latin original was translated into a variety of European languages and printed in multiple editions before the end of the fifteenth century.

35. The letter *qāf* is identified by a *nuqta* above the letter, and *fā'* receives a *nuqta* below the letter.

36. Roper 2002, 133.

37. Ibid., 134. Arabic alphabets were reproduced in a variety of Italian books throughout the sixteenth century.

38. Ibid.

39. Krek 1979.

40. Later editions added a Latin preface dated 1517. Roper 2002, 131.

41. The orthography of *qaf* and *fa* follow Eastern orthography, much like Pedro de Alcalá's book *Arte para ligeramente saber la lengua araviga*: the letter *qāf* is identified by a *nuqta* above the letter, and *fā'* receives a *nuqta* below the letter.

42. Abdulrazak 1990, 67–68.

43. Nuovo 1990.

44. Bobzin 1999, 151. A Latin translation of the Qur'an was printed in 1543, exactly one hundred years after its translation was completed in Spain by Robert of Ketton. For an accessible discussion of the context surrounding Ketton's translation, see Menocal 2002.

45. Mahdi 1995, 1–2; cf. Nuovo 1990.

46. Blair 2006, 28–29. Blair highlights and isolates focused images and passages that demonstrate the errors.

47. Bobzin 1999, 6.

48. Birnbaum et al. 1989, 2: "Unlike the European Manuscript tradition which was generally confined to the monastery environment, the Islamic manuscript, with its associated arts, was an integral part of the education of Ottoman elites."

49. Lawson 1990, 147. According to Lawson, Stanley Morrison described Granjon as "unquestionably the greatest master of italics of his age."

50. Lawson 1990, 355.

51. Vervliet 1981; Lunde 1981; Bloom 2001.

52. Interestingly, *alif* is listed as the equivalent of the Hebrew *aleph,* rather than the Latin letter A. All the other characters receive Latin letter equivalencies.

53. The isolated forms are presented as variant final forms, and they can be typeset as such.

54. For discussion of how Tipographia Medicea revitalized Arabic scholarship in northern Europe, see Jones 1994.

55. The Venetian Senate often granted specific printers exclusive rights to print or distribute particular books, especially those with non-Latin typefaces. Steinberg 1996, 53; Krek 1979, 208–209.

56. Leaman 2004, 37: "Because calligraphy is writing we stress its relationship to the language in which it operates. But it may not be language which is important to calligraphy, paradoxically it may be that this is the least important aspect."

57. Messick 1993, 240.

58. Clanchy 1979, 98–105.

59. Case layouts arranged by individual letters gave rise to new forms of information organization, such as the alphabetical list and the index. Bell 2001, 18–19: "The art of indexing was not very highly developed before 1550. . . . By the end of the 18th century, indexes were recognized as instruments in their own right for the systemization of knowledge." See also Eisenstein 2005, 80–107; Illich 1993.

60. The ASCII character set of 1963 contains 128 characters, only 52 of which are letters. This represents a more than 50 percent reduction of total sorts and an almost 80 percent reduction of lettering sorts when compared to Gutenberg's 292.

61. Wagner and Reed 2009, 11.

62. Ibid. See also AbiFarès 2001; Hanebutt-Benz, Glass, and Roper 2002.

63. Roper 2002, 134.

64. Faroqhi 2000, 94.

65. Ibid., 95; Gdoura 1985, 99–97.

66. W. Wright 1896, 3.

67. Niebuhr 1792, 2: 261.

68. Milo 2011b.

69. Mustafa Izzet Efendi's *meshk* exercises also provided the model for Armenian Ottoman type-designer Ohanis Mühendisoğlu's *yeni hurufat* (new letters) typeface in 1870 C.E. Thomas Milo commends the design as "calligraphically extremely sophisticated," as it does not reproduce any of Eurabic features that haunt European Arabic type. Milo 2002a, 122–123.

70. Milo 2011b, 2013.

71. Milo 2011b.

72. See Elias 2012, 238–243, 335n16

73. Elias 2012, 281.

74. Ibid., emphasis in original.

75. Ingold 2007, 124.

76. The written word establishes an intellectual and communicative relationship with the viewer, regardless of whether the visual phrase is immediately decipherable or legible. Erzen 2000, 288.

77. Ja'far 2002.

78. Ibid., 5.

79. Ibid., 19.

80. Ibid., 22.

81. See also T. F. Mitchell 1953 on *ruq'ah* script. Mitchell, like Ja'far, emphasizes multiple connections and variable forms of the cursive line.

82. Thomas Milo contrasts the attention to subtle scribal detail exhibited by Ottoman scribes with the incredible precision of architectural and natural detail exhibited by European illustrators. When the Swiss architects Gaspare and Giuseppe Fossati were hired to renovate the Hagia Sophia, they accurately depicted the building's spatial organization and architectural depth through refined techniques of linear perspective. But the same level of detail did not translate to the calligraphic roundels that decorate the space. The architectural engraving depicts a space; it does not copy a text or reproduce script. Milo comments: "It is as if the artist lacks the mental machinery to understand what he is seeing, and so is unable to depict it. . . . Conversely, this kind of realistic depiction of the building would likely have been impossible for an artists of the Middle-Eastern tradition, lacking an understanding of the visual culture of Europe." Milo 2002a, 118.

83. Connell 2015, 24, 99n3; Gilmont and Maag 1998, 1. For the original passage in Latin, see Luther 1912, 1:153 (no. 1038).

4. Print in Ottoman Lands

1. When the Orthodox Christian patriarch in Constantinople submitted a profession of allegiance to the conquering sultan, Mehmet requested a Turkish translation. The Turkish text was later printed in Basel using the Greek alphabet to phonetically represent Turkish. Kut 1960, 800, cites Salaville and Dalleggio 1958.

2. Saoud 2004, 3. The architect's name is recorded as Atık Sinan (not to be confused with Mimar Sinan, the most famous of Ottoman architects).

3. For a number of sources on Bellini's career, see S. E. Roberts 2013, 250n171.

4. Ibid., 153–154. Ottoman ambassadors recruited engravers, along with other artists, from the Florentine court. The term Roberts uses is "intaglio," which likely refers to engravers of metal ornamentation. But such engravers were also known to cut metal type.

5. Abdulrazak 1990, 80: "Given his big appetite for Western artifacts, it seems reasonable that if he [Sultan Mehmet] had wanted or needed printing he would have purchased the machine, hired the people necessary to run it, and used it as a propaganda tool himself."

6. Shaw and Shaw 1976, 1:58–60, 151–153.

7. Strauss 2003, 456–457. These linguistic and scribal differences were not hard and fast. The Arab Melkite community, for instance, also employed Arabic script.

8. Over the course of centuries, Turkish has been written with Arabic, Armenian, Cyrillic, Greek, Hebrew, and Latin characters.

9. Finkel (2005, 88) quotes Bayezid II as saying, "By impoverishing his own kingdom, [Ferdinand] has enriched our own."

10. Tamari 2001, 9.

11. The Soncino Hebrew press marks the first printing with movable type in Egypt. Hebrew printers were also the first to print in Salonika, Fez, Adrianople (Edirne), and Safed. Hill 2016b.

12. Krek 1979, 209.

13. Nicolay 1585, 130; Ghobrial 2005, 4–5.

14. Hacikyan 2000, 90n4.

15. Sanjian, Little, and Ottenbreit 2012; Sanjian 2014.

16. Lucaris's life is covered in Runciman 1968; R. J. Roberts 1967; Pektas 2014.

17. R. J. Roberts 1967, 13–43.

18. Ibid. In a letter dated February 22, 1627, Roe records helping Lucaris pass the books through customs.

19. Ibid., 30.

20. Runciman 1968, 272; Faroqhi 2000, 70.

21. Runciman 1968, 273.

22. Green 2009; Sabev 2007b, 316.

23. Rivlin and Szyliowicz 1965, 118. The equipment was given to Abgar Dpir, who used it to publish less-controversial Greek texts.

24. The Ottomans' "delay" in adopting print is often contrasted to their quick adoption of cannon and military machinery. See, for example, Coşgel, Thomas, and Rubin 2009. Yet no technology is purely utilitarian. All technologies are adopted and *applied*. Print adoption could just as easily be contrasted to ethnobotany or the guillotine.

25. Gdoura 1985, 99–97; Mukerji 2006, 655n2. Gdoura cites Michaud's *Biographie Universelle* (1841) as the source of this claim.

26. Ersoy 1959.

27. Firmin-Didot's reference to Sultan Bayezid in *Essai sur la typographie* is incredibly brief. His correspondence and letters written during his time in Constantinople may provide additional insight.

28. The bans are yet to be located, and their exact wording remains unknown. Turkish scholars began questioning the existence and veracity of the bans in the early twentieth century. The absence of the bans becomes especially conspicuous given the frequency with which they continue to be cited in scholarly literature. The alleged bans con-

tinue to provide the scaffolding for numerous studies of Arabic script and media. Citation trails, when they exist, typically point to Kut 1960. Kut wrote the article "Matba'a: In Turkey" for the first edition of Brill's *Encyclopedia of Islam,* and it has not been updated. The article does indeed mention the bans, but it references neither specific archival documents nor further studies.

29. Levey 1975, 57; Erünsal 2000.

30. S. E. Roberts 2013.

31. Frasca-Spada and Jardine 2000, 40–45.

32. S. E. Roberts 2013, 149. Guillaume Carousin's name is signed as "William" in English-language editions.

33. Ibid., 150–151.

34. Darnton 1982, 72–73.

35. Eisenstein 1979, 405.

36. Kreiser 2001, 13; Kunt 2008, 4–5; Erginbaş 2005, 14.

37. Kunt 2008.

38. Sarıcaoğlu and Yılmaz 2012, 160–163.

39. Ibid., 162.

40. Ibid., 164.

41. Unless otherwise stated, translations of *Vesiletü-t Tibaa* are taken or adapted from Christopher Murphy's English translation. Murphy 1995, 286–292.

42. Sabev 2004, 298.

43. Çelebi had risen through the ranks of the Twenty-Eighth Battalion of the Janissary corps. Thus, he received the titular epithet Yirmisekiz, or "Twenty-Eight," in Turkish.

44. Saint-Simon and St. John 1888.

45. Barber 1969, 8; 1986.

46. Morrison (2000, 23) describes Romain du Roi as "a complete break with the humanist calligraphic tradition." The typeface did not attempt to model the forms of handwritten lettering. The new system replaced organic principles with quantified proportions and rationalized aesthetics. According to Bringhurst (1997, 7.2.6:128), the letters were "dictated by an idea, not the truth of human anatomy."

47. Kunt 2008, 4; Berkes 1964, 34.

48. Sarıcaoğlu and Yılmaz 2012, 146. Ottoman patrons commonly drafted similar trade agreements. If the endeavor proved successful, the patrons would share in its glory; if things went awry, they could easily absolve themselves from direct involvement.

49. Necatioğlu 1982.

50. Haiman 1983.

51. Sabev 2007b, 297. In an interview with the author, Thomas Milo (2012) commented that Kis may have been a colleague or teacher of Ibrahim Müteferrika.

52. Kunt 2008. Kunt notes that Müteferrika follows the modern practice of citing other sources.

53. The translation is adapted from ibid.

54. Writers such as Polidoro Virgili (1470–1555) and Francis Bacon (1561–1626) advanced similar arguments on the benefits of printing during the sixteenth and early seventeenth centuries.

55. Murphy 1995, 286.

56. Ibid., 287.

57. Boogert 2005, 275.

58. Larsson 2011, 31.

59. Murphy 1995, 289.

60. Eisenstein 2005, 80–107.

61. Messick 1997, 300–301. Messick draws a distinction between person-to-person transmission of the Qur'an and the religious sciences and auxiliary sciences that do not follow such a model. Müteferrika asked to print only works of the second category.

62. Müteferrika's request for a religious *fatwa* resembles the process of requesting an imprimatur from the Catholic Church. Like an imprimatur, the *fatwa* and *ferman* do not specifically endorse the contents of the books to be published. They simply authorize their publication.

63. Skovgaard-Petersen 1997, 73.

64. Murphy 1995, 292.

65. Messick 1997, 308: "Correctors applied old scholarly skills to two new necessities of the print era, the standardization of language and the certification of accuracy in printed works."

66. Erginbaş 2005, 24.

67. According to François Baron de Tott, the Müteferrika press struggled because "printing could not express the varieties and niceties of [*naskh*] ligatures." Tott 1786, 147. See also Sabev 2007b, 318.

68. Berkes 1964, 198.

69. Shaw and Shaw 1976, 2:236; Sabev 2004; Erginbaş 2005, 13.

70. Carleson 1979, 21; Kreiser 2001, 14.

71. For foreigners such as Carleson, Jonah's name, Ashkenazi, identifies him as from Eastern or Central Europe, and thus a speaker of Yiddish (or Judeo-German). Brad Sabin Hill, curator of the I. Edward Kiev Judaica Collection at the George Washington University, Washington, DC, explicitly made this connection and drew it to my attention.

72. Bornstein-Makovetsky 2012. Interestingly, Bornstein-Makovetsky's article makes no mention of Jonah's alleged connection with Müteferrika.

73. Carleson 1979, 24.

74. Sarıcaoğlu and Yılmaz 2012, 150. Sarıcaoğlu and Yılmaz also provide a transcription of Ibrahim's original letter on page 361.

75. The partnership of Said Çelebi and Ibrahim Müteferrika received its authorizing *ferman* during the month of Dhu'l Ka'da in 1139 A.H. (July 1727 C.E.). Publication of the first book occurred during the month of Receb 1141 A.H. (February 1729 C.E.).

76. For a useful and brief bibliographic list of the press output, see Watson 1968. See also Kut and Türe 1996.

77. Sabev argues that comparisons between the Müteferrika print runs and European printers operating during the same period are faulty and suggests that Müteferrika's output be compared to the era of incunabula printing in Europe. Sabev 2007b, 304–305.

78. Abdulrazak (1990, 81–85) presents Katip Çelebi as an important influence on and intellectual predecessor to Ibrahim Müteferrika.

79. Sarıcaoğlu and Yılmaz 2012, 87.

80. Ibrahim's additions drew on Edmund Pourchot's Latin book *Institutiones Philosophicae* (1695). Ibrahim also translated *Harmonia Macrocosmica* (1660), the star atlas of Dutch

astronomer Andreas Cellarius, under the Turkish title *Mecmua-i Heyet-i Kadime ve Cedide.* Sarıcaoğlu and Yılmaz 2012, 98–99.

81. Ibid., 318.

82. Ibid., 94–96.

83. For extended discussion and a partial English-language translation of *Tarih-i Hind-i Garbi,* see Goodrich 1990.

84. Sarıcaoğlu and Yılmaz 2012, 236.

85. Erginbaş 2005, 38–39.

86. Berkes 1964, 46n37. The work may be based on William Whiston's 1719–1721 book *The Longitude and Latitude Found by the Inclinatory or Dipping Needle.*

87. Berkes 1964, 42–45; B. Lewis 1961, 47; Shaw and Shaw 1976, 237. Müteferrika's treatise was translated into French in 1761 under the title *Traite de la Tactique,* and it was later translated into German and Russian as well.

88. Berkes 1964, 43–44.

89. Sarıcaoğlu and Yılmaz 2012, 91.

90. Ibid., 74. What was being talked about was not Westernization but Islamic preservation.

91. Ibid., 339.

92. Ibid., 244. A book printed by Jonah and sons in 1740 is unique for displaying two words in Latin type. The book is *Privileǧos del poderozo rey Karlo,* and the words "in Constantinople" appear at the bottom of the title page. I am grateful to Brad Sabin Hill, curator of the I. Edward Kiev Judaica Collection at George Washington University, Washington, DC, for drawing to my attention Yerushalmi's study, in which the title page of the unique copy in the Harvard Library is reproduced. Yerushalmi 1971.

93. Sarıcaoğlu and Yılmaz 2012, 105. Yahya Erdem discovered a note by Langlès (1763–1824) in which he transcribed the opening page of the dictionary.

94. Nuhoğlu 2000, 85.

95. Sarıcaoğlu and Yılmaz 2012, 339.

96. Ayalon 2010b, 575–577. Government ventures mark most early ventures of Arabic printing in the Middle East. In Egypt, Muhammad Ali similarly followed suit when he founded the Egyptian El-Amiriya government press by political decree in 1820. The deployment of the Müteferrika press for state purposes, however, was much more limited in scope than European state presses of the same period.

97. The distinction between the "mode" of print and the "means" of print is borrowed from Hesse 1996.

5. Questions of Script Reform

1. Mahdi 1995, 6.

2. Comrie, Stone, and Polinsky 1996.

3. Fraktur, a variety of Latin black letter, was commonly used in northern Europe until the twentieth century. Initially, the German Nazi party promoted Fraktur as a display of the "true spirit of German soul." Later, in a push toward quicker and more legible communications, Fraktur was denounced in anti-Semitic terms as a vehicle preventing German advancement. Bain and Shaw 1998.

4. B. Anderson 1991.

5. Geoffrey Wheeler outlines four broad phases of modernization in the Muslim world: (1) the adoption of military and communication techniques, (2) partial reforms of medieval modes of government, (3) new Islamist movements, and (4) the open call to become "modern industrialized states." Wheeler 1974, 157.

6. Szyliowicz 1992, 252.

7. Shaw and Shaw 1976, 2:59–61. Secularization of society and the *millet* system was bolstered by the Reform Decree of 1856. Ibid., 2:123–136.

8. Strauss 2003. Istanbul-based presses continued to produce large quantities of materials in Greek, Armenian, Hebrew, Cyrillic, and Syriac during the eighteenth and nineteenth centuries.

9. Szyliowicz 1992, 253.

10. Gitelman 2013.

11. Berkes 1964, 171; Messick 1993, 54–58; Liebesny (1975, 65) describes the Ottoman Mecelle code as "Islamic in content but European in form."

12. Ertürk 2011.

13. Diringer 1968, 428: Whereas the alphabet followed religion, printing followed the flag. See also Deringil 1993.

14. B. Anderson 1991. Anderson highlights the importance of the printed newspaper in the creation of imagined national communities. Johannes Pedersen also notes the role that newspapers played in introducing readers in the Arabic world to printed versions of Arabic script. Pedersen 1984, 137.

15. McLuhan 1994, 212. McLuhan describes the newspaper as a "mosaic form" in which disparate texts are collected together within a homogeneous space. The shared space of a newspaper indexes the nation on any particular day.

16. Ertürk 2011, 35. Modern Arabic, however, unlike Turkish, remains intimately tied to the language of Qur'anic revelation. This posed a unique set of challenges for those wishing to modernize Arabic. Niloofar Haeri provides a series of pertinent questions that faced Arabic newspaper editors: Was Classical Arabic a language in which to give street addresses or advertisements? Was it an appropriate language for jokes? Could it present a weather report without appearing awkward? Haeri 2003, 73–74.

17. Mardin (1962, 252–275) discusses Şinasi's contributions to Turkish secularization and modernization.

18. G. L. Lewis 1999, 13; Ertürk 2011, 35. Ertürk describes the new language as "a simplified written register distinct from the lofty prose compositions of court literature."

19. Tansel 1953, 248.

20. Similar movements toward popular accessibility and textual modernization were afoot in the Ottoman Arabic Press. The Arabic printer Faris al-Shidyaq, a contemporary of Şinasi's, incorporated typographic features such as running page headers, tables of contents, title pages, publication information, errata pages, and wider margins to assist legibility. While working with the Church Missionary Society press in Malta, al-Shidyaq consulted on the design of an Arabic typeface. Roper 1995; Blair 2006, 604.

21. G. L. Lewis 1999, 5–26. See also Ertürk 2011; Seely 1998; Özmen 1968.

22. Ertürk 2011, 4.

23. Mardin 1961, 268–269.

24. Özmen 1968, 10.

25. Ertürk 2011, 10.

26. Kologlu 1992, 242. Kologlu notes that a Latin-based script was adopted for Albanian.

27. Berkes 1964, 196.

28. G. L. Lewis 1999, 32.

29. Acar 1999, 30n2: "nations which accepted Islam had to leave their own alphabets gradually and had to adapt their language within the limits of the Arabic [script], because the Koran was revealed in Arabic and written in Arabic."

30. G. L. Lewis 1999, 29.

31. In 1932, the first complete recitation of the Qur'an in Turkish translation occurred. And the call to prayer was required to be in Turkish until 1950. Ertürk 2011, 88n42; Seely (1968), 53.

32. B. Lewis 1961, 272. In 1927, the Soviet government announced plans to replace Arabic script with a Unified Latin Alphabet for phonetic representation of the languages spoken by Soviet Muslims. This announcement preceded Modern Turkey's adoption of Latin script, but Atatürk did not reference it in his speech. In 1940, the Soviets replaced Unified Latin with modified Cyrillic alphabets for the same languages. Wheeler 1974, 157–160.

33. Messick 1993, 24–32. Drawing on Derrida, Messick describes a particularly Islamic notion of "recitational logocentrism" in Yemen.

34. Seely 1968, 59.

35. Özmen 1968, 11.

36. Wheeler 1974, 158. The shift to Latin script realigned networks of education and textual exchange. With the adoption of the new orthography, Turkish students began studying in Europe rather than Egypt, Syria, and Persia. Seely 1968, 63.

37. As much as Arabic script may struggle with Turkish phonemes, this perceived weakness does not imply that Latin-derived letters are necessarily ideal. Germanus 1951, 13: "the absolute phonetic value of the Latin script is mere illusion." See also Al-Toma 1961, 407–408.

38. Levey 1975, 144.

39. Tracy (1975, 121) describes how simple the Arabic writing system is. The complexity lies with the typesetting, not the script itself.

40. Meynet 1971.

41. Nammour 2014, 44.

42. A frequently quoted aphorism states, "In the West, one reads in order to understand, but Arabic speakers must understand in order to read." Whereas readers of the Latin alphabet could voice written words directly in speech, Arabic readers required familiarity with a text in order to decipher words with proper vocalization marks. Hunziker 1985, 3; Al-Toma 1961, 405.

43. Haralambous 2006, 2.

44. Landau 2008, 185: "Romanization projects have generally been only one aspect of the drive towards modernization of national symbols and the increase of cultural receptivity. . . . To this are added specific arguments against continuing to use the old alphabets." The spread of Latin script demonstrates the colonial and geopolitical power of the states that employed it, rather than any inherent benefit in the script itself.

45. The Academy of Arabic Language in Cairo ultimately reviewed more than 250. It received 35 new submissions between 1958, the initial deadline, and 1960. Hunziker 1985, 16–17; Moginet 2009, 93; Nammour 2014, 48–51.

46. Hunziker 1985, 17; AbiFarès 2001, 73–74.

47. Nammour 2014, 50.

48. Yannis Haralambous has reconstructed and implemented three proposals submitted to the Cairo Academy using the OMEGA typesetting system: the seventy-two-form ACADEMY proposal of 1959, Ahmad Lakhdar's ASV-Codar system, and the Latin-script-inspired set of Yayha Boutemène. Haralambous 2006.

49. Landau 2008, 191. All the Turkic countries that successfully transitioned to Latin script (i.e., Turkey and the former Soviet Turkic republics) adopted "authoritarian methods" of enforcing script reform.

50. Nadim's sample sheet shows only the opening parenthesis and guillemet, and his list of numerals inadvertently omits the number 8.

51. Khattar was not the first to propose this strategy. Yusif Ghassub proposed a similar strategy in 1930. Al-Toma 1961, 409.

52. Nammour 2014, 14.

53. Ibid., 20.

54. Ibid., 16.

55. Ibid., 17

56. Ibid., 48–51.

57. Ibid., 88. Khattar filed his patent for an "Arabic Alphabet" on June 21, 1947, and received U.S. patent 157,982 on April 4, 1950. He also registered patents in Canada, France, Iran, India, Syria, and Egypt.

58. Khattar 1955.

59. Yara Khoury Nammour designates Khattar as a "typotect." She draws the term from Piet Zwart, who coined it as a combination of "typographer" and "architect." Typotects design textual spaces through which readers move. Nammour 2014, 71.

60. Hunziker 1985, 18.

61. Al-Toma 1961, 413.

62. Hunziker 1985, 20. Hunziker provided training for type designers and prepared Arabic fonts for the workshop, while Stefan Moginet demonstrated commercial and industrial uses of the ASV-Codar system. Moginet's notes and examples from the workshop may have formed the foundation of his book *Writing Arabic: From Script to Type* (2009).

63. Moginet 2009, 96–101, contains examples of the ASV-Codar system in use.

64. In Arabic scribal practice, a horizontal extension between connecting letters is referred to as *kashidah.*

65. Critics were quick to dismiss Fahmi's suggestions as a practical improvement with regard to low rates of Arabic literacy. For an article written by one of Fahmi's contemporaries, who specifically criticized the proposal, see Germanus 1951.

66. Haralambous 2006, 11.

67. Derrida 1976, 89: "Every graphic form may have a double value—ideographic and phonetic."

68. Abu-Shayeb 2005.

69. The Armani company employs a similar strategy for branding its logo across scripts. The undotted letter j of the Latin typeface used for Armani's primary logo forms the Arabic letter *rā'* in the company's Arabic logo.

70. The bold modern design of the Ahmad font spread quickly, often through piracy and unauthorized duplication. Arabic font choices were extremely limited in the early 1990s, and Ahmad offered a novel aesthetic choice that departed from more traditional, and clunky, alternatives. Humeid 2005, minute 18; AbiFarès 2001, 209.

71. Yaghan 2008.

72. Shrivtiel 1998.

73. Al-Toma 1961, 408.

74. Strikingly similar rhetoric, in which a "backward"-looking Islamic and Arab world confronts the future-oriented West, remains a powerful and frequently repeated trope of twenty-first-century cultural and political battles.

75. Humeid 2005.

76. Shaw 2012, 23–24.

77. Ingold 2007, 124.

78. Messick 1997, 309. Cf. Shaw 2012, 24: "Lithography accommodates the full range of Arabic cursive connections and stylistic variety, something which typography could never achieve."

79. Scribes who learned to write in reverse quickly overcame the issue of printing in mirror image. Mirror-image writing was also a popular trick of calligraphic skill, as exemplified in Turkey by Mustafa Rakim. The nineteenth century saw a rise in the popularity of mirror writing. This rise may be related to the development of mirror writing in support of lithography, which spread across the Islamic world during the same period.

80. Senefelder 1819, 65. Senefelder suggested that the new method might be useful for reproducing musical notation. Western musical notation requires a large set of complex ligatures that relate vertically as well as horizontally. Musical notation, like Arabic, is a complex script, and it did not transfer to movable type. See also Proudfoot 1997, 173.

81. Proudfoot 1997, 179.

82. Ibid., 164.

83. Marzolph 2007, 206–210.

84. Ibid.; Proudfoot 1997, 165.

85. Bringhurst 1997, 7.3.3: 138–139: "With the development of lithography, at the end of the eighteenth century, printing moved another step back toward the two-dimensional world of the medieval scribe."

86. Hirsch 1978.

87. Kreiser 2001.

88. Proudfoot 1997, 172; 1995, 217.

89. Proudfoot 1997, 165.

90. In Eurocentric histories of print, lithography is often positioned as an extension of the already apparent benefits of movable type printing. Lithography assisted multicolor printing, which had significant influence, for example, on advertising design and picture books.

91. Green 2009.

92. Skovgaard-Petersen 1997, 76; Ayalon 2010b.

93. Lunde 1981.

94. Notable exceptions include the first Qur'an printed in Tehran in 1826 and the al-Azhar Qur'an of 1924, both of which were set with movable type. The first of these is covered in Marzolph 2007. For extensive discussion of the latter, see Suit 2014, 73–106.

95. Messick 1997, 310.

96. Berkes 1964, 195n59.

97. Schimmel 1994, 154; Acar 1999, 197.

98. Kreiser 2001, 15.

99. Stanley 2004.

100. For a recent printing of Ali's book, see A. Y. Ali 1982.

101. A. Y. Ali 1982, iv. See also Blair 2006, 31–33.

102. Sproat 2010.

103. The incredibly brief account of Linotype in the current book cannot do justice to the influence that Linotype and similar machines exerted on non-Latin scripts. For a wonderful and thoroughly researched presentation of these changes, see Ross 1999, especially chaps. 8–10. Discussing Linotype on page 144 of that book, Ross writes: "The keying method indubitably governed the design of the characters. Its size determined the number of sorts, and thereby the fount conspectus. Its manner of composition, in this case linear, affected the actual shape of the letterforms, as well as their spacing, which was also governed by the channel sizes. Conversely, the layout itself was determined by the widths of some of the typeforms occasioning cross-lugging, where due to the excessive width of a character the adjacent sort needed to be narrow. . . . Duplexing also required letterforms occupying the same channel to be identical width. Channel positions were therefore crucial to matrix manufacture. In short, *until the keyboard was conceived at least in draft form, no artwork should be designed; until it was completed, no fount could be manufactured.*" Emphasis added.

6. Arabic Script on Computers

1. Cf. Blair 2006, 608: "Many of these modernist attempts at systems of printing Arabic [e.g., reformed or simplified Arabic script] were rendered moot by the advent of digital technology." A similar claim is made in Nammour 2014, 20.

2. Tracy 1975, 122–125.

3. Moran 1960; Ross 1999, 180. See also Moholy-Nagy 1946.

4. Bringhurst 1997, 7.3.3: 138–139: "Since the middle of the twentieth century, most commercial printing has been by two-dimensional means. The normal method is offset photolithography."

5. Warde 1963. For discussion of these implications on the design and printing of non-Latin scripts, see Ross 1999, chapters 10 and 11.

6. J. Lewis 1963, 68.

7. Tracy 1975, 125: "The benefits are of the same kind as those achieved, for instance, by the Linotype-Paul 505C mathematics program."

8. One of the Mac's innovations, which attracted designers and artists, was the replacement of horizontal pixels with square pixels. Hertzfeld and Capps 2005, 32–33.

9. Drucker 2013, 79: "The choice of what to store—a glyph outline, curves and points, or a pile pattern—had consequences at every step of the font's life cycle."

10. Ross 1999, 197: "The trueness of the digital output to the original letter-drawing depended, to some extent, on the nature of the design, but it also relied on the resolution of the machine, and the size of its writing spot [or pixels]."

11. The binary sequence is usually transcribed from right to left, the same direction as the Latin alphabet.

12. ASCII contains only 2^7 or 128 distinct code points rather than 2^8 or 256, because only 7 bits of the 8-bit byte were originally used to encode characters. The eighth bit served as a parity bit for error detection. If the total arrived at by adding the other 7 bits equaled an odd number, the parity bit was 1. If the total was even, the parity bit was 0. This was a simple check that reduced the chance of transmission error by 50 percent. Improvements in memory and transmission allowed 8-bit encoding schemes to utilize the entire range of 256 code points.

13. Accented letters, like scripts, are powerful ethnic and cultural symbols. When the European community sought to remove the "ñ" key from keyboards distributed in Spain, Gabriel García Márquez fired back: "The 'ñ' is not an archaeological piece of junk, but just the opposite: a cultural leap of a Romance language that left the others behind in expressing with only one letter a sound that other languages continue to express with two." Rojo 2007.

14. Hence the need for an "escape" character, which escaped the current scheme.

15. ISO 2022 was based on ECMA-35, an earlier standard published by the European Computer Manufacturers Association (ECMA) in 1971.

16. Latin script was encoded by a variety of ISO 8859 schemes, divided by region and language: Western European, Eastern European, Southern European, Northern European, and, later, Turkish, Baltic, and Celtic.

17. The Iran System Corporation also created a distinct encoding scheme specifically for Persian-language support.

18. Boutros 2005, 50. Macintosh computers incorporated Diwan, an Arabic system initially designed by an independent company for the Apple II in 1982. Diwan included a word processor and four specially designed fonts for screen and laser printing.

19. *The Unicode Standard 7.0*, 4; cf. *The Unicode Standard 1.0*, 1.

20. Gillam 2003, 7; John 2013, 326–327.

21. *The Unicode Standard 1.0;* "What Is Unicode?" (Unicode.org).

22. UTF-32 only uses 21 of the 32 available bits, the rest of the bits are padded with zeros.

23. *The Unicode Standard, Version 7.0* includes a total of 137,468 private-use code points. In addition to the 6,400 private-use points located in Unicode's Basic Multilingual Plane (BMP), another 131,068 points are available for private use outside the BMP. *The Unicode Standard 7.0*, 3.

24. Unicode characters can be represented in one of three encoding forms: a 32-bit form (UTF-32), a 16-bit form (UTF-16), and an 8-bit form (UTF-8). UTF-16, which is optimized for characters in the Basic Multilingual Plane (BMP) forms the basis for the subsequent examples in this chapter. For an explanation of why the multiple forms were adopted, see Gillam 2003, 80–81. For instructions on converting across the three forms, see Comstock 2011.

25. *The Unicode Standard 7.0*, 15.

26. Gillam 2003, 62–64.

27. *Lām-alif* (U+FEFB) is also encoded as a distinct Unicode character in the Arabic Presentation Forms-A Block.

28. Gillam 2003, 21.

29. Details of Unicode's allocation of code points can be found in section 2.9 of the Unicode Standard. *The Unicode Standard 7.0*, 48–52.

30. Ibid., 29–30.

31. Ibid., 353. Phoenician Script is encoded in Middle East -II: Ancient Scripts, which also includes the Old North Arabian, Old South Arabian, Imperial Aramaic, Manichaean, Pahlavi and Parthian, Avestan, Nabatean, and Palmyrene scripts.

32. For examination of the ways in which Arabic script adapted to the representation of African languages, see Mumin and Versteegh 2014.

33. Unlike Latin letters, individual strokes of CJK ideographs are also coded separately for specific semantic uses such as indexing. And a Unicode mechanism exists for describing the stroke characters that construct ideographic characters. *The Unicode Standard 7.0*,708, 891–898.

34. Ibid., 800.

35. The encoding width, however, is non-zero. The zero-width non-joiner and the zero-width joiner are encodes like any other Unicode character with a fixed width of 16 bits.

36. These characters can also influence the cursivity of non-Arabic scripts, including Latin script typefaces such as Newlywed script and Zapfin.

37. John 2013, 324.

38. UAX#9 annex specifies fourteen different types of directionality in addition to over-ride characters and code points that reference explicit directional formatting. Gillam 2003, 223–238; Davis 2014.

39. Collections of *nuqta* are encoded as separate characters in the unfavored block of Arabic Presentation Forms.

40. Nemeth 2008, 18.

41. *The Unicode Standard 7.0*, 14.

42. Unicode encodes all Arabic diacritics and vocalization marks, including specialty marks necessary for the representation of the Qur'an. These modifying marks are displayed in the Unicode charts by a dotted circle and the relative location of the character's glyph. *Fathah* (U+064E), for example, is shown in the charts above a dotted circle. This indicates that placement of *fathah* is rendered above the glyph of the modified letter.

43. *The Unicode Standard 7.0*, 362.

44. Choueiry (2009) advises that adapting Latin forms is a good starting point for beginning Arabic font designers. Designing a font from scratch requires a greater degree of typographic expertise.

45. Google Noto Fonts are a recent entry into these discussions. The name Noto is from "not more tofu," with "tofu" referring to the empty boxes displayed by a computer when it does not have the required Unicode glyph. Noto aims to "support all languages with a harmonious look and feel." Google, Inc. 2014.

46. Khera 2003. For discussion and analysis of the design of Frutiger, see Osterer and Stamm 2014.

47. Papazian 2004, 15. For thoughtful reflection on various methods of harmonizing Arabic script and Latin script, see Nemeth 2006.

48. AbiFarès 2007.

49. Ibid., 19.

50. Ibid., 21.

51. Ibid., 17. The term "Dutch flavor" references both the technical proficiency of contemporary Dutch design and the long history of Dutch designers working with Arabic script typography.

52. Ibid., 114–117: Chahine and Unger's original concept was to design an Arabic companion for the Latin font Capitolium. Outside of the Typographic Matchmaking project, Chahine has also worked on Arabic extensions of Frutiger, Palatino, and the calligraphic Latin typeface Zapfino.

53. Ibid., 2007, 21–22.

54. The Typographic Matchmaking character set did not support Urdu, nor did it support any of the Arabic script languages covered by Unicode's Arabic Supplement and Arabic Extended blocks.

55. Typeset polyglot and polyscript Bibles, for example, were printed as early as the sixteenth century.

56. Dixon 2012.

57. AbiFarès 2007, 42.

58. Nemeth 2006, 6–7.

59. Alternatively, if visual sizing is matched, the line spacing, or leading, of the Latin text appears exaggerated.

60. Microsoft Arabic Typesetting adopted the opposite approach. Nemeth (2006, 10) quotes John Hudson and Mamoun Sakkal, who designed Microsoft's Arabic Typesetting typeface: "In designing typefaces with coordinated Arabic and Latin scripts, the trend has been to adjust the Arabic proportions to match the Latin. In Arabic Typesetting, we tried for the first time to design the Latin to match the Arabic by providing longer ascenders and descenders, and reducing the impact of capital letters since Arabic does not have such a feature."

61. AbiFarès 2007, 32.

62. The list includes four, rather than five, fonts because the process of designing TheMix Arabic was quite different from the other four.

63. For the complete set of designed characters, see AbiFarès 2007, appendix B, 170–172.

64. Ibid., 168–169.

65. Ibid., 131.

66. Ibid., 100. The quote is from Fred Smeijers, the Dutch partner on the team that designed the Fresco Arabic font.

67. Ibid., 101. The quote is from Lara Assouad, the Arabic partner on the team that designed the Fresco Arabic font.

68. Ross 1999, 48. During the era of movable type, printers paired foreign typesetting expertise with local linguistic and scribal knowledge.

69. AbiFarès 2007, 163.

70. Ibid., 8.

71. Ibid., 7. Per the project's subtitle, "Building cultural bridges with typeface design."

72. Ibid., 15.

73. Ibid., 12. AbiFarès insightfully notes that "the internet has returned textual information to its front-row importance" after twentieth-century challenges to textual dominance in the form of audiovisual media.

74. Ibid., 11.

75. Ibid., 13.

76. Ibid., 14–15.

77. Milo 2016b: "The origin of the project was the urgent need in 1981 to produce a phrase book and grammar of the lightly-documented South Lebanese Arabic dialect for Dutch UNIFIL troops. Even with a good budget, the typographic industry was unable to provide a product that matched everyday Middle Eastern practice. This observation eventually led to a solution (in 1985, too late for the Lebanese manual and too early for the industry to be understood), based on principles outlined by Pierre MacKay (combining authoritative script expertise with a minimal set of composition elements) and T. F. Mitchell's *Writing Arabic: A Practical Introduction to Ruqʿah Script* (which is in fact the only known 'script grammar' to date of any Islamic script). The resulting technology was therefore initially based on the requirements for *ruqʿah*, not *naskh*—and certainly not simplified *naskh*."

78. Ibid.: "In the early 1990s Microsoft considered this novel technology for the emerging Windows platform, but found it too complicated and invited DecoType to make a simplified *naskh* typeface instead. This typeface became the now ubiquitous DecoType Naskh in Windows. In second instance, DecoType were invited to turn the *ruqʿah* machine into an Object Linking and Embedding (OLE) server for MS Office. Subsequently, the Arab MS team urged DecoType to tackle *naskh* in the same manner, with another OLE server as a result. This script-grammar inspired *naskh* typeface has been developed and expanded ever since. After a comprehensive overhaul and technical redesign, it was deployed as the typeface of choice for the Omani web Qur'an."

79. Ibid.

80. Ibid. ACE's handling of *nastaʾliq* addresses "the extraordinary challenges of full Unicode coverage, correct and exhaustive *kashidah* handling and, the most difficult of all, kerning." Milo 2016b.

81. Nemeth 2008, 18.

82. Gruendler 2012, 101; Daniels 2014, 30.

83. Mumin 2014, 59.

84. Nemeth 2008, 14.

85. Milo 2016a.

86. These new letters occur in languages as diverse as Persian, Urdu, Kurdish, Pashto, Sindhi, Hausa, Bosnian, Saraiki, Kalami, Ormuri, and Shina.

87. Celebrated typographer Robert Bringhurst describes the DecoType system as "a wonderful tool for [typesetting classical] work. [The ACE-driven *naskh* typeface] is based on a very close and careful study of classical Arabic script. At the same time, it's a modern tool—an extremely sophisticated piece of applied analysis. . . . It approaches typography as digital calligraphy—and with Arabic, that is a very productive approach. It restores diplomatic relations between the present and the past." Bringhurst does not suggest typesetting the poems of Michelangelo or the plays of Shakespeare in a modernist sans-serif font such as Helvetica and Univers. Nor would he suggest typesetting classical Arabic without the affordances of ACE technology: "When we edit and typeset works of the European Renaissance

or Baroque, we meet them part way. When we edit and typeset works of classical Arabic, Persian, or Turkish literature, we need to do the same." Bringhurst 2010.

88. For an example of the note, see Fudge 2016, 399.

89. Mahdi 1995, 4.

90. The award was named after its first recipient, Dr. Peter Karow, who developed the Ikarus typography software. Milo was the second recipient of the award for pioneering the concept of smart font technology. Donald Knuth, who developed TEX and Metafont, was the third recipient for pioneering digital methods of line and page layout.

91. Gillam (2003, 52–53) details five levels of abstraction that occur in the digital coding of characters. All the levels occur on the computational backstage and have little direct bearing on the visual design of perceivable glyphs.

92. *The Unicode Standard 7.0*, 19.

93. Milo 2011, 245: "For the foreseeable future our world will be multilingual, exactly *because* of the Internet."

94. Jules-Rosette 1990, 101: "Computers recode cultural expression and social activity. This modeling process occurs in at least three ways with relationship to computers. (1) The computer operates with a fixed program or coded text into which information (a natural language) is entered. (2) The computer, including its hardware and software, constitute a macrostructure about which discourse is developed. (3) The entire narrative program of computer adoption is a structure within which process of technological change are reflected." Consideration of Arabic script alters debates at all three levels: (1) the character-glyph coding model of the Unicode Standard; (2) discourses surrounding the digital representation of scripts and writing systems; and (3) the application and global adoption of programs that support non-Latin scripts.

Coda

1. Dodd 2006, 172.

2. Milo 2016a.

3. Lupton 2014, 165.

4. Marks 2011, 319.

5. Ross 2012, 125.

6. John 2013, 332.

7. Nemeth 2006, 5.

8. Ross 1999, 222.

9. Tracy 1975, 125.

10. Knuth 1986b. Drucker (2013, 83–85) examines the "metaphysical" and philosophical implications of Knuth's software.

11. Fahmy 2006. Hossam Fahmy's AlQalam system applies TeX to assist complex Arabic typesetting, with a specific focus on accurate Qur'anic representation. Fahmy subsequently applied Knuth's MetaFont language to parameterize Arabic fonts. MetaFont, like DecoType's ACE, models pen strokes rather than complete characters. Fahmy 2007.

12. Rich text is also referred to as "styled text," "formatted text," and "fancy text."

13. *The Unicode Standard 7.0*, 19.

14. Abulhab (2006) suggests that only *naskh* is a purely "Arabic" script, while both *nasta'liq* and *naskh* are "Arabetic" scripts.

15. *The Unicode Standard 7.0,* 737.

16. Bolter 2001, 48.

17. The term "design writing" is borrowed from V. Kirschenbaum 2005. Similar ideas are expressed in Heim 1999, xviii, and Bolter 2001, 23.

18. Heim 1999, *E45*: "The words on the computer screen are illuminated, charged phosphorescently, and glow from within. The word obtains a new kind of power in the electric element."

BIBLIOGRAPHY

Abbott, Nabia. 1939a. "The Contribution of Ibn Muklah to the North-Arabic Script." *American Journal of Semitic Languages and Literatures* 56(1): 70–83.

————. 1939b. *The Rise of the North Arabic Script and Its Kur'ânic Development, with a Full Description of the Kur'ân Manuscripts in the Oriental Institute.* Chicago: University of Chicago Press.

Abdel-Hakeem, M. A. S. 1994. "Qur'ānic Orthography: The Written Representation of the Recited Text of the Qur'ān." *Islamic Quarterly* 38(3): 171–192.

Abdel-Malek, Kamal, and Wael Hallaq, eds. 2000. *Tradition, Modernity, and Postmodernity in Arabic Literature: Essays in Honor of Professor Issa J. Boullata.* Boston: Brill.

Abdulrazak, Fawzi A. 1990. "The Kingdom of the Book: The History of Printing as an Agency of Change in Morocco between 1865 and 1912." Ph.D. diss., Boston University.

AbiFarès, Huda Smitshuijzen. 1998. "Arabic Type: A Challenge for the 2nd Millennium." *Baseline International TypoGraphics Magazine* 26.

————. 2001. *Arabic Typography: A Comprehensive Sourcebook.* London: Saqi.

————, ed. 2007. *Typographic Matchmaking: Building Cultural Bridges with Typeface Design.* Amsterdam: BIS Publishers & Khatt Foundation.

————. 2008. "Arabic Type as Cultural Identity." In *Printing and Publishing in the Middle East: Papers from the Second Symposium on the History of Printing and Publishing in the Languages and Countries of the Middle East, Bibliothèque nationale de France, Paris . . . 2005. Contributions au deuxième colloque sur l'Histoire de l'imprimé dans les langues et les pays du Moyen Orient, Bibliothèque nationale de France, Paris . . . 2005 (Journal of Semitic Studies Supplement, 24),* edited by Philip Sadgrove, 233–239. Oxford: Oxford University Press.

————. 2011. *Typographic Matchmaking in the City.* Amsterdam, Netherlands: Khatt Foundation.

Abulhab, Saad D. 2006. "Typography: Behind the Arabetic Calligraphic Veil." *Visible Language* 40.3: 294–307.

Abu-Shayeb, Zuhair. 2005. Interview with author. August 27. Amman, Jordan.

Acar, M. Şinasi. 1999. *Turk Hat Sanati: Araç, Gereç, and Formlar (Turkish Calligraphy: Materials, Tools, and Forms)*. Istanbul, Turkey: Antik, A.S.

Akbar, Ali. 2015. "The Influence of Ottoman Qur'ans in Southeast Asia through the Ages." In *Proceedings of the British Academy 200: From Anatolia to Aceh: Ottomans, Turks, and Southeast Asia)*, edited by Andrew Peacock and Annabel Teh Gallop, 311–334. Oxford: Oxford University Press.

Al-Bagdadi, Nadia. 2005. "From Heaven to Dust: Metamorphosis of the Book in Premodern Arab Culture." *Medieval History Journal* 8(1): 83–107.

Albin, Michael W. 1993. "Early Arabic Printing: A Catalogue of Attitudes." *Manuscripts of the Middle East: The Role of the Book in the Civilizations of the Near East* 5: 114–122.

———. 1995. "The Book in the Islamic World: A Selective Bibliography." In *The Book in the Islamic World: The Written Word and Communication in the Middle East*, edited by George N. Atiyeh, 273–282. Albany: State University of New York Press.

al-Faruqi, Isma'il Raji, and Lois Lamya al-Faruqi. 1986. *The Cultural Atlas of Islam*. New York: Macmillan.

Ali, Abdullah Yusuf, trans. 1982. *The Holy Qur-an: Text, Translation & Commentary*. Lahore, Pakistan: Sh. Muhammad Ashraf. First published in 1938.

Ali, Wijdan. 1996. *What Is Islamic Art?* Mafraq, Jordan: Al-Bayt University Press.

———. 1997. *Modern Islamic Art: Development and Continuity*. Gainesville: University Press of Florida.

———. 2005. Interview with author. August 25. Amman, Jordan.

Allehaiby, Wid H. 2013. "Arabizi: An Analysis of the Romanization of the Arabic Script from a Sociolinguistic Perspective." *Arab World English Journal* 4(3): 52–62.

Alnadji, Khaled. 2001. "Reforming Arabic Calligraphy for Computer Art and Design in Kuwaiti Art Education." Ph.D. diss., Pennsylvania State University.

Alparslan, Ali. 1960. "Khatt." In *The Encyclopedia of Islam*, 4:1122–1126. Leiden: Brill.

———. 2002. "The Art of Calligraphy in the Turkish World." In *The Turks*, edited by Hasan Celâl Güzel, C. Cem Oğuz, and Osman Karatay, 4:25–32. Ankara, Turkey: Yeni Türkiye Publications.

———. 2003. "The Art of Calligraphy and the Ottomans." In *Ottoman Civilization*, edited by Halil Inalcik and Günsel Rend, 2:824–839. Istanbul, Turkey: Republic of Turkey, Ministry of Culture.

Alphabetum Arabicum. 1592. Rome: Tipographia Medicea.

Al-Toma, Salih J. 1961. "The Arabic Writing System and Proposals for Its Reform." *Middle East Journal* 15(4): 403–515.

Anderson, Benedict. 1991. *Imagined Communities: Reflections on the Origin and Spread of Nationalism*. New York: Verso.

Anderson, Donald M. 1992. *Calligraphy: The Art of Written Forms*. New York: Dover.

Antoon, Sinan. 2007. *I'jaam: An Iraqi Rhapsody*. San Francisco: City Lights Publishers.

Asad, Talal. 1986. *The Idea of an Anthropology of Islam*. Washington, DC: Center for Contemporary Arab Studies, Georgetown University.

———. 2003. *Formations of the Secular: Christianity, Islam, Modernity*. Palo Alto, CA: Stanford University Press.

Atıl, Esin. 1987. *The Age of Sultan Süleyman the Magnificent.* Washington, DC: National Gallery of Art.

Atiyeh, George N., ed. 1995a. *The Book in the Islamic World: The Written Word and Communication in the Middle East.* Albany: State University of New York Press.

———. 1995b. "The Book in the Modern Arab World: The Cases of Lebanon and Egypt." In *The Book in the Islamic World: The Written Word and Communication in the Middle East,* edited by George N. Atiyeh, 233–254. Albany: State University of New York Press.

Avakian, H. A. 1978. "Islam and the Art of Printing." *Uit bibliotheektuin en informatieveld,* 256–269. Utrecht. Reprinted in *The History of the Book in the Middle East,* edited by Geoffrey Roper, 407–420. Surrey, England: Ashgate.

Ayalon, Ami. 1995. *The Press in the Arab Middle East: A History.* New York: Oxford University Press, 1995.

———. 2010a. "Arab Booksellers and Bookshops in the Age of Printing, 1850–1914." *British Journal of Middle Eastern Studies* 37(1): 73–93. Reprinted in *The History of the Book in the Middle East,* edited by Geoffrey Roper, 277–298. Surrey, England: Ashgate.

———. 2010b. "The Press and Publishing." In *The New Cambridge History of Islam.* Vol. 6, *Muslims and Modernity: Culture and Society since 1800,* edited by Robert W. Hefner, 572–596. Cambridge: Cambridge University Press.

Ayvazoğlu, Beşir. 2000. "A Review of the Ottoman World Aesthetic." In *The Great Ottoman-Turkish Civilization,* edited by Kemal Çiçek, 4:263–272. Ankara, Turkey: Yeni Türkiye Publications.

Babinger, Franz. 1919. *Stambuler Buchwesen im 18. Jahrhundert.* Leipzig, Germany: Deutscher Verein für Buchwesen und Schrifttum.

Baer, Eva. 2004. *The Human Figure in Islamic Art: Inheritances and Islamic Transformations.* Bibliotheca Iranica. Islamic Art and Architecture Series. Vol. 11. Costa Mesa, CA: Mazda Publishers.

Bagheri, Mohammad. 1998. "Siyaqāt Accounting: Its Origin, History and Principles." *Acta Orientalia Academiae Scientiarum Hungaricae* 51(3): 297–301.

Bain, Peter, and Paul Shaw, eds. 1998. *Blackletter: Type and National Identity.* New York: Princeton Architectural Press.

Baker, Colin F. 2007. *Qur'an Manuscripts: Calligraphy, Illumination, Design.* London: British Library.

Balagna, Josée. 1984. *L'imprimerie arabe en occident (XVIe, XVIIe et XVIIIe siècles).* Paris: Maisonneuve & Larose.

Barber, Giles. 1969. *French Letterpress Printing: A List of French Printing Manuals and Other Texts in French Bearing on the Technique of Letterpress Printing, 1567–1900.* Oxford: Oxford Bibliographical Society.

———. 1986. "Martin-Dominique Fertel and His *Science pratique de l'imprimerie, 1723.*" *The Library: Transactions of the Bibliographic Society* s6–8(1): 1–17.

Bauer, Thomas. 1996. "Arabic Writing." In *The World's Writing Systems,* edited by Peter Daniels and William Bright, 559–564. New York: Oxford University Press.

Bayar, Abdelouahad, and Khalid Sami. 2009. "How a Font Can Respect Basic Rules of Arabic Calligraphy." *International Arab Journal of E-Technology* 1(1): 1–18.

Beheri, Muhammad. 2005. Interview with author. August 24. Amman, Jordan.

Bell, Hazel K. 2001. *Indexers and Indexes in Fact and Fiction.* Toronto, ON, Canada: University of Toronto Press.

Benjamin, Walter. 2008. *The Work of Art in the Age of Its Mechanical Reproducibility, and Other Writings on Media.* Edited by Michael W. Jennings, Brigid Doherty, and Thomas Y. Levin. Cambridge, MA: The Belknap Press of Harvard University.

Berk, Süleyman. 2003. *Hattat Mustafa Rakim Efendi.* Istanbul, Turkey: Kaynak Kitaplığı Yayınları.

Berkes, Niyazi. 1964. *The Development of Secularism in Turkey.* Montreal, QC, Canada: McGill University Press.

Berque, Jacques. 1995. "The Koranic Text: From Revelation to Compilation." In *The Book in the Islamic World: The Written Word and Communication in the Middle East,* edited by George N. Atiyeh, 17–32. Albany: State University of New York Press.

Berry, John. 2012. "Afterword: The Shapes of Language." In *Non-Latin Scripts: From Metal to Digital Type,* edited by Fiona Ross and Graham Shaw, 155–156. London: St. Bride Library.

Berry, John D., ed. 2002. *Language, Culture, Type: International Type Design in the Age of Unicode.* New York: Association Typographique Internationale (ATypI).

Bierman, Irene. 1998. *Writing Signs: The Fatamid Public Text.* Berkeley: University of California Press.

Bigelow, Charles, and Kristen Holmes. 1993. "The Design of a Unicode Font." *Electronic Publishing* 6(3): 999–1015.

Birnbaum, Eleazar, et al. 1989. *From Manuscript to Printed Book in the Islamic World: Catalogue of an Exhibition at the Thomas Fisher Rare Book Library.* Toronto, ON, Canada: University of Toronto Press.

Black, M. H. 1963. "The Printed Bible." In *The Cambridge History of the Bible,* edited by S. L. Greenslade, 3:408–475. Cambridge: Cambridge University Press.

Blair, Sheila S. 2006. *Islamic Calligraphy.* Edinburgh: Edinburgh University Press.

Blair, Sheila, and Jonathan Bloom. 2000. *Islam: A Thousand Years of Faith and Power.* New York: TV Books.

Bloom, Jonathan M. 2001. *Paper before Print: The History and Impact of Paper in the Islamic World.* New Haven, CT: Yale University Press.

Bobzin, Hartmut. 1999. "Between Imitation and Imagination: The Beginnings of Arabic Typography." Lecture given at the Orient-Institut Beirut in 1997. 2nd ed. Beirut, Lebanon.

———. 2002. "From Venice to Cairo: On the History of Arabic Editions of the Koran (16th–Early 20th Century)." In *Middle Eastern Languages and the Print Revolution: A Cross-Cultural Encounter,* edited by Eva Hanebutt-Benz, Dagmar Glass, and Geoffrey Roper, 151–176. Westhofen, Germany: WVA-Verlag Skulima.

Bolter, Jay David. 2001. *Writing Space: The Computer, Hypertext, and the History of Writing.* 2nd ed. Mahwah, NJ: Lawrence Erlbaum Associates.

Bolter, Jay David, and Richard Grusin. 1999. *Remediation: Understanding New Media.* Cambridge, MA: MIT Press.

Boogert, Maurits H. van den. 2005. "The Sultan's Answer to the Medici Press? Ibrahim Müteferrika's Printing House in Istanbul." In *The Republic of Letters and the Levant,* edited by Alastair Hamilton, Maurits H. van den Boogert, and Bart Westerweel, 265–291. Leiden: Brill.

Bornstein-Makovetsky, Leah. 2010. "Ashkenazi, Jonah ben Jacob." In *Encyclopedia of Jews in the Islamic World,* executive editor Norman A. Stillman, 4:271–272. Leiden: Brill.

Boullatta, Kamal. 2000. "Visual Thinking and the Arab Semantic Memory." In *Tradition, Modernity, and Postmodernity in Arabic Literature: Essays in Honor of Professor Issa J. Boullata,* edited by Kamal Abdel-Malek and Wael Hallaq, 284–303. Boston: Brill.

Boutros, Mourad. 2005. *Arabic for Designers.* London: Mark Batty Publisher.

Boutros, Mourad, et al. 2009. *Talking about Arabic.* London: Mark Batty Publisher.

Bowker, Geoffrey, and Susan Leigh Star. 1999. *Sorting Things Out: Classification and Its Consequences.* Cambridge, MA: MIT Press.

Brend, Barbara. 2003. *Perspectives on Persian Painting: Illustrations to Amīr Khusrau's Khamsah.* London: Routledge.

Breydenbach, Bernhard von. 1488. *Des sainctes peregrinations de Iherusalem.* Lyons: Michel Topié and Jacques Heremberck.

Bringhurst, Robert. 1997. *The Elements of Typographic Style.* 2nd ed. Vancouver: Hartley & Marks, Publishers.

———. 2010. "Robert Bringhurst and Arabic Typography." Saint-Martin-le-Vinoux, France: WinSoft International.

Brown, Norman O. 1983. "The Apocalypse of Islam." *Social Text* 8: 155–171.

Bulliet, Richard W. 1987. "Medieval Arabic *Tarsh:* A Forgotten Chapter in the History of Printing." *Journal of the American Oriental Society* 107(3): 427–438.

Burckhardt, Titus. 1976. *Art of Islam: Language and Meaning.* London: World of Islam Festival Trust Publishing.

Carey, James. 1989. *Communication as Culture.* New York: Routledge.

Carleson, Edvard. 1979. *İbrahim Müteferrika Basımevi ve bastığı ilk eserler (Ibrahim Müteferrika's Printing House and Its First Printed Works).* Edited by Mustafa Akbulut. Ankara, Turkey: Türk Kütüphaneciler Derenği.

Carter, Thomas Francis. 1955. *The Invention of Printing in China and Its Spread Westward.* 2nd ed. New York: L. C. Goodrich.

Chartier, Roger. 1995. *Forms and Meanings: Texts, Performances, and Audiences from Codex to Computer.* Philadelphia: University of Pennsylvania Press.

Chiarello, Mark, and Todd Klein. *The DC Comics Guide to Coloring and Lettering Comics.* New York: Watson-Guptill.

Choueiry, Halim. 2009. "Teaching Arabic Type Design in a Global Context." In *Talking about Arabic,* by Mourad Boutros et al., 18–25. London: Mark Batty Publisher.

Clanchy, Michael T. 1979. *From Memory to Written Record: England 1066–1307.* London: Edward Arnold.

Clogg, Richard. 1979. "An Attempt to Revive Turkish Printing in Istanbul in 1799." *International Journal of Middle Eastern Studies* 10: 67–70.

Cohen, Anouk. 2011. "Fabriquer le livre à Rabat et à Casablanca: une ethnographie." Ph.D. diss., Université Paris Ouest Nanterre La Défense.

Coles, Stephen. 2012. *The Anatomy of Type: A Graphic Guide to 100 Typefaces.* New York: Harper Design.

Comrie, Bernard, Gerald Stone, and Maria Polinsky. 1996. *The Russian Language in the Twentieth Century.* Oxford: Clarendon Press.

Comstock, Steve. 2011. *An Introduction to Unicode.* Denver: The Trainer's Friend, Inc.

Connell, Martin. 2015. *Hear the Word of the Lord: The Lectionary in Catholic Ritual.* Chicago: Liturgy Training Publications.

Coşan, Mahmud Esâd. 1982. *Matbaaci Ibrâhîm-i Müteferrika ve Risâle-i Islâmiye.* Ankara, Turkey: Elif Matbaacılık.

Coşgel, Metin M., Thomas J. Miceli, and Jared Rubin. 2009. "Guns and Books: Legitimacy, Revolt, and Technological Change in the Ottoman Empire." Department of Economics Working Paper Series, Working Paper 2009–12. Mansfield: University of Connecticut.

———. 2012. "The Political Economy of Mass Printing: Legitimacy and Technological Change in the Ottoman Empire." *Journal of Comparative Economics* 40(3): 357–371.

Dane, Joseph A. 2003. *The Myth of Print Culture: Essays on Evidence, Textuality and Bibliographical Method.* Toronto, ON, Canada: University of Toronto Press.

———. 2011. *Out of Sorts: On Typography and Print Culture.* Philadelphia: University of Pennsylvania Press.

Daniels, Peter T. 1990. "Fundamentals of Grammatology." *Journal of the American Oriental Society* 110(4): 727–731.

———. 2014. "The Type and Spread of Arabic Script." In *The Arabic Script in Africa: Studies in the Use of a Writing System,* edited by Meikal Mumin and Kees Versteegh, 25–39. Leiden: Brill.

Daniels, Peter T., and William Bright, eds. 1996. *The World's Writing Systems.* New York: Oxford University Press.

Darling, Linda T. 2012. "Ottoman Turkish: Written Language and Scribal Practice, 13th to 20th Centuries." In *Literacy in the Persianate World: Writing and the Social Order,* edited by Brian Spooner and William L. Hanaway, 171–195. Philadelphia: University of Pennsylvania Museum of Archaeology and Anthropology.

Darnton, Robert. 1982. "What Is the History of Books?" *Daedalus* 111(3): 65–83.

Davis, Mark, ed. 2014. *Unicode Standard Annex #9: Unicode Bidirectional Algorithm: Version 7.0.* Mountain View, CA: The Unicode Consortium.

Debray, Régis. 1996. "The Book as Symbolic Object." In *The Future of the Book,* edited by Geoffrey D. Nunberg, 139–151. Berkeley: University of California Press.

DecoType. 1995. "The DecoType Professional Font Series™ for Microsoft Windows™." Amsterdam, Netherlands: DecoType.

———. 2006. *Tasmeem™ Manual: The Spirit of Arabic Writing.* Saint-Martin-le-Vinoux, France: WinSoft International and DecoType.

DeFrancis, John. 1989. *Visible Speech: The Diverse Oneness of Writing Systems.* Honolulu: University of Hawai'i Press.

Deringil, Selim. 1993. "The Invention of Tradition as Public Image in the Late Ottoman Empire, 1808 to 1908." *Comparative Studies in Society and History* 35(1): 3–29.

Derman, M. Uğur. 1998. *Letters in Gold: Ottoman Calligraphy from the Sakıp Sabancı Collection.* New York: Metropolitan Museum of Art.

———. 2002. "The 'Celi' (jeli) Concept in Turkish Calligraphy." In *The Turks,* edited by Hasan Celâl Güzel, C. Cem Oğuz, and Osman Karatay, 4:15–24. Ankara, Turkey: Yeni Türkiye Publications.

Derman, M. Uğur, and Nihad M. Çetin. 1998. *The Art of Calligraphy in the Islamic Heritage.* Istanbul, Turkey: IRCICA.

Déroche, François, et al. 2006. *Islamic Codicology: An Introduction to the Study of Manuscripts in Arabic Script.* London: Al-Furqān Islamic Heritage Foundation.

Derrida, Jacques. 1976. *Of Grammatology [De la grammatologie].* Translated and with an introduction by Gayatri Chakravorty Spivak. Baltimore, MD: Johns Hopkins University Press.

———. 2002. *Acts of Religion.* Edited by Gil Anidjar. New York: Routledge.

de Vries, Hent, and Samuel Weber, eds. 2001. *Religion and Media: Cultural Memory in the Present.* Palo Alto, CA: Stanford University Press.

Dichy, Joseph. 2014. "Conjecture: How the First Comprehensive Dictionary in History Was Invented." In *Arab and Arabic Linguistics: Traditional and New Theoretical Approaches,* edited by Manuela E. B. Giolfo, 43–68. New York: Oxford University Press.

Diringer, David. 1968. *The Alphabet: A Key to the History of Mankind.* New York: Funk and Wagnalls.

Dixon, Catherine. 2012. "'From the Inside, from the Heart': Type Designer Nadine Chahine." *Print Magazine,* April 17.

Dodd, Robin. 2006. *From Gutenberg to OpenType: An Illustrated History of Type from the Earliest Letterforms to the Latest Digital Fonts.* Vancouver: Hartley and Marks Publishers.

Donner, Fred McGraw. 2010. *Muhammad and the Believers: At the Origins of Islam.* Cambridge, MA: Harvard University Press.

Drucker, Johanna. 2013. "From A to Screen." In *Comparative Textual Media: Transforming the Humanities in the Postprint Era,* edited by Katherine N. Hayles and Jessica Pressman, 71–96. Minneapolis: University of Minnesota Press.

Dutton, Yassin. 1999. "Red Dots, Green Dots, Yellow Dots and Blue: Some Reflections on the Vocalisation of Early Qur'anic Manuscripts—Part I." *Journal of Qur'anic Studies* 1(1): 115–140.

Eco, Umberto. 1976. *A Theory of Semiotics.* Advances in Semiotics. Bloomington: Indiana University Press.

Edwards, David B. 1995. "Print Islam: Media and Religious Revolution in Afghanistan." *Anthropological Quarterly* 68(3): 171–184.

Edwards, Mark U. 1994. *Printing, Propaganda, and Martin Luther.* Berkeley: University of California Press.

Eickelman, Dale F. 1995. "Mass Higher Education and the Religious Imagination in Contemporary Arab Societies." In *The Book in the Islamic World: The Written Word and Communication in the Middle East,* edited by George N. Atiyeh, 255–272. Albany: State University of New York Press.

Eisenstein, Elizabeth L. 1979. *The Printing Press as an Agent of Change: Communications and Cultural Transformations in Early Modern Europe.* Cambridge: Cambridge University Press.

———. 1997. "From The Printed Word to the Moving Image." *Social Research* 64(3): 1049–1066.

———. 2005. *The Printing Revolution in Early Modern Europe.* 2nd ed. Cambridge: Cambridge University Press.

———. 2011. *Divine Art, Infernal Machine: The Reception of Printing in the West from First Impressions to the Sense of an Ending.* Philadelphia: University of Pennsylvania Press.

Elias, Jamal J. 2012. *Aisha's Cushion: Religious Art, Perception, and Practice in Islam.* Cambridge, MA: Harvard University Press.

Erduman, Deniz. 2004. *Geschreibene Welten: Arabische Kalligraphie und Literatur in Wandel der Zeit/A Written Cosmos: Arabic Calligraphy and Literature throughout the Centuries.* Exhibition catalog. Museum für Angewandte Kunst (Museum of Applied Arts). Frankfurt, Germany: DuMont Litteratur und Kunst.

Erginbaş, Vefa. 2005. "Forerunner of the Ottoman Enlightenment: İbrahim Müteferrika and His Intellectual Landscape." Master's thesis, Sabancı University, Istanbul, Turkey.

Ergürbüz, Şefik. 1947. *Matbaacılık Tarihi.* İzmit, Turkey: Işıl Kitabevi.

Ersoy, Osman. 1959. *Türkiye'ye Matbaanın Girişi ve Ilk Basılan Eserler.* Ankara, Turkey: Ankara Üniversitesi Dil ve Tarih Coğrafya Fakültesi.

Ertürk, Nergis. 2011. *Grammatology and Literary Modernity in Turkey.* Oxford: Oxford University Press.

Erünsal, Ismail E. 2000. "Ottoman Libraries and the Ottoman Librarian Tradition." In *The Great Ottoman-Turkish Civilization,* edited by Kemal Çiçek, 4:867–885. Ankara, Turkey: Yeni Türkiye Publications.

Erzen, Jale Nejdet. 1991. "Aesthetics and Aisthesis in Ottoman Art and Architecture." *Journal of Islamic Studies* 2(1): 1–24.

———. 2000. "Ottoman Aesthetics." In *The Great Ottoman-Turkish Civilization,* edited by Kemal Çiçek, 4:287–298. Ankara, Turkey: Yeni Türkiye Publications.

Fahmy, Hossam A. H. 2006. "AlQalam for Typesetting Traditional Arabic Texts." *TUGboat* 27(2): 159–166.

———. 2007. "Parameterized Arabic Font Development for AlQalam." *TUGboat* 29(1): 79–88.

Faroqhi, Suraiya. 2000. *Subjects of the Sultan: Culture and Daily Life in the Ottoman Empire.* New York: I. B. Tauris Publishers.

Febvre, Lucien, and Henri-Jean Martin. 1958. *The Coming of the Book: The Impact of Printing, 1450–1800.* London: NLB.

Fekete, Louis. 1955. *Die Siyāqat-schrift in der türkischen Finanzverwaltung: Beitrag zur türkischen Paläographie.* Budapest: Akadémiai Kiadó.

Feldbusch, Elizabeth. 1986. "The Communicative and Cognitive Functions of Written Language." *Written Communication* 3(1): 81–89.

Felton, John. 2006. *The Ten Commandments of Typography/Type Heresy.* New York: Merrell.

Finkel, Caroline. 2005. *Osman's Dream: The Story of the Ottoman Empire, 1300–1923.* London: John Murray.

Firmin-Didot, Ambroise. 1855. *Essai sur la typographie.* Paris: Firmin Didot frères.

Frasca-Spada, Marina, and Nick Jardine, eds. 2000. *Books and the Sciences in History.* Cambridge: Cambridge University Press.

Fudge, Bruce, ed. and trans. 2016. *A Hundred and One Nights.* New York: New York University Press.

Fujita, Haruhiko, ed. 2007–2010. *Words for Design: Comparative Etymology of Design and Its Equivalents.* 3 vols. Osaka: Japan Society for the Promotion of Science.

Füssel, Stephan A. 2003. *Gutenberg and the Impact of Printing.* Burlington, VT: Ashgate.

Gacek, Adam. 2001. *The Arabic Manuscript Tradition: A Glossary of Technical Terms and Bibliography.* Leiden: Brill.

———. 2008. *The Arabic Manuscript Tradition: A Glossary of Technical Terms and Bibliography—supplement.* Leiden: Brill.

———. 2009. *Arabic Manuscripts: A Vademecum for Readers.* Leiden: Brill.

Garfield, Simon. 2011. *Just My Type: A Book about Fonts.* New York: Gotham Books.

Gdoura, Wahid. 1985. *Le début de l'imprimerie arabe à İstanbul, Turkey et en syrie: Évolution de l'environnement culturel (1706–1787).* Tunis, Tunisia: Institut Superieur de Documentation.

Geertz, Clifford. 1971. *Islam Observed: Religious Development in Morocco and Indonesia.* Chicago: University of Chicago Press.

———. 1983. "Art as a Cultural System." In *Local Knowledge: Further Essays in Interpretive Anthropology,* 94–120. New York: Basic Books.

Gelb, Ignace J. 1952. *A Study of Writing: The Foundations of Grammatology.* London: Routledge and Kegan Paul.

Gencer, Yasemin. 2010. "İbrahim Müteferrika and the Age of the Printed Manuscript." In *The Islamic Manuscript Tradition: Ten Centuries of Book Arts in Indiana University Collections,* edited by Christiane Gruber, 154–193. Bloomington: Indiana University Press.

George, Alain. 2010. *The Rise of Islamic Calligraphy.* Berkeley, CA: Saqi.

Gerçek, Selim Nüzhet. 1939. *Türk Matbaaciligi, 1: Müteferrika Matbaası.* Istanbul, Turkey: Devlet Basımevi.

Germanus, 'Abdul Karim. 1951. "Observations on the Arabic Alphabet." *Islamic Review* 39 (November): 13–14.

Ghaly, Mohammed. 2009. "The Interplay of Technology and Sacredness in Islam: Discussions of Muslim Scholars on Printing the Qur'an." *Studies in Ethics, Law, and Technology* 3(2): Article 3.

Ghobrial, John-Paul. 2005. "Diglossia and the 'Methodology' of Arabic Print." Presented at the 2nd International Symposium on the History of Printing and Publishing in the Languages and Countries of the Middle East, Paris, November 2–4.

Ghulam, Yousif Mahmud. 1982. *The Art of Arabic Calligraphy.* Lafayette, CA: Y. M. Ghulam.

Gillam, Richard. 2003. *Unicode Demystified: A Practical Programmer's Guide to the Encoding Standard.* San Francisco: Addison-Wesley.

Gilmont, Jean François, and Karin Maag, eds. 1998. *The Reformation and the Book: St. Andrews Studies in Reformation History.* Burlington, VT: Ashgate.

Gitelman, Lisa. 1999. *Scripts, Grooves, and Writing Machines: Representing Technology in the Edison Era.* Stanford, CA: Stanford University Press.

———. 2013. "Print Culture (Other than Codex): Job Printing and Its Importance." In *Comparative Textual Media: Transforming the Humanities in the Postprint Era,* edited by Katherine N. Hayles and Jessica Pressman, 183–197. Minneapolis: University of Minnesota Press.

Glass, Dagmar, Geoffrey Roper, and Hrant Gabeyan. 2002. "Arabic Book and Newspaper Printing in the Arabic World." In *Middle Eastern Languages and the Print Revolution: A Cross-Cultural Encounter,* edited by Eva Hanebutt-Benz, Dagmar Glass, and Geoffrey Roper, 177–226. Westhofen, Germany: WVA-Verlag Skulima.

Gonzales, Valérie. 2001. *Beauty and Islam: Aesthetics in Islamic Art and Architecture.* New York: I. B. Tauris.

Goodrich, Thomas D. 1990. *The Ottoman Turks and the New World: A Study of Tarih-i Hind-i Garbi and Sixteenth-Century Ottoman Americana*. Near and Middle East Monographs. Vol. 3. Wiesbaden, Germany: O. Harrassowitz.

Goody, Jack. 2000. *The Power of the Written Tradition*. Smithsonian Series in Ethnographic Inquiry. Washington, DC: Smithsonian Institution Press.

Google, Inc. 2014. "Google Noto Fonts." www.google.com/get/noto/.

Grabar, Oleg. 1973. *The Formation of Islamic Art*. New Haven, CT: Yale University Press.

———. 1992. *The Mediation of Ornament*. The A. W. Mellon Lectures in the Fine Arts, 35:38. Princeton, NJ: Princeton University Press.

Graham, William A. 1987. *Beyond the Written Word: Oral Aspects of Scripture in the History of Religion*. Cambridge: Cambridge University Press.

Green, Nile. 2009. "Journeymen, Middlemen: Travel, Transculture, and Technology in the Origins of Muslim Printing." *International Journal of Middle Eastern Studies* 41: 203–224.

Greimas, Algirdas Julien. 1987. *On Meaning: Selected Writings in Semiotic Theory [Du Sens]*. Translated by Paul J. Perron and Frank H. Collins. Minneapolis: University of Minnesota Press.

Gruber, Christiane, ed. 2010. *The Islamic Manuscript Tradition: Ten Centuries of Book Arts in Indiana University Collections*. Bloomington: Indiana University Press.

Gruendler, Beatrice. 1993. *The Development of the Arabic Scripts: From the Nabatean Era to the First Islamic Centuries*. Atlanta, GA: Scholars Press.

———. 2012. "Stability and Change in Arabic Script." In *The Shape of Script: How and Why Writing Systems Change*, edited by Stephen D. Houston, 93–118. Santa Fe, NM: School for Advanced Research Press.

Guar, Albertine. 1984. *A History of Writing*. London: The British Library.

Hacikyan, Agop J., ed. 2000. *The Heritage of Armenian Literature*. Detroit: Wayne State University Press.

Haeri, Niloofar. 2003. *Sacred Language, Ordinary People: Dilemmas of Culture and Politics in Egypt*. New York: Palgrave Macmillan.

Haiman, György. 1983. *Nicholas Kis: A Hungarian Punch-Cutter and Printer, 1650–1702*. San Francisco: J. W. Stauffacher / Greenwood Press in association with J. Howell-Books.

Haleem, M. A. S. Abdel. 1994. "Quranic Orthography: The Written Representation of the Recited Text of the Quran." *Islamic Quarterly* 38(3): 171–192.

Hamilton, Alastair, Maurits H. van den Boogert, and Bart Westerweel. 2005. *The Republic of Letters and the Levant*. Leiden: Brill.

Hamm, Roberto. 1975. *Pour une typographie Arabe*. Paris: Sindbad.

Hanebutt-Benz, Eva, Dagmar Glass, and Geoffrey Roper, eds., in collaboration with Theo Smets. 2002. *Middle Eastern Languages and the Print Revolution: A Cross-Cultural Encounter*. Westhofen, Germany: WVA-Verlag Skulima.

Hanna, Nelly. 2003. *In Praise of Books: A Cultural History of Cairo's Middle Class, Sixteenth to the Eighteenth Century*. Syracuse, NY: Syracuse University Press.

Haralambous, Yannis. 1992. "Typesetting the Holy Qur'an with TEX." In *Proceedings of the 2nd International Conference on Multilingual Computing (Latin and Arabic script)*, Durham, UK.

———. 2006. "Simplification of the Arabic Script: Three Different Approaches and Their Implementation." In *Electronic Publishing, Artistic Imaging, and Digital Typography*, edited by Roger D. Hersch, Jacques André, and Heather Brown, 138–156. Berlin: Springer-Verlag.

Harris, Roy. 1995. *Signs of Writing.* New York: Routledge.

Hayles, Katherine N., and Jessica Pressman, eds. 2013. *Comparative Textual Media: Transforming the Humanities in the Postprint Era.* Minneapolis: University of Minnesota Press.

Healey, John F. 1993. "Nabataean to Arabic: Calligraphy and Script Development among the Pre-Islamic Arabs." *Manuscripts of the Middle East: The Role of the Book in the Civilizations of the Near East* 5: 41–52.

Heim, Michael. 1999. *Electric Language: A Philosophical Study of Word Processing.* 2nd ed. New Haven, CT: Yale University Press.

Hertzfeld, Andy, and Steve Capps. 2005. *Revolution in The Valley: The Insanely Great Story of How the Mac Was Made.* Sebastopol, CA: O'Reilly.

Hesse, Carla. 1996. "Books in Time." In *The Future of the Book,* edited by Geoffrey D. Nunberg, 21–36. Berkeley: University of California Press.

Hill, Brad Sabin. 2016a. Interviews with author. Washington, DC.

———. 2016b. "Printing." In *Encyclopedia of Hebrew Language and Linguistics,* edited by Geoffrey Khan et al., 3:233–262. Leiden: Brill.

Hindman, Sandra, and James Douglas Farquhar. 1977. *Pen to Press: Illustrated Manuscripts and Printed Books in the First Century of Printing.* Baltimore, MD: Johns Hopkins University Press.

Hiromoura, Masaaki. 2009. *Ji Born: A Book of Letters and Characters.* Tokyo: ADP.

Hirsch, Rudolf. 1978. *The Printed Word: Its Impact and Diffusion.* London: Variorum Reprints.

Holdermann, Jean Baptiste Daniel. 1730. *Grammaire Turque: Ou méthode courte et facile pour apprendre la langue Turque.* Constantinople: Müteferrika Matbaası.

Hourani, C. 1982. "The Arab Typographical Revolution: The Work of Nasri Khattar." In *The Arab Cultural Scene, a Literary Review Supplement.* London.

Houston, Stephen D., ed. 2004. *The First Writing: Script Invention as History and Process.* New York: Cambridge University Press.

———. 2012. *The Shape of Script: How and Why Writing Systems Change.* Santa Fe, NM: School for Advanced Research Press.

Hudson, John. 2002. "Unicode, from Text to Type." In *Language, Culture, Type: International Type Design in the Age of Unicode,* edited by John D. Berry, 24–44. New York: Association Typographique Internationale (ATypI).

Humeid, Ahmad. 2004. "TypoClash: Arabic Script and Western Technologies." Presented at Bauhaus-Universität Weimar, Weimar, Germany, June 8.

———. 2005. Interviews with author. August 1 and 7. Amman, Jordan.

Hunziker, Hans Jürg. 1985. "Aspects of Arabic Script Reform." *Typographische Monatsblätter: Schweizer Graphische Mitteilungen / Swiss Typographic Monthly Magazine* 104(4): 1–36.

Hurgronje, C. Snouck. 1931. *Mekka in the Latter Part of the 19th Century.* Leiden: Brill.

Husayn, Muhammad Ahmad. 1972. *Origins of the Book: Egypt's Contribution to the Development of the Book from Papyrus to Codex.* Norwalk, CT: New York Graphic Society.

Hustwit, Gary (director). 2007. *Helvetica.* Brooklyn: Swiss Dots Limited.

Ibn al-Bawwab, Ali ibn Hilal. ca. 1030. "Manzume fi Hüsni'l-hat ve Usulih." Süleymaniye Kütüphanesi, Istanbul, Turkey. Index number AyaSofya 002002.

Ibn al-Nadim, Abu'l-Faraj M. 1970. *The Fihrist of al-Nadim: A 10th Century Survey of Muslim Culture.* Edited and translated by Bayard Dodge. 2 vols. New York: Columbia University Press.

Ibn 'Ata'Allah, Ahmad ibn Muhammad. 1978. *The Book of Wisdom.* Translated with notes by Victor Danner. New York: Paulist Press.

Ibn Khaldūn. 1967. *The Muqaddimah: An Introduction to History.* Edited and translated by Franz Rosenthal. London: Routledge.

Ibn Khallikan. 1970. *Ibn Khallikan's Biographical Dictionary.* Translated from the Arabic by Bn. Mac Guckin de Slane. Beirut: Librairie du Liban.

İhsanoğlu, Ekmeleddin, and Hatice Aynur. 2007. "The Birth of the Tradition of Printed Books in the Ottoman Empire: Transition from Manuscript to Print (1729–1848)." *Archivum Ottomanicum* 24: 165–196.

Illich, Ivan. 1993. *In the Vineyard of the Text: A Commentary to Hugh's Didascalion.* Chicago: University of Chicago Press.

İnal, İbnülemin Mahmut Kemal. 1955. *Son Hattatlar.* Istanbul, Turkey: Maarif Basımevi.

Ingold, Timothy. 2007. *Lines: A Brief History.* New York: Routledge.

Innis, Harold Adams, and Mary Innis. 1972. *Empire and Communications.* Toronto, ON, Canada: University of Toronto Press.

Ja'far, Mustafa. 2002. *Arabic Calligraphy: Naskh Script for Beginners.* San Francisco: McGraw-Hill.

Jahn, Karl. 1970: "Paper Currency in Iran: A Contribution to the Cultural and Economic History of Iran in the Mongol Period." *Journal of Asian History* 4(2): 101–135.

John, Nicholas A. 2013. "The Construction of the Multilingual Internet: Unicode, Hebrew, and Globalization." *Journal of Computer-Mediated Communication* 18: 321–338.

Johns, Adrian. 1998. *The Nature of the Book: Print and Knowledge in the Making.* Chicago: University of Chicago Press.

Johnson, William A. 2013. "Bookrolls as Media." In *Comparative Textual Media: Transforming the Humanities in the Postprint Era,* edited by Katherine. N. Hayles and Jessica Pressman, 101–124. Minneapolis: University of Minnesota Press.

Jones, Robert. 1994. "The Medici Oriental Press (Rome 1585–1614) and the Impact of Its Publications on Northern Europe." In *The "Arabick" Interest of the Natural Philosophers in Seventeenth-Century England,* edited by G. A. Russell, 88–108. Leiden: Brill.

Jules-Rosette, Bennetta. 1984. *The Messages of Tourist Art: An African Semiotic System in Comparative Perspective.* Topics in Contemporary Semiotics. New York: Plenum Press.

———. 1990. *Terminal Signs: Computers and Social Change in Africa.* Approaches to Semiotics. Vol. 90. New York: Mouton de Gruyter.

———. 1993. "Semiotic Modeling Systems: The Contribution of Thomas A. Sebeok." *Semiotica* 96(3-4): 269–283.

Karabacek, Josef Ritter von. 1991. *Arab Paper.* Translated with additional notes by Don Baker and Suzy Dittmar. London: Islington Books.

Kaye, Alan S. 1996. "Adaptations of Arabic Script." In *The World's Writing Systems,* edited by Peter Daniels and William Bright, 743–762. New York: Oxford University Press.

———. 2013. "Arabic Alphabet for Other Languages." In *Encyclopedia of Arabic Language and Linguistics,* edited by Kees Versteegh et al., 133–147. Leiden: Brill.

Kennedy, Hugh. 2015. "Baghdad as Center of Learning and Book Production." In *By the Pen and What They Write: Writing in Islamic Art and Culture,* edited by Sheila Blair and Jonathan Bloom. The Sixth Biennial Hamad Bin Khalifa Symposium on Islamic Art, November 7–9, Doha, Qatar.

Khatibi, Abdelkhatibi, and Mohammed Sijelmassi. 1976. *The Splendour of Islamic Calligraphy.* New York: Rizzoli.

Khattar, Nasri. 1950. "Arabic Alphabet." US patent 157,982, filed June 21, 1947, and issued April 4, 1950.

———. 1955. "Unified Arabic: A Weapon against Illiteracy." *Al-Kulliyah* 30: 5.

Khera, Paul. 2003. "Abbar: Building Bridges—Has Yassar Abbar Developed the Arab World's Answer to Univers?" *Eye* 50.

Kinross, Robin. 2004. *Modern Typography: An Essay in Critical History.* London: Hyphen Press.

Kirschenbaum, Matthew G. 2004. "Extreme Inscription: Towards a Grammatology of the Hard Drive." *TEXT Technology* 2: 91–125.

———. 2013. "The .txtual Condition." In *Comparative Textual Media: Transforming the Humanities in the Postprint Era,* edited by Katherine. N. Hayles and Jessica Pressman, 53–69. Minneapolis: University of Minnesota Press.

Kirschenbaum, Valerie. 2005. *Goodbye Gutenberg: Hello to a New Generation of Readers and Writers.* New York: Global Renaissance Society.

Knuth, Donald E. 1986a. *The METAFONTbook.* Reading, MA: Addison-Wesley.

———. 1986b. *The TeXbook.* Reading, MA: Addison-Wesley.

Kologlu, Orhan. 1992. "The Penetration and Effects of the Printing Techniques on the Muslim Societies." In *Transfer of Modern Science & Technology to the Muslim World,* edited by Ekmeleddin İhsanoğlu, 239–249. Istanbul, Turkey: IRCICA.

Kreamer, Christine Mullen, Mary Nooter Roberts, Elizabeth Harney, and Allyson Purpura, eds. 2007. *Inscribing Meaning: Writing and Graphic Systems in Art History.* Exhibition catalog. Washington, DC: National Museum of African Art, Smithsonian Institution.

Kreiser, Klaus. 2001. "Causes of the Decrease of Ignorance? Remarks on the Printing of Books in the Ottoman Empire." In *The Beginnings of Printing in the Near and Middle East: Jews, Christians and Muslims,* edited by the Lehrstuhl für Türkische Sprache, Geschichte und Kultur, Universität Bamberg, 13–17. Wiesbaden, Germany: Harrassowitz Verlag.

Krek, Miroslav. 1977. *A Gazetteer of Arabic Printing.* Weston, MA: M. Krek.

———. 1979. "The Enigma of the First Arabic Book Printed from Movable Type." *Journal of Near Eastern Studies* 38(3): 203–212.

Kunt, I. Metin. 2005. Interview with author. October 18. Istanbul, Turkey.

———. 2008. "Reading Elite, Elite Reading." In *Printing and Publishing in the Middle East: Papers from the Second Symposium on the History of Printing and Publishing in the Languages and Countries of the Middle East, Bibliothèque nationale de France, Paris . . . 2005. Contributions au deuxième colloque sur l'Histoire de l'imprimé dans les langues et les pays du Moyen Orient, Bibliothèque nationale de France, Paris . . . 2005 (Journal of Semitic Studies Supplement, 24),* edited by Philip Sadgrove, 89–100. Oxford: Oxford University Press.

Kut, Günay Alpay. 1960. "Matba'a: In Turkey." In *The Encyclopaedia of Islam*, 6:799–803. Leiden: Brill.

Kut, Turgut, and Fatma Türe. 1996. *Yazmadan basmaya: Müteferrika, Mühendishane, Üsküdar*. Istanbul, Turkey: Yapı Kredi Kültür Merkezi.

Lagally, Klaus. 1992. "ArabTEX—Typesetting Arabic with Vowels and Ligatures." In *EuroTEX 92: Proceedings of the 7th European TEX Conference*, edited by Jiří Zlatuška, 153–172. Brno, Czechoslovakia: Masarykova Universita.

Landau, Jacob M. 2008. "Attempts at Romanization in the Middle East and Central Asia." In *Printing and Publishing in the Middle East: Papers from the Second Symposium on the History of Printing and Publishing in the Languages and Countries of the Middle East, Bibliothèque nationale de France, Paris . . . 2005. Contributions au deuxième colloque sur l'Histoire de l'imprimé dans les langues et les pays du Moyen Orient, Bibliothèque nationale de France, Paris . . . 2005 (Journal of Semitic Studies Supplement, 24)*, edited by Philip Sadgrove, 185–192. Oxford: Oxford University Press.

Larsson, Göran. 2011. *Muslims and the New Media: Historical and Contemporary Debates*. Burlington, VT: Ashgate.

Latour, Bruno. 1986. "Visualization and Cognition: Thinking with Eyes and Hands." *Knowledge and Society: Studies in the Sociology of Culture Past and Present* 6: 1–40.

Lawson, Alexander. 1990. *Anatomy of a Typeface*. Boston: David R. Goodine.

Leaman, Oliver. 2004. *Islamic Aesthetics: An Introduction*. Notre Dame, IN: University of Notre Dame Press.

Leroi-Gourhan, André. 1993. *Gesture and Speech [Le geste et la parole]*. Translated by Anna Bostock Berger. Cambridge, MA: MIT Press.

Levey, Michael. 1975. *The World of Ottoman Art*. London: Thames and Hudson.

Levy, David M. 2001. *Scrolling Forward: Making Sense of Documents in the Digital Age*. New York: Arcade Publishers.

Lewis, Bernard. 1961. *The Emergence of Modern Turkey*. London: Oxford University Press.

Lewis, Geoffrey L. 1999. *The Turkish Language Reform: A Catastrophic Success*. New York: Oxford University Press.

Lewis, John. 1963. *Typography/Basic Principles: Influences and Trends since the 19th Century*. London: Studio Books.

Liebesny, Herbert J. 1975. *The Law of the Near and Middle East: Readings, Cases, and Materials*. Albany: State University of New York Press.

Lunde, Paul. 1981. "Arabic and the Art of Printing." *Saudi Aramco World* 32(2): 20–35.

Lupton, Ellen. 2004. *Thinking with Type: A Critical Guide for Designers, Writers, Editors, & Students*. Princeton, NJ: Princeton Architectural Press.

———. 2014. *Type on Screen: A Critical Guide for Designers, Writers, Developers, & Students*. Princeton, NJ: Princeton Architectural Press.

Lupton, Ellen, and Jennifer Cole Phillips. 2015. *Graphic Design: The New Basics*. Princeton, NJ: Princeton Architectural Press.

Luther, Martin. 1912. *D. Martin Luthers Werke, Kritische Gesamtausgabe. Tischreden*. 6 vols. Weimar: Hermann Böhlau.

———. 1952. *The Table Talk of Martin Luther*. Edited by Thomas S. Kepler. New York: World Publishing Company.

MacDonald, M. C. A. 2009. *The Development of Arabic as a Written Language: Papers from the Special Session of the Seminar for Arabian Studies Held on 24 July, 2009.* Oxford: Archaeopress.

MacKay, Pierre A., ed. 1990a. *Computers and the Arabic Language.* Washington, DC: Hemisphere Publishing Corporation.

———. 1990b. "The Internationalization of TEX with Special Reference to Arabic." In *Proceedings of the IEEE International Conference on Systems, Man and Cybernetics,* 481–484. New York: Institute of Electrical and Electronics Engineers.

Madigan, Daniel A. 2001. *The Qur'ân's Self-Image: Writing and Authority in Islam's Scripture.* Princeton, NJ: Princeton University Press.

Mahdi, Mushin. 1995. "From the Manuscript Age to the Age of Printed Books." In *The Book in the Islamic World: The Written Word and Communication in the Middle East,* edited by George N. Atiyeh, 1–15. Albany: State University of New York Press.

Mahir, Banu. 1999. *Turkish Calligraphy.* Edited by Nestern Refioğlu. Istanbul, Turkey: N. Refioğlu Publishers.

Mahmoud, Youssef. 1981. "The Arabic Writing System and Deliberate Orthographic Change." *Al'Arabiyya* 14: 79–84.

Male, Lydia Sharman. 1990. "In the Mind of the Beholder." *Saudi Aramco World* 41(3): 10–15.

Mandel Khan, Gabriele. 2001. *Arabic Script: Styles, Variants, and Calligraphic Adaptations.* New York: Abbeville.

Manguel, Alberto. 1996. *A History of Reading.* New York: Viking.

Mansour, Nassar. 2010. *Sacred Script: Muhaqqaq in Islamic Calligraphy.* London: I. B. Tauris.

Mardin, Şerif. 1961. "Some Notes on an Early Phase in the Modernization of Communications in Turkey." *Comparative Studies in Society and History* 3(3): 250–71.

———. 1962. *The Genesis of Young Ottoman Thought: A Study in the Modernization of Turkish Political Ideas.* Princeton Oriental Studies. Vol. 21. Princeton, NJ: Princeton University Press.

Marks, Laura. 2010. *Enfoldment and Infinity: An Islamic Genealogy of New Media Art.* Cambridge, MA: MIT Press.

———. 2011. "Calligraphic Animation: Documenting the Invisible." *Animation: An Interdisciplinary Journal* 6(3): 307–323.

Martin, Henri-Jean. 1994. *The History and Power of Writing.* Chicago: University of Chicago Press.

Marzolph, Ulrich. 2007. "Persian Incunabula: A Definition and Assessment." *Gutenberg-Jahrbuch* 82 (2007): 205–220.

McCloud, Scott. 1993. *Understanding Comics: The Invisible Art.* Northampton, MA: Kitchen Sink Press.

McLuhan, Marshall. 1962. *The Gutenberg Galaxy: The Making of Typographic Man.* Toronto, ON, Canada: University of Toronto Press.

———. 1994. *Understanding Media: The Extensions of Man.* MIT Press edition. Cambridge, MA: MIT Press.

Meggs, Philip B., and Alston W. Purvis. 2006. *Meggs' History of Graphic Design.* Hoboken, NJ: J. Wiley & Sons.

Ménage, V. L. 1958. "The Map of Hajji Ahmed and Its Makers." *Bulletin of the School of Oriental and African Studies* 21(3): 291–314.

Menocal, Maria Rosa. 2002. *The Ornament of the World: How Muslims, Jews, and Christians Created a Culture of Tolerance in Medieval Spain.* Boston: Little, Brown.

Messick, Brinkley. 1993. *The Calligraphic State: Textual Domination in a Muslim Society.* Los Angeles: University of California Press.

———. 1997. "On the Question of Lithography." *Culture & History* 16: 158–176. Reprinted in *The History of the Book in the Middle East,* edited by Geoffrey Roper, 299–317. Surrey, England: Ashgate, 2013.

Meynet, Roland. 1971. *L'écriture arabe en question: Les projets de l'Académie de Langue Arabe du Caire de 1938 à 1968.* Beirut: Dar el-Machreq.

Milo, Thomas. 2002a. "Arabic Script and Typography: A Brief Historical Overview." In *Language, Culture, Type: International Type Design in the Age of Unicode,* edited by John D. Berry, 112–127. New York: Association Typographique Internationale (ATypI).

———. 2002b. "Authentic Arabic: A Case Study. Right-to-Left Font Structure, Font Design, and Typography." *Manuscripta Orientalia* 8(1): 49–61.

———. 2011a. "Balancing Arabic and Latin Typography." *Book 2.0* 1(2): 239–254.

———. 2011b. "The Rôle of Dutch Arabic Typography in Middle Eastern Printing." Presented at ATypI (Association Typographique Internationale) Reykjavík, September 14–18, Reykjavík, Iceland. Filmed by River Valley TV.

———. 2012. Interview with author. July 16. Amsterdam, Netherlands / Washington, DC.

———. 2013. "Arabic Typography." In *Encyclopedia of Arabic Language and Linguistics,* edited by Kees Versteegh et al. Leiden: Brill.

———. 2016a. Interview with author. February 12. Amsterdam, Netherlands / Washington, DC.

———. 2016b. Written correspondence with author. October 21.

Milo, Thomas, and Mohamed Zakariya. 2005. "Smithshuijzen AbiFarès, H.—Arabic Typography: A Comprehensive Sourcebook." *Bibliotheca Orientalis* 42(1–2): 161–166.

Mitchell, T. F. 1953. *Writing Arabic: A Practical Introduction to Ruq'ah Script.* London: Oxford University Press.

Mitchell, W. J. T. 1994. *Picture Theory: Essays on Verbal and Visual Representation.* Chicago: University of Chicago Press.

Moginet, Stefan F. 2009. *Writing Arabic: From Script to Type.* Cairo: The American University in Cairo Press.

Moholy-Nagy, László. 1946. *The New Vision.* 4th rev. ed. New York: Wittenborn and Company.

Moran, James. 1960. "Filmsetting: Bibliographical Implications." *The Library: Transactions of the Bibliographic Society* s5-15: 231–245.

Moreh, Schmuel. 2003. "Napoleon and the French Impact on Egyptian Society in the Eyes of al-Jabarti." In *Napoleon in Egypt,* edited by Irene Bierman, 77–98. Reading, UK: Ithaca Press.

Morison, Stanley. 1936. *First Principles of Typography.* New York: Macmillan. Reprinted in *Texts on Type: Critical Writings on Typography,* edited by Steven Heller and Philip B. Meggs, 170–177. New York: Allworth Press, 2001.

———. 2000. *Letter Forms.* Typophile Chap Books, 45. New York: Hartley and Marks Publishers. First published in 1968.

Moxon, Joseph. 1962. *Mechanick Exercises on the Whole Art of Printing.* Edited by Herbert David and Harry Carter. Oxford: Oxford University Press.

Mukerji, Chandra. 1983. *From Graven Images: Patterns of Modern Materialism.* New York: Columbia University Press.

———. 2006. "Printing, Cartography and Conceptions of Place in Renaissance Europe." *Media, Culture & Society* 28(5): 651–669.

Mulder, Eildert. 2007. "Keyboard Calligraphy." *Saudi Aramco World* 58(4): 34–39.

Mumin, Meikal. 2014. "The Arabic Script in Africa: Understudied Literacy." In *The Arabic Script in Africa: Studies in the Use of a Writing System,* edited by Meikal Mumin and Kees Versteegh, 41–62. Leiden: Brill.

Mumin, Meikal, and Kees Versteegh, eds. 2014. *The Arabic Script in Africa: Studies in the Use of a Writing System.* Leiden: Brill.

Munro, John M. 1981. "Facing the Future." *Saudi Aramco World* 32(2): 30–35.

Murphy, Christopher M. 1995. "Ottoman Imperial Documents Related to the History of Books and Printing." In *The Book in the Islamic World: The Written Word and Communication in the Middle East,* edited by George N. Atiyeh, 283–292. Albany: State University of New York Press.

Müteferrika, Ibrahim. 1995. "Vesiletü-t Tibaa." Translated by Christopher M. Murphy. In *The Book in the Islamic World: The Written Word and Communication in the Middle East,* edited by George N. Atiyeh, 285–292. Albany: State University of New York Press.

Mystakidis, B. A. 1911. "Osmanlı Hükümeti Tarafından Ilk Kurulan Matbaa ve Bunun Neşriyatı." Tarih-i Osmanlî Encümeni Mecmuası.

Nammour, Yara Khoury. 2014. *Nasri Khattar, a Modernist Typotect.* Amsterdam: Khatt Books.

Nasr, Seyyed Hossein. 1987. *Islamic Art and Spirituality.* Albany: State University of New York Press.

———. 1994. *Ideals and Realities of Islam.* San Francisco: Aquarian Press.

Naveh, Joseph. 1982. *Early History of the Alphabet: An Introduction to West Semitic Epigraphy and Paleography.* Jerusalem: Magnes Press.

Necatioğlu, Halil. 1982. *Matbaacı İbrahim-i Müteferrika ve Risâle-i İslâmiye adlı eserinin tenkidli metni.* Ankara, Turkey: Elif Matbaacılık Tesisleri.

Necipoğlu, Gülru. 2005. *The Age of Sinan: Architectural Culture in the Ottoman Empire.* Princeton, NJ: Princeton University Press.

Nelson, Kristina. 1985. *The Art of Reciting the Qur'an.* Austin: University of Texas Press.

Nemeth, Titus. 2006. "Harmonization of Arabic and Latin Script: Possibilities and Obstacles." M.A. thesis, Department of Typography & Graphic Communication, University of Reading, UK.

———. 2008. "A Primer for Arabic Typeface Design for the DecoType Arabic Calligraphic Engine in WinSoft Tasmeem." Version 1.1.1 ACE Tools. Nottuln, Germany: Karsten Lücke.

Netton, Ian R. 1989. *Allâh Transcendent: Studies in the Structure and Semiotics of Islamic Philosophy, Theology, and Cosmology.* New York: Routledge.

Neuman, Christoph. 2002. "Book and Newspaper Printing in Turkish, 18th–20th Centuries." In *Middle Eastern Languages and the Print Revolution: A Cross-Cultural Encounter*, edited by Eva Hanebutt-Benz, Dagmar Glass, and Geoffrey Roper, 227–248. Westhofen, Germany: WVA-Verlag Skulima.

Nicolay, Nicolas de. 1585. *The navigations, peregrinations and voyages, made into Turkie*. London: T. Dawson.

Niebuhr, Carsten. 1792. *Travels through Arabia and other countries in the East [Reisebeschreibung nach Arabien und andern umliegenden Ländern]*. Translated by Robert Heron. 3 vols. Belfast: William Macghie.

Noordzij, Geert. 2005. *The Stroke: Theory of Writing*. Translated by Peter Enneson. London: Hyphen Press.

Nuhoğlu, Hidayet Y. 2000. "Müteferrika's Printing Press: Some Observations." In *The Great Ottoman-Turkish Civilization*, edited by Kemal Çiçek, 3:83–90. Ankara, Turkey: Yeni Türkiye Publications.

Nunberg, Geoffrey, ed. 1996. *The Future of the Book*. Berkeley: University of California Press.

Nuovo, Angela. 1990. "A Lost Arabic Koran Rediscovered." *The Library: Transactions of the Bibliographic Society* s6–12(4): 273–292.

Olson, David R. 1994. *The World on Paper: The Conceptual and Cognitive Implications of Reading and Writing*. Cambridge: Cambridge University Press.

Oman, G. 1960. "Matba'a." In *The Encyclopaedia of Islam*, 6:794–799. Leiden: Brill.

Ong, Walter J. 1982. *Orality and Literacy: The Technologizing of the Word*. New York: Methuen.

Osborn, J.R. 2005. "Islamic Calligraphy as Recitation: The Visual Expansion of Divine Words." *Humanities and Technology Review* 24: 15–30.

———. 2006. "Islamic Traditions of the Book: Calligraphy, Performance, and Print." *International Journal of the Book* 3(3): 33–38.

———. 2007. *Newberry Library Holdings Related to Arabic Script, the Printing of Arabic Characters, and Middle Eastern Print*. Chicago: Newberry Library.

———. 2008. "The Type of Calligraphy." Ph.D. diss., University of California, San Diego, La Jolla.

———. 2009. "Narratives of Arabic Script: Calligraphic Design and Modern Spaces." *Design and Culture* 1(3): 289–306.

Osterer, Heidrun, and Philipp Stamm. 2014. *Adrian Frutiger Typefaces: The Complete Works*. Basel, Switzerland: Birkhauser Architecture.

Oweis, Fayeq. 2005. *Pocket Guide to Arabic Script: [al-lughah al-'Arabīyah]*. New York: Hippocrene Books.

Özdalga, Elisabeth, ed. 2005. *Late Ottoman Society: The Intellectual Legacy*. London: Routledge.

Özdemir, İbrahim Söner. 2009. "Design Words of Turkey: A Concise History of Turkish Modernization." In *Words for Design: Comparative Etymology of Design and Its Equivalents*, edited by Haruhiko Fujita, 2:80–86. Osaka: Japan Society for the Promotion of Science.

———. 2010. "Tasarım and 'Design': Reflections on a Semantic Gap." In *Words for Design: Comparative Etymology of Design and Its Equivalents*, edited by Haruhiko Fujita, 3:52–59. Osaka: Japan Society for the Promotion of Science.

Özmen, Yücel. 1968. "A Sociolinguistic Analysis of Language Reform in Turkey 1932–1967 (with special reference to the activities of the Turk Dil Kurumu)." M.S. thesis, George-town University, Washington, DC.

Pamuk, Orhan. 2001. *My Name Is Red [Benim adım Kırmızı]*. Translated by Erdağ M. Göknar. New York: Alfred A. Knopf.

Panossian, Razmik. 2006. *The Armenians: From Kings and Priests to Merchants and Commissars*. New York: Columbia University Press.

Papazian, Hrant. 2004. "Latinization: Prevention and Cure." *Spatium Magazin für Typografie* 4: 10–20.

Parkes, M. B. 1993. *Pause and Effect: An Introduction to the History of Punctuation in the West*. Berkeley: University of California Press.

Parlatir, Ismail. 2002. "The 19th-Century Ottoman Turkish Language." In *The Turks,* edited by Hasan Celâl Güzel, C. Cem Oğuz, and Osman Karatay, 4:152–172. Ankara, Turkey: Yeni Türkiye Publications.

Peçewi, İbrahim. 1981. *Peçevi tarihi*. Edited by Bekir Sıtkı Baykal. Ankara, Turkey: Kültür Bakanlığı.

Pedersen, Johannes. 1984. *The Arabic Book*. Princeton, NJ: Princeton University Press.

Pektas, Nil Ozlem. 2014. "The First Greek Printing Press in Constantinople (1625–1628)." Doctor of philosophy thesis, University of London, Royal Holloway and Bedford New College.

Porter, Venetia, ed. 2008. *Word into Art: Artists of the Modern Middle East*. Exhibition catalog. The British Museum / Dubai International Financial Centre. Dubai, UAE: Dubai Holdings.

Proudfoot, Ian. 1995. "Early Muslim Printing in Southeast Asia." *Libri* 45: 216–223.

———. 1997. "Mass Producing Houri's Moles, or Aesthetics and Choice of Technology in Early Muslim Book Printing." In *Islam: Essays on Scripture, Thought, and Society: A Festscrift in Honour of Anthony H. Johns,* edited by Peter G. Riddell and Tony Street, 161–184. Leiden: Brill.

———. 1998. "Lithography at the Crossroads of the East." *Journal of the Printing Historical Society* 27: 113–131.

Qadi, Ahmad. 1959. *Calligraphers and Painters: A Treatise by Qāḍī Ahmad, Son of Mīr-Munshī*. Translated by V. Minorsky. Freer Gallery of Art Occasional Papers. Vol. 4339. Washington, DC: Smithsonian Institution Press.

Reichmuth, Stefan. 2001. "Islamic Reformist Discourse in the Tulip Period (1718–30): Ibrahim Müteferriqa and His Arguments for Printing." In *International Congress on Learning and Education in the Islamic World, Istanbul 12–15 April 1999,* edited by Ali Cakşu, 149–161. Istanbul, Turkey: Research Center for Islamic History, Art, and Culture (IRCICA). Reprinted in *The History of the Book in the Middle East,* edited by Geoffrey Roper, 201–213. Surrey, England: Ashgate, 2013.

Revell, E. J. 1975. "The Diacritical Dots and the Development of the Arabic Alphabet." *Journal of Semitic Studies* 20: 178–190.

Rice, David Storm. 1955. *The Unique Ibn al-Bawwab Manuscript in the Chester Beatty Library*. Dublin: E. Walker.

Rivlin, Benjamin, and Joseph S. Szyliowicz, eds. 1965. *The Contemporary Middle East: Tradition and Innovation*. New York: Random House.

Roberts, R. J. 1967. "The Greek Press at Constantinople in 1627 and Its Antecedents." *The Library: The Transactions of the Bibliographic Society* s5–XXII(1): 13–43.

Roberts, Sean E. 2013. *Printing a Mediterranean World: Florence, Constantinople, and the Renaissance of Geography.* Cambridge, MA: Harvard University Press.

Robertson, Edward. 1920. "Muhammad Ibn Abd Al-Rahman on Calligraphy." In *Studia Semitica et Orientalia,* edited by the University of Glasgow Oriental Society, 57–83. Glasgow, Scotland: University of Glasgow Oriental Society.

Robertson, Frances. 2013. *Print Culture: From Steam Press to Ebook.* London: Routledge.

Robinson, Francis. 1993. "Technology and Religious Change: Islam and the Impact of Print." *Modern Asian Studies* 27(1): 229–251.

Rogers, Henry. 1995. "Optimal Orthographies." In *Scripts and Literacy: Reading and Learning to Read Alphabets, Syllabaries and Characters,* edited by Insup Taylor and David R. Olson, 31–43. Boston: Kluwer Academic Publishers.

Rogers, J. M., and R. M. Ward. 1988. *Süleyman the Magnificent.* London: British Museum Publications.

Rojo, Luis Durán. 2007. "El triunfo de la Ñ—Afirmación de Hispanoamérica." *Reflexiones sobre el Perú. El Derecho, La Cultura, La Filosofía, La Política, La Teología:* http://blog.pucp.edu.pe/blog/luisduran/.

Romano, Frank. 2014. *History of the Linotype Company.* Rochester, NY: RIT Press.

Roper, Geoffrey. 1995. "Faris al-Shidyaq and the Transition from Scribal to Print Culture in the Middle East." In *The Book in the Islamic World: The Written Word and Communication in the Middle East,* edited by George N. Atiyeh, 209–232. Albany: State University of New York Press.

———. 2002. "Early Arabic Printing in Europe." In *Middle Eastern Languages and the Print Revolution: A Cross-Cultural Encounter,* edited by Eva Hanebutt-Benz, Dagmar Glass, and Geoffrey Roper, 129–150. Westhofen, Germany: WVA-Verlag Skulima.

———. 2007. "The Printing Press and Change in the Arab World." In *Agent of Change: Print Culture Studies after Elizabeth Eisenstein,* edited by Sabrina Alcorn Baron, Eric N. Lindquist, and Eleanor F. Shevlin, 250–267. Boston: University of Massachusetts Press, in association with the Center for the Book, Library of Congress. Reprinted in *The History of the Book in the Middle East,* edited by Geoffrey Roper, 389–406. Surrey, England: Ashgate, 2013.

———, ed. 2013. *The History of the Book in the Middle East.* Surrey, England: Ashgate.

———, ed. 2014. *Historical Aspects of Printing and Publishing in Languages of the Middle East: Papers from the Third Symposium on the History of Printing and Publishing in the Languages and Countries of the Middle East, University of Leipzig, September 2008.* Leiden: Brill.

Rosenthal, Franz. 1971. *Four Essays on Art and Literature in Islam.* Leiden: Brill.

———. 1995. "'Of Making Books There Is No End': The Classical Muslim View." In *The Book in the Islamic World: The Written Word and Communication in the Middle East,* edited by George N. Atiyeh, 33–55. Albany: State University of New York Press.

Ross, Fiona. 1999. *The Printed Bengali Character and Its Evolution.* Surrey, England: Curzon. First published in Dhaka, Bangladesh, by the Bangala Academy.

———. 2002. "An Approach to Non-Latin Type Design." In *Language, Culture, Type: International Type Design in the Age of Unicode,* edited by John D. Berry, 65–75. New York: Association Typographique Internationale (ATypI).

————. 2012. "The Type Design Process for Non-Latin Scripts." In *Non-Latin Scripts: From Metal to Digital Type*, edited by Fiona Ross and Graham Shaw, 125–153. London: St. Bride Library.

Ross, Fiona, and Graham Shaw, eds. 2012. *Non-Latin Scripts: From Metal to Digital Type*. London: St. Bride Library.

Roxburgh, David J. 2003. "On the Transmission and Reconstruction of Arabic Calligraphy: Ibn al-Bawwab and History." *Studia Islamica* 96 (Écriture, Calligraphie, et Peinture): 39–53.

Ruder, Emil. 2013. *Emil Ruder: Fundamentals, Four Lectures from the 1950s by the Master of Timeless Typography*. Tokyo: Seibundo Shinkosha Publishing.

Runciman, Steven. 1968. *The Great Church in Captivity: A Study of the Patriarchate of Constantinople from the Eve of the Turkish Conquest to the Greek War of Independence*. Cambridge: Cambridge University Press.

Sabbagh, Ramiz. 2005. Interview with author. August 3. Amman, Jordan.

Sabev, Orlin (Orhan Salih). 2004. *First Ottoman Journey in the World of Printed Books: A Reassessment [Pürvoto osmansko püteshestvie v sveta na pechatnata kniga (1726–1746): nov pogled]*. Sofia, Bulgaria: Avangard Prima.

————. 2007a. "The First Ottoman Turkish Printing Enterprise: Success or Failure (A Reassessment)." In *Ottoman Tulips, Ottoman Coffee: Leisure and Lifestyle in the Eighteenth Century*, edited by Dana Sajdi, 63–89. New York: Tauris Academic Studies.

————. 2007b. "Formation of Ottoman Print Culture (1726–1746): Some General Remarks." In *New Europe College: Regional Program 2003–2004, 2004–2005*, edited by Irina Vainovski-Mihai, 293–333. Bucharest: New Europe College.

————. 2009. "Rich Men, Poor Men: Ottoman Printers and Booksellers Making Fortune or Seeking Survival (Eighteenth–Nineteenth Centuries)." *Oriens* 37: 177–190. Reprinted in *The History of the Book in the Middle East*, edited by Geoffrey Roper, 319–332. Surrey, England: Ashgate, 2013.

————. 2010. "A Virgin Deserving Paradise or a Whore Deserving Poison: Manuscript Tradition and Printed Books in Ottoman Turkish Society." In *Friars, Nobles and Burghers—Sermons, Images and Prints: Studies of Culture and Society in Early-Modern Europe in Memoriam István György Tóth*, edited by Jaroslav Miller, 389–409. Budapest: Central European University Press. Reprinted in *The History of the Book in the Middle East*, edited by Geoffrey Roper, 143–163. Surrey, England: Ashgate.

————. 2014. "Waiting for Godot: The Formation of Ottoman Print Culture." In *Historical Aspects of Printing and Publishing in Languages of the Middle East: Papers from the Third Symposium on the History of Printing and Publishing in the Languages and Countries of the Middle East, University of Leipzig, September 2008*, edited by Geoffrey Roper, 101–120. Leiden: Brill.

Saenger, Paul Henry, and Kimberly Van Kampen, eds. 1999. *The Bible as Book: The First Printed Editions*. New Castle, DE: Oak Knoll Press.

Safadi, Yasin Hamid. 1979. *Islamic Calligraphy*. Boulder, CO: Shambala.

————. 1980. "Printing in Arabic: 'Monotype' Distinguished Naskh Characters Have Set the Standard to Be Emulated." *Monotype Recorder*, 2 (September 1980): 2–7.

Saint-Simon, Louis de Rouvroy, and Bayle St. John. 1888. *The Memoirs of the Duke of Saint-Simon on the Reign of Louis XIV and the Regency*. Translated by Bayle St. John. London: S. Sonnenschein, Lowrey & Company.

Sakkal, Mamoun. 1993. "An Islamic Image: Calligraphy as Graphics." Bothell, WA: Sakkal Design. www.sakkal.com.

———. 2004. "Modern Arabic Typography: Challenges and Opportunities." Interview conducted by Stuart Taylor, December 17. Transcript provided via personal correspondence with Mamoun Sakkal.

Salaville, Sévérien, and Eugene Dalleggio D'Alessio. 1958. *Karamanlidika: Bibliographie analytique d'ouvrages en langue turque imprimés en caractères grecs.* Athens: Institut français d'Athènes.

Salomon, Richard. 2012. "Some Principles and Patterns of Script Change." In *The Shape of Script: How and Why Writing Systems Change,* edited by Stephen D. Houston, 119–133. Santa Fe, NM: School for Advanced Research Press.

Sampson, Geoffrey. 1985. *Writing Systems: A Linguistic Introduction.* Palo Alto, CA: Stanford University Press.

Sanjian, Ara. 2014. "Armenian Printing in Constantinople and Venice." In *Celebrating the Legacy of Five Centuries of Armenian-Language Book Printing, 1512–2012,* edited by Ara Sanjian, Daniel Little, and Gerald Ottenbreit. Dearborn: Armenian Research Center, University of Michigan-Dearborn.

Sanjian, Ara, Daniel Little, and Gerald Ottenbreit, eds. 2012. *Celebrating the Legacy of Five Centuries of Armenian-Language Book Printing, 1512–2012.* Dearborn: Armenian Research Center, University of Michigan-Dearborn.

Santo Domingo, Nuria Torres, Juan Manuel Vizcaíno, and Miren Ibarra Ibaibarriaga. 2013. *Catálogo de fondo antiguo con tipografía árabe: Una colección singular en la Biblioteca Islámica Félix Ma Pareja.* Edited by Luisa Mora Villarejo. Madrid: Agencia Española de Cooperación Internacional para el Desarrollo.

Saoud, Rabah. 2004. "Muslim Architecture under Ottoman Patronage (1326–1924)." Manchester, UK: Foundation for Science Technology and Civilisation.

Sarıcaoğlu, Fikret, and Coşkun Yılmaz. 2012. *Müteferrika: Basmacı İbrahim Efendi ve Müteferrika Matbaası / Basmacı İbrahim Efendi and the Müteferrika Press.* 3rd edition. Istanbul, Turkey: Esen Ofset.

Şarikavak, Kazim. 2000. "An Unknown Enlightenment Movement in the Ottoman Empire." In *The Great Ottoman-Turkish Civilization,* edited by Kemal Çiçek, 3:77–82. Ankara, Turkey: Yeni Türkiye Publications.

Sauvaget, Jean. 1951 "Suggestions pour un reform de la typographie Arabe." *Revue des études Islamiques* 19: 127–132.

Schaefer, Karl. 2002. "Arabic Printing before Gutenberg—Block-Printed Arabic Amulets." In *Middle Eastern Languages and the Print Revolution: A Cross-Cultural Encounter,* edited by Eva Hanebutt-Benz, Dagmar Glass, and Geoffrey Roper, 123–238. Westhofen, Germany: WVA-Verlag Skulima.

———. 2014. "Mediæval Arabic Block Printing: State of the Field." In *Historical Aspects of Printing and Publishing in Languages of the Middle East: Papers from the Third Symposium on the History of Printing and Publishing in the Languages and Countries of the Middle East, University of Leipzig, September 2008,* edited by Geoffrey Roper, 1–16. Leiden: Brill.

Schimmel, Annemarie. 1970. *Islamic Calligraphy: Iconography of Religions.* Leiden: Brill.

———. 1984. *Calligraphy and Islamic Culture.* Hagop Kevorkian Series on Near Eastern Art and Civilization. New York: New York University Press.

———. 1994. *Deciphering the Signs of God: A Phenomenological Approach to Islam.* Albany: State University of New York Press.

Schneider, Manfred. 2001. "Luther with McLuhan." In *Religion and Media,* edited by Hent de Vries and Samuel Weber, 198–215. Palo Alto, CA: Stanford University Press.

Seely, Jonathan F. 1968. "The New Turkish Orthography of 1928: Its Effect on the Lexical Turkification of Ottoman Turkish." M.S. thesis, Georgetown University, Washington, DC.

Sells, Michael Anthony. 1999. *Approaching the Qur'an: The Early Revelations.* Ashland, OR: White Cloud Press.

Senefelder, Alois. 1819. *A Complete Course in Lithography.* London: R. Ackerman.

Shabout, Nada. 1999. *Modern Arab Art: Formation of Arab Aesthetics.* Gainesville: University Press of Florida.

Shaw, Graham. 2012. "Non-Latin Scripts and Printing Technologies: Triumphs and Tribulations." In *Non-Latin Scripts: From Metal to Digital Type,* edited by Fiona Ross and Graham Shaw, 11–33. London: St. Bride Library.

Shaw, Stanford J. 1991. *The Jews of the Ottoman Empire and the Turkish Republic.* New York: New York University Press.

Shaw, Stanford J., and Ezel Kural Shaw. 1976. *History of the Ottoman Empire and Modern Turkey.* 2 vols. Cambridge: Cambridge University Press.

Shenyurek, Eleanor West. 1972. "The Introduction of Printing into Turkey: A Bibliographic Paper." M.S. thesis, The Catholic University of America, Washington, DC.

Shrivtiel, Shraybom. 1998. "The Question of Romanisation of the Script and the Emergence of Nationalism in the Middle East." *Mediterranean Language Review,* 179–196.

Siegel, James T. 2000. *The Rope of God.* Ann Arbor: University of Michigan Press.

Simon, Rachel. 2010. "Printing and Printers." In *Encyclopedia of Jews in the Islamic World,* executive editor Norman A. Stillman, 100–112. Leiden: Brill.

Skovgaard-Petersen, Jakob. 1997. "Fatwas in Print." *Culture & History* 16: 73–88.

Smitshuijzen, Edo. 2009. *Arabic Font Specimen Book.* Amsterdam: Uitgeverij De Buitenkant.

Sourdel-Thomine, J. 1960. "Khatt." In *The Encyclopedia of Islam,* 4:1113–1122. Leiden: Brill.

Spiekermann, Erik. 2011. "Graphic Design Can Change Your Life." Berlin: Gestalten TV.

Spooner, Brian, and William L. Hanaway, eds. 2012. *Literacy in the Persianate World: Writing and the Social Order.* Philadelphia: University of Pennsylvania Museum of Archaeology and Anthropology.

Sproat, Richard William. 2010. *Language, Technology, and Society.* Oxford: Oxford University Press.

Stanley, T. 2004. "Page-Setting in Late Ottoman Qur'āns: An Aspect of Standardization." *Manuscripta Orientalia* 10(1): 56–63.

Steinberg, S. H. 1996. *Five Hundred Years of Printing.* London: The British Library and Oak Knoll Press.

Stolow, Jeremy. 2005. "Religion and / as Media." *Theory, Culture & Society* 22(4): 119–45.

———. 2010. *Orthodox by Design: Judaism, Print Politics, and the ArtScroll Revolution.* Berkeley: University of California Press.

Stone, Caroline. 1981. "On Paper." *Saudi Aramco World* 32(2): 30–35.

Strauss, Johann. 2003. "Who Read What in the Ottoman Empire (19th–20th Centuries)?" *Middle Eastern Literatures* 6(1): 39–76. Reprinted in *The History of the Book in the Middle East,* edited by Geoffrey Roper, 455–492. Surrey, England: Ashgate, 2013.

———. 2005. "'Kütüp ve Resail—i Mevkute': Printing and Publishing in a Multi-Ethnic Society." In *Late Ottoman Society: The Intellectual Legacy,* edited by Elisabeth Özdalga, 225–253. London: Routledge.

Suit, Natalia Kasprzak. 2014. "Quranic Matters: Media and Materiality." Ph.D. diss., University of North Carolina at Chapel Hill.

Szyliowicz, Joseph S. 1992. "Functionalist Perspectives on Technology: The Case of the Printing Press in the Ottoman Empire." In *Transfer of Modern Science & Technology to the Muslim World,* edited by Ekmeleddin İhsanoğlu, 251–260. Istanbul, Turkey: IRCICA.

Tabbaa, Yasser. 1999. "Canonicity and Control: The Sociopolitical Underpinnings of Ibn Muqla's Reform." *Ars Orientalis* 29: 91–100.

———. 2002. *The Transformation of Islamic Art during the Sunni Revival.* London: I. B. Tauris Publishers.

Takikawa, Mio. 2012. "Hagia Sophia and Sinan's Mosques: Structure and Decoration in Suleymaniye Mosque and Selimye." *Seijo University Departmental Bulletin of Aesthetics and Art History* 17 / 18: 103–119.

Tamari, Ittai Joseph. 2001. "Jewish Printing and Publishing Activities in the Ottoman Cities of Constantinople and Salonika at the Dawn of Early Modern Europe." In *The Beginnings of Printing in the Near and Middle East: Jews, Christians and Muslims,* edited by the Lehrstuhl für Türkische Sprache, Geschichte und Kultur, Universität Bamberg, 9–10. Wiesbaden, Germany: Harrassowitz Verlag.

Tansel, Fevziye Abdullah. 1953. "Arap Harflerinin Islahı ve Değiştirilmesi Hakkında İlk Teşebbüsler ve Neticeleri (1862–1884)." *Belleten* 17(66): 223–249.

Thevet, André. 1670. *Histoire des plus illustres et scavans hommes de leurs siecles: Tant de l'europe que de l'asie, afrique & amerique.* Paris: François Mauger.

Toderini, Giambatista. 1990. *İbrahim Müteferrika Matbaası ve Türk Matbaacılığı.* Edited by Şevket Rado. Istanbul, Turkey: Yayın Matbaacılık Ticaret.

Tott, François, Baron de. 1786. *Memoirs of Baron de Tott. Containing the state of the Turkish empire & the Crimea, during the late war with Russia. With numerous anecdotes, facts, & observations, on the manners & customs of the Turks & Tartars.* London: G. G. J. & J. Robinson.

Tracy, Walter. 1964. "The Flourishing Reed: Arabic Scripts." In *Alphabet 1964: International Annual of Letterforms,* edited by R. S. Hutchings, 139–146. London: James Moran.

———. 1975. "Arabic without Tears." *Penrose Annual* 68: 121–126.

Ülker, Muammer. 1987. *Başlangıctan Günümüze Türk Hat Sanatı (The Art of Turkish Calligraphy from the Beginning up to the Present).* Ankara, Turkey: Türkiye Iş Bankası Kültür Yaıyınlari.

The Unicode Consortium. 1991. *The Unicode Standard: Worldwide Character Encoding, Version 1.0, Volume 1.* San Francisco: Addison-Wesley.

———. 2014. *The Unicode Standard: Version 7.0—Core Specification.* Mountain View, CA: The Unicode Consortium.

———. 2015. "What Is Unicode?" www.unicode.org/standard/WhatIsUnicode.html.

Verdery, Richard N. 1971. "The Publications of the Bulaq Press under Muhammad ʿAli of Egypt." *Journal of the American Oriental Society* 91(1): 129–132.

Versteegh, C. H. M. 1997. *The Arabic Language.* New York: Columbia University Press.

Vervliet, Hendrik D. L. 1981. *Cyrillic & Oriental Typography in Rome at the End of the Sixteenth Century: An Inquiry into the Later Work of Robert Granjon (1578–90) [Robert Granjon à Rome].* Berkeley, CA: Poltroon Press.

Wagner, Bettina, and Marcia Reed, eds. 2009. *Early Printed Books as Material Objects.* Proceeding of the Conference Organized by the IFLA Rare Books and Manuscripts Section, Munich, August 19–21. Berlin: De Gruyter.

Walsh, Robert. 1828. *Narrative of a Journey from Constantinople to England.* 2nd ed. London: Frederick Westley and A. H Davis.

Warde, Beatrice. 1955. *The Crystal Goblet: Sixteen Essays on Typography.* Edited by H. Jacob. London: Sylvan Press.

———. 1963. "Type Design in the New Cold-Type Age," supplement, *Print in Britain,* 9–10.

Watson, William J. 1968. "Ibrahim Müteferrika and Turkish Incunabula." *Journal of the American Oriental Society* 88(3): 435–441.

Welch, Anthony. 1979. *Calligraphy in the Arts of the Muslim World.* Austin: University of Texas Press.

Wheatcroft, Andrew. 1995. *The Ottomans: Dissolving Images.* London: Penguin.

Wheeler, Geoffrey. 1974. "Modernization in the Muslim East: The Role of Script and Language Reform." *Asian Affairs* 61: 157–164.

White, Alex. 2011. *The Elements of Graphic Design: Space, Unity, Page Architecture, and Type.* 2nd ed. New York: Allworth Press.

Williams, Raymond. 1961. *The Long Revolution.* New York: Columbia University Press.

Wittek, Paul. 1948. "Notes sur la turgha ottomane (I)." *Byzantion* 18: 311–334.

———. 1950. "Notes sur la turgha ottomane (I)." *Byzantion* 20: 267–293.

Wright, Elaine Julia. 2012. *The Look of the Book: Manuscript Production in Shiraz, 1303–1452.* Washington, DC: Freer Gallery of Art and Arthur M. Sackler Gallery, Smithsonian Institution.

Wright, William. 1896. *A Grammar of the Arabic Language: Translated from the German of Caspari and Edited with Numerous Additions and Corrections.* 3rd ed. Cambridge: Cambridge University Press.

Yaari, Avraham. 2007. "Ashkenazi, Jonah ben Jacob." In *Encyclopedia Judaica.* 2nd ed. Detroit: Macmillan Reference.

Yaghan, Mohammad Ali. 2008. "ʿArabizi': A Contemporary Style of Arabic Slang." *Design Issues* 24 (2): 39–52.

Yerushalmi, Yosef Hayim. 1971. "Privilegos del poderozo rey Karlo [1740]; a Neapolitan Call for the Return of the Jews and Its Ladino Translation." In *Studies in Jewish Bibliography, History and Literature in Honor of I. Edward Kiev,* edited by Charles Berlin, 517–541. New York: Ktav Publishing House.

Yılmaz, Malik. 2001. "Osmanlı Hükümeti Tarafından Ilk Kurulan Matbaa ve Bunun Neşriyatı." *Türk Kütüphaneciliği* 15, 4: 436–442.

Zakariya, Mohamed. 2000. "Becoming a Calligrapher: Memoirs of an American Student of Calligraphy." Zakariya Calligraphy. www.mohamedzakariya.com.

————. 2002. "The Hilye of the Prophet Muhammad." Zakariya Calligraphy. www
.mohamedzakariya.com.

————. 2003. "Rhyming in R." Zakariya Calligraphy. www.mohamedzakariya.com.

Zapf, Herman, and John Dreyfus. 1991. *Classical Typography in the Computer Age.* Los Angeles: William Andrews Clark Memorial Library.

Zoghbi, Pascal. 2013. "Nasri Khattar's Typographic Journey." 29Letters: www.29lt.com.

ACKNOWLEDGMENTS

This book is the result of many years of research, writing, and imagination. My interest in Arabic script began more than twenty years ago, and many worlds have come since I first left home. The book you hold would not have been possible without a wealth of support from individuals and institutions alike. I thank all those who have taken time to discuss the ideas and share their insights. The work has benefited from the contributions of helpful characters everywhere. Some of those dialogues occurred face-to-face in attics and cafés around the world. Others were mediated across time by dusty books and rusty machines. Thanks to all the librarians, archivists, and curators who prevent these historic artifacts from becoming *too* dusty and *too* rusty.

I started down the path of this research in the Department of Communication at the University of California, San Diego (UCSD), and I completed it with the Program of Communication, Culture & Technology at Georgetown University. Both these departments are wonderfully supportive of this type of interdisciplinary work. I am grateful to have developed the book alongside such diverse colleagues and stimulating students. I also thank the Süleymaniye Yazma Eser Kütüphanesi, The Newberry Library, The American Institute of Yemeni Studies (AIYS), The Catholic University of America, and the American University in Dubai for the times that they hosted me. The work was financially supported by research grants and fellowships from UCSD, The Newberry Library, and Georgetown University. The knowledgeable staff and special collections of the Islâm Arıştırmaları Merkezi (ISAM), the Research Centre for Islamic History, Art, and Culture (IRCICA), the Institute of Christian Oriental Research (ICOR) at the Catholic University, and the I. Edward Kiev Judaica Collection at George Washington University were also incredibly helpful.

Portions of the work have been presented at meetings and symposia sponsored by the Middle East Studies Association (MESA), the American Anthropological Association (AAA), the National Communication Association (NCA), the Humanities and Technology

Association (HTA), the Georgetown University Roundtable on Language and Linguistics, the Khatt Foundation, the International Conference on the Book, and the Thirteenth Annual Berkeley Graduate Symposium: Interdisciplinary Approaches to the Study of Visual Representation. I appreciate all who listened attentively, questioned, criticized, and challenged the work in progress. I reserve a special depth of gratitude for UCSD's Art, Culture, and Knowledge (ACK) Group, organized by Professor Bennetta Jules-Rosette. Iterations of the ACK Group have read, dissected, and provided incredibly useful feedback on numerous versions of the project. An Outstanding Dissertation award from the UCSD African and African-American Studies Research Center (AAASRC) recognized the work's early potential, and a Travel Fellowship from the Hamad bin Khalifa Symposium on Islamic Art allowed me to reflect on the nearly completed book alongside a diverse group of scholars dedicated to the study of Arabic script.

I am indebted to my mentors and colleagues for their guidance, suggestions, and advice (both practical and conceptual). Bennetta Jules-Rosette, in particular, is a source of inspiration in her analyses of art, culture, knowledge, signs, and technology, as well as her tireless dedication to academia as a profession. Her insights have shaped this book in countless ways. I also recognize Mehmet Fatsa, who introduced me to the secrets that hide within Arabic script, and Carol Padden, who guided the research in its early phases and whose acumen continues to influence the way I approach and present the topic. I am incredibly grateful for my family, who have blessed me with love, kindness, and understanding. Among the countless others who have helped on the way, I offer special thanks to Elizabeth Eisenstein, Paul Gehl, Brad Sabin Hill, Thomas Milo, Huda Smitshuijzen AbiFarès, Yannis Haralambous, Marcelo Lima, Mohamed Zayani, Nevzat Kaya, Carole Sargent, Carl Sachs, Anthony Scotto, Abdurahman Kaya, Natalia Suit, Ghazi Abu Hakema, David Groppe, AleXander Jacobs, Jason Browning, K.C. Jones, Carrie Casillas, Jen Manthei, Evan Barba, Bill Marsh, Gordon Chang, the Khoury family, Nasreen Alkhateeb, and Jack Axe.

I thank my research assistants at Georgetown University, Bentley Brown and Mark Visonà, both of whom read early versions and flagged potential problems. Mark was especially helpful with the standardization of transliterated terms and bibliographic references. Sharmila Sen and Heather Hughes of Harvard University Press are a fantastic team and incredibly supportive. Their patience, guidance, and assistance helped ease the book to fruition. I am also deeply thankful for the anonymous reviewers, whose honest and direct comments helped define the scope of the book, correct inaccuracies, and strengthen the final product. The work is much improved due to their careful reading and attention to detail. I am honored that Mohamed Zakariya agreed to provide illustrations, and I thank all those who granted permission to reprint images. A wealth of support has elevated the book, and I share my thanks with all mentioned parties. Any scholarly, bibliographic, and typographic errors that remain are fully my own (although I am equally willing to share those if anyone finds them helpful). Finally, I recognize, with deep gratitude, the written characters themselves, who make this all possible.

INDEX

Abbar, Yassar, 179–180

Abbasid era, 5–7, 15, 32, 36, 40–41, 114; adoption
of paper, 22–23, 79; explosion of writing
during, 6, 22; Qur'anic *masahif,* 20, 28, 30,
38–39, 205n26; scribal tradition, 45, 70; *tawqi'*
as authoritative style of, 58, 61, 208n30;
varieties of script style, 16–17, 21–22

Abdullah, Yusuf Ali, 19, 161

Abdullah Efendi, Ottoman Şeyhülislam, 112,
116–119

AbiFarès, Huda Smitshuijzen, 180–185, 226n73.
See also Khatt Foundation for Arabic
Typography

abjad, Arabic, ix, 23–28, 183, 188–190; computer
encoding of, 165, 169–172, 177–178, 190; and
script reform, 137, 144, 148, 153. *See also*
Arabic letters

Abu Bakr, 49, 97

Academy of Arabic Language in Cairo, 132,
140–142, 145, 147, 158, 220n45

Acar, M. Şinasi, 51, 67, 219n29

Advanced Composition Engine (ACE). *See*
DecoType

Africa, 5, 76, 85, 170, 203n4; Arabic script in,
8, 85, 173, 204n6, 224n32; languages of, 4,
172–173, 190, 226n86

al-aqlam al-sittah, 8, 43, 52–53, 73; comparisons
with other styles, 60–63; in *hilye* designs,
48–51, 56; in Ottoman practice, 52–59, 70–71;
Yaqut's mastery of, 39–40. *See also names of
specific styles*

alif, 23, 25, 150–154, 172, 208n35, 212n52;
khanjariya, 29; *maddah,* 150; *maqsurah,* 144,
148, 152–153; as measuring device, 34–35, 45;
in Ottoman *tughra,* 67; in various styles of
script, 20, 55–58, 60–61, 64

Alphabetum Arabicum. See Tipographia
Medicea

Amiriya Press, El-, 143–144, 159, 217n96

Amsterdam. *See* Holland / Dutch

Andalusia, 9, 85, 104, 114, 118. *See also*
Spain / Spanish

animation, 2, 196–197, 207n4

Arabe Standard Voyellé-Codage Arabe
(ASV-Codar), 11, 147–151, 162,
220n48

Arabic language, 26, 43, 134, 142, 181, 203n5;
dictionaries of, 119–120, 125, 205n37;
European studies of, 85–86, 89–91, 226n77;
and Ottoman Turkish, 135–138; Qur'an as
necessarily, 9, 43, 70, 81, 136–137, 155, 218n16.
See also abjad, Arabic; Arabic letters

Gutenberg, Johannes, 8, 79–80, 102, 104, 158; mentioned in Ottoman sources, 113; printings of, 76–77, 93, 157, 212n60; Ottoman print trajectory in relation to, 10, 102, 129, 133

Habsburgs, 109, 122
hadith, 48–49, 116, 208n30
Hagia Sophia, 66, 213n82
Hamdullah, Şeyh, 43, 49, 99, 103; as figurehead of Ottoman *khatt*, 45–47, 48; as "font" designer, 48, 51–52; and Hafiz Osman, 47–48, 51–52; legendary exploits of, 47; *mushaf* templates of, 48, 53, 56, 160–161; refinements of *thuluth* and *naskh*, 46–47, 56, 103, 207n13; and Sultan Bayezid II, 45–46, 106; and Yaqut al-Musta'simi, 45–47, 52, 70
hamza, ix, 23, 31, 138; and script reform, 144, 148, 150, 152–153; in Unicode, 177–178
Hanyu Pinyin, 132
harakat. See tashkil
Hebrew script, 16, 212n52; computer handling of, 169, 172, 175–177; European printing of, 83–84, 86; in the Ottoman *millet* system, 42–43, 73, 104; Ottoman printing of, 5, 10, 104–107, 118–119, 127–128, 218n8; representing languages other than Hebrew, 42–43, 105, 214n8; and script reform, 132, 134. *See also* Jews / Judaism
Hekmioğlu Ali Pasha, 122
Helvetica, 18, 68, 146, 165, 171, 226n87; Arabic letters made from, 153–154
Hill, Brad Sabin, 216n71, 217n92
hilye, 48, 52, 73, 139, 161, 207n17; Ottoman template for, 48–51, 56; symbolic associations of, 72, 207n15
Holdermann, Jean Baptiste, 124
Holland / Dutch, 104, 109, 119, 157, 216n80, 226n77; type design, 12, 180–185, 225n51
Hudson, John, 225n60
Humeid, Ahmed, 153, 221n70
Hungary, 112–114

Ibn al-Bawwab, 7, 32, 36–40, 45, 206n50
Ibn al-Nadim, 7, 16–20, 30–31, 33
Ibn Khallikan, 36, 205n40

Ibn Muqlah, 7, 15–16, 194, 207n6; and Arabic scribal tradition, 33, 40, 45, 206n56; contributions to *al-khatt al-mansub*, 33–34, 205n40, 206nn41–42; and Ibn al-Bawwab, 36–37; political career of, 32–33, 36; and Yaqut al-Musta'simi, 206n54
Ibrahim Müteferrika, 10, 104, 129, 131, 136, 146; books printed by, 119–126, 157, 216n61, 216n77; early life of, 112–113, 128–129, 215n51; European descriptions of, 118, 216n67; familiarity with European scholarship, 113, 117, 121–123, 215n52; and Jonah (Yonah) ben Jakob Ashkenazi, 118–119, 120–121, 124, 216n72; maps printed by, 109–110, 120–121, 128, 133; *Risale-i Islamiye*, 112; and Said Çelebi, 112–113, 160, 216n75; scholarly interests, 123, 125, 216n61, 216n78; service to the state, 125, 129, 133–135, 159–160; translations by, 121–122, 124–125; *Usül ul-hikem nizam il-umem*, 122–123, 217n87; *Vesiletü-t Tibaa*, 110, 113–121, 123, 215n4
Ibrahim Pasha, Nevşehirli Damat, 109, 110, 112, 119, 121, 123
Ibrahim Peçevi, 112–113
i'jaam, 26–29, 31, 71; mistakes in printing of, 88; pen used for, 55–56; texts without, 30, 63, 177, 192, 205n30; in Unicode, 177–178, 188–189. *See also nuqta*
illumination: of computer screens, 200, 228n18; in manuscripts, 37, 39, 49, 114, 206n46
indexing, 115–116, 119–120, 122, 199, 212n59, 224n33
India, 123, 157, 220n57
International Business Machines (IBM), 140, 145, 169–170
International Standards Organization (ISO): ISO 8859, 169–170, 172, 223n16; ISO 2022, 169, 223n15
Iran, 60, 220n57, 223n17. *See also* Persia
Iraq, 121, 159, 205n30. *See also* Baghdad
Islam, 106, 114, 137, 218n11, 219n29; Arabic script as symbol of, 104, 131, 137–138, 155; art, 13, 161, 221n79 (*see also* calligraphy); authority, 19, 129, 160; conversion to, 40, 112; Islamic glory, 9, 115–116, 125, 217n90; and printing,